ALSACE WINES

The fortified church at Hunawihr, supposedly founded by Hunon and his saintly wife, Huna, who, at the domestic wash pool after several bad vintages, prayed and transformed the water into wine

Alsace Wines
& Spirits

Pamela Vandyke Price
with Christopher Fielden

SOTHEBY PUBLICATIONS

© Pamela Vandyke Price 1984
First published in 1984 for
Sotheby Publications by
Philip Wilson Publishers Ltd
Russell Chambers, Covent Garden,
London WC2E 8AA

Available to the USA book trade from
Sotheby Publications
Harper & Row, Publishers, Inc
10 East 53rd Street
New York
NY 10022, USA

Exclusive distribution to the wine trade
in the USA:
THE WINE APPRECIATION GUILD
155 Connecticut Street
San Francisco
California 94107, USA

(415) 864-1202

ISBN 0 85667 183 5

Library of Congress Catalog Number 84-50547

Designed by Mary Osborne
Typeset by Modern Text Typesetting, Southend
Printed in England by the Pitman Press Ltd, Bath

Endpapers
A sixteenth-century wood-cut with a caption in Latin which says: 'A picture of the
town of Colmar and surrounding countryside drawn from life' (not shown)

For
Andrew Henderson
who shares my love of wine
especially the wines of Alsace
'the lovely land'
with much affection

Contents

List of Colour Plates   8

Acknowledgements   9

Introduction   13

1   The Alsace Vineyard   17
     The Climate of the Vineyard   22

2   The History of the Alsace Vineyard   27

3   The Grapes, Wines and Vines   59
     The Main Grape Varieties   59
     The Wines   77
     Vineyard Routine   82
     The Vintage   86
     Making the Wine   88
     Pressing   93
     Fermentation   95
     Casks   96
     Treatment and Malolactic Fermentation   99
     Bottling   100

4   Some Special Wines   101

5   The Sparkling Wines   105

6   The Alsace Wine Trade   111
     The Alsace Wine Law   113
     The Alsace Bottle   121

7   A Who's Who of the Main Firms   125

8   Gastronomy   149

9   Serving and Drinking the Wines   157

10   The Confrérie Saint Etienne   167

11   Spirits and Liqueurs   171
12   The Route du Vin   183
      Map   184-5
Bibliography   199
Appendices
   I   *Exports of Alsace Wines – Trends in 1983*   202
  II   *Alsace Vintages 1969-82*   203
 III   *Plantations of Appellation Contrôlée Wines 1969-82*   204
  IV   *Sales of Bottled Appellation Contrôlée Wines 1976-82*   205
   V   *The Alsace Crop According to the Types of Grower 1981-82*   206
  VI   *The 1982 crop in hectolitres in relation to the thirteen preceding years*   207
 VII   *Details of Vendange Tardive and Sélection de Grains Nobles Wines*   208
VIII   *Law governing Vendange Tardive and Sélection de Grains Nobles Wines*   209
  IX   *The 1983 Vintage*   210
Index   211

List of Colour Plates

	Between pages
Riquewihr (*Patrick Eagar*)	72 and 73
The Alsace grapes (*C.I.V.A.*)	72 and 73
Vineyards (*C.I.V.A.*)	72 and 73
Rodern (*C.I.V.A.*)	112 and 113
Vintage (*C.I.V.A.*)	112 and 113
Hugel's sign in Riquewihr (*Hugel*)	112 and 113
Vintaging with *hottes (C.I.V.A.)*	128 and 129
Picking the grapes (*C.I.V.A.*)	128 and 129
The 'tulipes des vignes' (*C.I.V.A.*)	128 and 129

Acknowledgements

Those who have contributed to this book by help, advice, information, the providing of material, recommendation of places to see, wines and foods to try, plus general hospitality and kindness are numerous. Even if space permitted the naming of them all, some omissions might occur so I trust that the many individuals in official bodies, hotels, restaurants, vineyards, shops, museums, libraries and information bureaux in both Alsace and the U.K. on whose services Christopher Fielden and I have drawn will accept a general expression of our gratitude.

My own indebtedness starts with the late Allan Sichel, who first took me to 'the lovely land', whose wines he had loved, bought and promoted and where he had many friends who still remember him with affection and respect. Then I am grateful to Patrick Grubb, M.W., who prompted the commissioning of this book, Mrs. Aileen Trew, M.W., who kindly allowed me to have a copy of her teaching notes for the Institute of Masters of Wine, Peter Hallgarten, who gave me the latest edition of his father's book, and the many members of the British wine trade who encouraged my interest in Alsace wines, among them especially the firm of O.W. Loeb, who have been especially patient – as always – at helping me with various details.

The French Government Tourist Office in London, where Mrs Pauline Hallam has long been a friend, has arranged many introductions through contacts in Alsace and I wish to thank the present head, M. René Bordy, also Mrs Florence Beddow in the photographic library. Food & Wine from France have been so helpful that I feel MM. Emmanuel Drion (now at S.O.P.E.X.A. in Paris) and Michel Girard, together with their delightful assistants, Miss Cathérine Manac'h and Miss Margaret Darke, are colleagues as well as friends; they have arranged many trips and visits for me, supplying much information and illustrated matter. It is impossible to over-estimate how much all my work owes to them.

In Alsace, I acknowledge the assistance of those who have been generous with their time and understandingly helpful at the co-operatives of Bennwihr, Cleebourg, Eguisheim, Ribeauvillé and Westhalten. M. Jean-Jacques Radmacher of La Wantzenau provided invaluable help with the section on spirits, as did M. and Mme Meyer at Villé, M. and Mme Mehr of the Lion d'Or, Breuschwickersheim and the Massenez shop in Riquewihr. David and Mimi Ling have given me a great deal of insight into Alsace – it

9

was good fortune that David, who is British but has gained valuable experience working in Alsace, married a girl from Eguisheim of a wine family. M. Jean-Claude Schoeni, of Ingersheim, also gave me a wine grower's point of view.

The Grandes Maisons d'Alsace were my collective hosts on one trip and each of them and their London representatives have been of lasting help and encouragement for many years. I can only thank them briefly, in alphabetical order, with my U.K. contacts given in brackets: M. Marc Beyer at Léon Beyer (Michael Druitt Wines), for an impressive visit; M. Guy Dopff of Dopff & Irion (J.B. Reynier), who showed me something of the organisation of a modern establishment; M. Pierre Dopff, Dopff 'Au Moulin' (Mentzendorff) who explained *crémants* and Pinot Blanc and provided much valuable additional material; M. and Mme Jean-Michel Bas and their family, of Kuentz-Bas (Rawlings Voigt), in whose beautiful house I was at once made to feel at home and whose *vendange tardive* wines were an education; M. Charles Baffié at G. Lorentz (Stowells of Chelsea) was particularly helpful in telling me about the red wines of Alsace; MM. Hubert and Bernard Trimbach of Trimbach (H. Parrot) whose wines and cellars I was fortunate enough to see on my first visit and which I have admired ever since; M. Jean-Jacques Preiss-Zimmer (Hatch, Mansfield) whose wines I have also admired and enjoyed for many years, has contributed many lively and pertinent views to my attempts at understanding Alsace.

To the late M. Jean Hugel, Mme. Hugel *mère* and the whole Hugel family I owe a very great deal. Over many years both they and Dreyfus Ashby in London have been endlessly patient and kind in dealing with my inquiries and, in Alsace, enlarging my experience both of their remarkable wines and of Alsace hospitality. 'Johnnie' Hugel has virtually organised several of my visits and his colleagues and competitors have bowed to the benevolent dynamism with which he has effected introductions, secured information, enabled me to pursue details of wine, gastronomy and Alsace life far beyond the scope of this book. Not only is his knowledge of the world's wines outstanding, but his encouragement both of myself and of all those who love Alsace has made him an outstanding personality among wine makers and wine lovers; to him, his charming wife and family I can only continue to raise an affectionate glass.

There have been many in other establishments who have assisted this book over many years. M. Schielé of Kuehn is another I met on my first visit, who has remained an appreciated source of information and a generous host on many occasions; M. and Mme. Jean Meyer of Jos. Meyer combine being delightful company with providing valuable insight into the Alsace wine scene. M. and Mme. Pierre Dreyer, of Sick-Dreyer are more recent friends, whose opinions, freely given over a superlative choucroute, have been of great use. M. and Mme. Zind-Humbrecht, together with their London representatives, Laytons, provided a most rewarding tasting and much useful information; Mlle. Muré of the Muré establishment is another enthusiast who combines energy with charm; she arranged a tasting and tour of the Clos St-Landelin that was of great interest. At Domaines Schlumberger M. Winter gave unstintingly of his time and provided a remarkable tasting of a long range of some of the greatest of the Schlumberger wines. In the U.K. I am grateful to those who introduced me to the wines of Louis Sipp, those of Faller Frères, Domaine Weinbach, Kaysersberg, also to Steven Spurrier of Caves de la Madeleine, who first showed me the wines of Jean Ziegler and Pierre Sparr.

To M. Pierre Bouard, of the C.I.V.A., a special expression of thanks – this book could not have been completed without his assistance. Not only has he kept me constantly informed as to events in the world of Alsace wine, but, being himself a fine photographer, many of the pictures generously contributed by his organisation are his own work. Mlle. Monique Rohrbach of the C.I.V.A. also gave up much time to helping with the selection of pictures. To the C.I.V.A. is owed the privilege of a visit to the Institut Vinicole Oberlin, where the director had not only prepared a most valuable short tasting and was able to explain the workings of the Institute at what must have been a busy time, but had arranged for the much respected M. Fernand Ortlieb to be present. To his knowledge and vast experience anyone writing on Alsace owes a great deal. The contribution of the C.I.V.A. is all the more appreciated because, at the time when our last visit was made there, the organisation had only just moved to their new premises and were in the midst of preparing for the official opening – everyone will understand how precious time and energy are at such periods.

In the practical preparation of the book I am grateful to Anne Jackson of Philip Wilson Publishers Ltd. and much indebted to the knowledge, competence and good sense of Heather Jones, who edited the copy.

Finally, it must be emphasised that this book has gained enormously in authority and scope because of the benevolence and generosity of Christopher Fielden, whose contributions are considerable. First, he offered me free use of material collected during his earlier researches into the history of the Alsace wine trade, then he accompanied me for part of a visit I recently paid to the region. Christopher has lived and worked in France, including Alsace, and he introduced me to many wines and producers whom I had not previously known. His experience as a member of the wine trade together with his knowledge of the wines of the world has been, therefore, doubly valuable, and we hope that this book will appeal both to visitors to Alsace and to students of wine.

In compliance with the wishes of the publisher and of Christopher himself I have written this book in the first person singular. But I wish to make it clear that, throughout, I have enjoyed the collaboration of a friend who is also a writer and a respected member of the British wine trade. Those who know us both – and our work – will I am sure agree that, although unaided I might have succeeded in producing a good book, the assistance given by Christopher has broadened its appeal and importance. And, as a tribute that is both professional and personal, I can say no more than that it is probably due to him that, during the researches and the writing, we never disagreed about anything!

Pamela Vandyke Price, January 1984

The Publishers would like to thank the following people and organisations for permission to use their photographs. The C.I.V.A. for pictures on pages 8, 20, 23, 24, 25, 31, 70, 78, 83, 85, 89, 90, 92, 142, 166 and 193; Food & Wine from France for pictures on pages 12, 196 and 198; The French Government Tourist Office for pictures on pages 26, 40, 41, 45, 54, 58, 87, 94, 110, 151, 156, 159, 182, 187, 189, 191 and 197; Patrick Eagar for pictures on pages 35 and 124; Domaines Schlumberger for the picture on page 144; Hugel for the picture on page 96 and Grants of St. James's for the picture on page 122.

Mittelwihr, with the storks' nest on the remains of the fifteenth-century church

Introduction

Alsace, which I have elsewhere referred to as 'the lovely land' is remarkable for many things. Indeed, it is rich in attractions. As a region it is both varied and outstandingly beautiful at all times of the year. Historically it is remarkable, having established and kept its individual character and traditions through many centuries that have involved fearful disasters, wars, invasions, economic vicissitudes, plagues and domination by a neighbour on more than one occasion, the last being within recent times. It is the consequence of this that 'l'Alsace ce n'est pas la France' as some Frenchmen would and do say; Alsace has managed to remain Alsace and is likely to do so for all time.

The works of art, from all periods, make this comparatively compact area a treasure-house. Indeed, the museums are both varied and packed with wonders; that of Colmar is second only to the Louvre in Paris for the large numbers of visitors who come to see the glorious exhibits. Even small villages often have exhibits that merit a detour and the craftsmanship and care devoted to the making of quite humble domestic utensils of the past and the decoration of the houses is impressive. It is as if, in this beautiful countryside – 'Quel beau jardin!' as Louis xiv is supposed to have remarked – man has also been inspired to create beautiful and handsome things and even in the design of many modern buildings, some of them purely utilitarian, there tends to be a discretion and quietness of taste that does not affront the eye; some of it may be exuberant, such as in the great supermarkets and shops in the big towns but it is agreeable, not strident. The artist Hansi, portrayer of so many Alsace occasions, whose peasants in national dress are shown on many of the postcards and whose delicate designs for shop signs make the main street skyline in many wine villages a wrought-iron picture-book, seems to have had the same defined, simple joy in depicting ordinary people and ordinary things.

Then, *Alsaciens,* insofar as one can generalise about any people of a particular region, are truly of Alsace. There is a gentleness about their gaiety that is not usually a part of typical French *esprit* or wit, a delicacy about the way they express their feelings that is not generally associated with Germany. There have been several English (note, English not merely 'British') friends who, lovers of Alsace as I am myself, have commented: 'They're far more like us!' intending the supreme compliment, with which, it must be admitted, many English people have infuriated and even insulted the inhabitants of other nations for a century or more. But there may be some truth in the statement. The *Alsacien* loves the countryside, he enjoys natural things and what, in the past, might be referred to as 'rustic pleasures', even if he cannot indulge in them at first hand as some form of landowner; he cultivates his garden and includes flowers here and in the decoration of his house or apartment. He enjoys a joke, often rather a simple one – the carvings in which the region is so rich often exemplify the same sort of sense of fun and humour that inspired many church carvings and misericords in England – cask carvings and decorations in Alsace and many details of the great paintings are comic, rather than satirical or crude; the beholder is encouraged to laugh rather than to snigger. The extraordinary delicacy of the detail in many of the great paintings often refers to quite ordinary objects: the glasses and tableware in the still lifes of the undeservedly little-known master, Stosskopf, the careful designs of the irons for making the wafers for use in church, the flowers and fruits framing many sacred subjects and the loving inclusion of the basic equipment for the Holy Child's bath in the great Issenheim altarpiece are indicative of the heightened perceptions not only of the artists and craftsmen, but also of the people themselves. Life is precious, the region is glorious, and in even the least communicative *Alsacien* there seems to be a sensitivity as well as a strength that has the power to appeal to and win the respect of many Anglo-Saxons.

There is also the unusual and agreeable acceptance of differences – between peoples and within ways of life as, for example, the way in which one village might be Roman Catholic, the next one Protestant but one does not hear of the two different sects fighting each other, not even in the days when a person's religion was, unfortunately, the spur to violence elsewhere in France. Nonetheless the *Alsaciens* have always been great fighters; the street names in the cities and towns read like a directory of French generals. The country gave them stamina – the inheritance of a hard-won independence (always maintained, even undercover) – and the ability to endure.

The site of the region also has, in my opinion, contributed something to the unique character of the *Alsacien*. It is small enough to know and love, but sufficiently large and varied to encourage an independence of mind, backed by the reassurance of certain traditions and past glories. The Alsace businessman may travel the world but, at home, he still walks down the street where he and his ancestors are known. He may still 'live above the shop' where his great-grandparents started a business and he may still employ men and women who can trace their ancestors back generations before he married into money or land and got a start up the ladder. If he is a new-comer (and the British would understand that this means perhaps within the last couple of generations or fifty years) then he has come to accept this somewhat stolid, planted in the earth, attitude towards him and will neither rush nor assail it, when needing to make changes.

What has this sketch of an outsider's view of Alsace and the Alsace character to do with a book about the region's wines?

They reflect the region, they are the standards of those who make them – who are *Alsaciens*. It may be that one or more of the great wine producers is in fact a foreigner; certainly no *Alsacien* is too proud to make use of the skills or friendship of wine experts from other regions and other countries. But I do not know of any firm whose wines are inconsistent with Alsace traditions. They are remarkably consistent, even when, as happens at times, it must be difficult for them to sell their wines on export markets without making at least some compromises as to style; this must have happened and is likely to happen again. But an Alsace wine is as individual as the region, the works of art and the people; although it might be a risk to wager that it would stand out at a blind tasting of a group of wines of similar style and price, made from similar grapes, I have the feeling and, indeed, the hope, that it might do so!

In this account of Alsace wines, it must be explained that, although I have long known and loved the region and have been fortunate enough to have enjoyed the hospitality and tuition of a number of the great firms, it would not have been possible for me to have included much of the business and technical aspects of the Alsace wine trade without the generous and unstinting help of Christopher Fielden. It is, I trust, a happy example of co-operation in that we were each able to defer to the other on some matters. We have never disagreed on our love for certain wines, although we did differ in our capacity for appreciating some of them, he as a member of the trade, I as a member of the public. This is why, in the chapter on wine-making firms, it seemed helpful to split the opinions – the reader will, we both hope, benefit by having the views of the two of us.

Certain words need explanation. In French, 'Gewurztraminer' does not have the umlaut over the 'u' as in German (Gewürztraminer) because in the French language the sound approximates to the German pronunciation. Throughout this book capital letters have been printed without accents, in accordance with French usage, although such words as Etienne and Emile may bear initial accents.

Then there is the difficulty of referring to 'Alsace' in terms both of wine and people. Christopher rightly says that you don't order a bottle of 'Bordeaux wine' or 'sparkling Champagne', so why not simply say 'Alsace'? Yes, but, alas, one *does* order a bottle of 'red Burgundy' or – for those non-English whose ancestors didn't own the Bordeaux region for 299 years and therefore still retain the right to say 'claret' – one says 'red Bordeaux'. Indeed, to order 'Alsace' is logical, but I think many will find it easier to understand 'Alsace wine'. So, in this book, I have used the term where it might otherwise not have seemed clear.

However, there is a further complication. 'Alsatian is ze dog', the late André L. Simon, founder of The International Wine & Food Society, used to growl. I admit that the word 'Alsation' also pulls me up. So I have, throughout this book, used the term 'Alsace wines' and, referring to the people, I have used *'Alsaciens'*, or 'the people of Alsace'. If this seems affected, my apologies.

There are a number of French terms and words in this book, which have been translated where the meaning is not immediately likely to be clear. Some, of course, are specifically in relation to wine, but it is one of the infuriating things in wine writing that the exact translation of a phrase or term in wine language is not always possible: there are many even among the most respected members of the British wine trade who use French and other foreign words freely, without being able to express themselves in that language at all – the words, making a direct impression, convey their significance and that's that – 'un vin fin' for example is not, really, at all the same thing as 'a fine wine'. I have done my best. The one thing I have not dared venture is to make any use of the special Alsace language! To hear two friends speaking it is amazing – total bafflement. The people of Alsace – perhaps prudently – do not provide any book on 'instant Alsace'. It is a true language, not merely a dialect. The names of some dishes are, obviously, 'Alsace'. No wonder that its use was forbidden during the occupation! But the only phrase I do know is one which, expressing greeting, may stand as an opening to this book about 'the lovely land' and the people and wines who are so delectable . . . *Allez-oop salut!*

1

The Alsace Vineyard

The Alsace vineyard is situated on the foothills of the Vosges, just west of the flatter country known as the Plaine d'Alsace and the meadows on the banks of the rivers Ill and Rhine. For about sixty miles the vineyards are predominant from north to south, extending only about two miles or a little more in width east to west. But the undulations of the ground are considerable: looking down on sections of the vineyard from a point of vantage, the vineyards are seen to cover the foothills, which project into them, as if giant hands on the summits were extending fingers. The stately, impressive, high Vosges mountains are imposing in outline and form and the foothill landscape is intensely varied, dipping and rising, sometimes sharply, sometimes in gradual curves, between the spoke-like projections of the *collines sous-vosgiennes* under the mountains. It is the extensive range of soil type and sub-soil of these hills within even quite small patches that makes the enormous variations within the Alsace wines, even those coming from a single named place.

People appraising a vineyard for study purposes often pay somewhat too much attention to the soil that they can see, either on the surface or as the earth is turned over in routine cultivation. But the tap or main root of a mature vine will penetrate to a depth of twelve to fifteen feet or more, with the auxiliary roots extending widely and horizontally from this so the soils not visible can contribute as much or far more to the nourishment of the vine than those nearer the surface; the water that the vine roots draw up is affected by the soils and substances through which it drains and runs before reaching the roots and, therefore, the soil content is one of the factors greatly affecting the quality of wine made from one patch, distinguishing it from that made almost alongside. In addition to the soil structure – which modern technology can often improve and knowledge of plant cultivation can assist by the processes of resting and replanting crops – there are the deposits of old vinestocks. It is obviously not possible to haul out every scrap of the roots when a vineyard is replanted and these contribute to the humus content of the soil.

What comes down from above, in terms of water, sunshine and the protective sprays and pesticides, is only of equal, not superior, importance to what comes up from below – water. The mineral deposits from the soil in this water affect the nourishment of the vine and, eventually, its fruit, just as diet affects the health of a human being.

The soils of the Alsace vineyard are very varied. They range from almost pure chalk to almost pure silex, with infinite permutations. This is because of the heaving and subsiding of the earth in this area in the far distant past.

About 600 million years ago, the mountains that are now the Vosges and the Black Forest thrust themselves up from the sea that then covered the whole of France. The Vosges are still mainly composed of what is known as the 'cristalline' and 'grèseuses' substances: the former is mainly granite, the latter a type of red sandstone (*grès rouge*) extremely useful as a building material because of its tightly packed composition. Then, gradually, the mountains became flooded once again, after having been covered with vegetation, traces of which remained even when seasonal plants and trees began. At the end of what is known as the secondary era, about 200 million years ago, the waters flowed back over the accumulations of the different soils on top of the basic substance, creating layers of many kinds, sandstone, limestone, marl, clay, chalk, pressing this all down on the foundation.

Then, in the tertiary period, about 60 million years ago, the mountains we know as the Alps were suddenly forced above the waters and, more gradually, the Vosges and Black Forest chains rose as well; but the section of land between these two big mountain ranges now subsided, leaving the high ground on either side permanently separating the two. This middle section was once more covered by the sea – so were the deposits that resulted from this recurrence of inundation. In the final phase of the settling down of the earth in this region, about a mere two million years ago, there was an age of ice, when glaciers covered the southern Vosges and, progressively, slid into the space they forced for themselves as they went down to the lower levels. When the ice melted, the deposits of these glaciers remained.

So it will be appreciated that what is Alsace today has been enriched over many millions of years by the folds formed by the rising and subsiding of the surface of the earth, by the deposits from pre-historic vegetation, seas and waters and the gradual erosion of the original rocks by rain, flood, ice, snow, all leaving traces behind them. In the Vosges foothills there is some loess, the fine, greyish-yellow loam deposited by rivers. There is chalk and limestone, good soil or subsoil for the types of vines that make fine, brisk white wines; granite that has been said to 'bleed into the vine' to remarkable effect – the schistous soils of vineyards as different as many of those of the Rhine, the Mosel, the port region of the Douro and the Dão area are, because of the contribution of this stone, of outstanding quality and character. Sand and gravel help drainage which clay can block; it is said with some truth that the vine 'likes to see the river, but not to get its feet wet'. This is why vineyards on the flat do not usually produce very fine wine and why a layer of clay high in the sub-soil can cause a vine's roots to get waterlogged. The minute but significant presence of many other deposits from prehistoric times, such as fossils, vegetative remains and minerals must not be forgotten; their presence, in a liquid largely consisting of water, as grapejuice is, can make the difference between an ordinary, albeit agreeable wine, and something exceptional.

DIAGRAM OF THE ALSACE VINEYARD

This diagram shows the different geological strata forming the Alsace vineyard and the Rhine flowing over all of them. It also indicates the Vosges and the Black Forest Mountains with their occasional outcrops of 'grès'

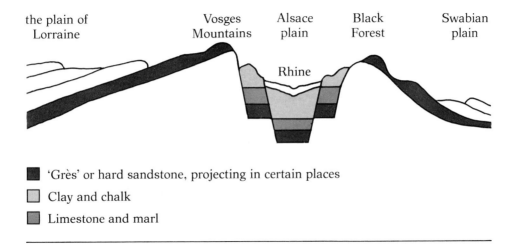

the plain of Lorraine — Vosges Mountains — Alsace plain — Black Forest — Swabian plain — Rhine

■ 'Grès' or hard sandstone, projecting in certain places

□ Clay and chalk

▨ Limestone and marl

The ribs of the Vosges foothills, sheltered from the worst rigours of the weather by the mountains themselves, extend mainly west to east towards the Rhine. This means that the majority of the vineyards face either directly south (if very fortunate), south-east and south-west. Even those with northern aspects are, these days, able to be assisted by the contours of the hills so that they are angled north-east, north-west, profiting by the slightest tilting of the terrain to enjoy more morning sun, more shelter, more contained warmth within a valley. Even on the flatter vineyards, verging on the Plaine d'Alsace, the vines can be so planted that they catch both light and warmth; anyone able to look down on a panorama of vines will see how the lines run along the contours of the landscape but are spaced and trained so that they profit to the full from the mini-climate of their particular plot. On the plain or flat they will be trained and pruned lower – to enjoy the shelter of the spot and not waste

19

Section of the Ammerschwihr vineyard, showing the different angles of the rows of vines according to the aspect and contours of the ground

growth on extending upwards. On slopes, the method behind the planting and training is intended to give the vines the maximum exposure to light (source of food for the leaves), sun to ripen the grapes and air, its circulation between the plants keeping them warm and free from any fungus diseases. It also makes sure they are sufficiently high above the earth to avoid any sudden chilling by frost.

THE GEOGRAPHICAL POSITION OF THE ALSACE VINEYARD

Two factors account for the unexpectedly dry climate: the west winds, blowing across France from the Atlantic, which are broken by the chain of the Vosges Mountains; and the sun which gives the vineyards on the slopes of the foothills the benefit of the first light and heat of the day

Look down, and see in the pattern of vines and vineyards the complexity that has directed some to be planted in straight lines, others sweeping round contours, some seemingly fanned out around a projection of land, rising in steep curves or wedged in blocks on little terraces or the crests of valleys. There is a reason for the precise positioning of each vinestock, whether this has been dictated by tradition – 'my great-grandfather always found that . . .' – or recent discoveries relating to soils, clones and the use of machines in the vineyard. (True, it is thought doubtful that mechanical harvesters will be able to work all the Alsace vineyards satisfactorily – but that was said about using tractors in them not so long ago!) Helicopters have a fairly limited use at present, mainly because of the fragmentation of holdings. Also, in many mountain regions, the currents of air can make this kind of flying difficult; they can be used for spraying but again, unless the patches of vineyard to undergo treatment are fairly extensive, the cost of putting them into operation is not always worthwhile. You will notice, in areas where they do work, that the vineyards are dilineated by conspicuous coloured metal tags at their boundries, to guide the pilots.

Essentially, the Alsace vineyard is a composite of little vineyard plots, owned, cultivated and picked by small proprietors; they may know the details of their holdings or they may merely trust in the worth of these, inherited from the past. Because of this and because of the variations in the composition of every chunk of soil on which the visitor may stand while surveying the vines, generalisations are impossible and unwise. But the wealth is both on the surface and below ground – impossible to assess and calculate exactly.

The Climate of the Vineyard

The climate of the Alsace vineyard is not exactly what might be expected by anyone looking at a map of the area. But it is mostly propitious to the vine and there are few years when total devastation by the weather occurs as it does in other, apparently milder, regions, where conditions do not generally indicate extremes of temperature.

The Vosges act as a protection against much torrential rain. Clouds may roll over from the west, but their arrival doesn't always signal rain. The sign to beware is when the Black Forest may be clearly seen on the German side of the Rhine, intensely blue with a touch of violet, almost mid-Mediterranean sea colour, while the high clouds whirl in grey-silver patterns above the Alsace vineyard like mother-of-pearl veils. . . this means rain. The day after such a view and such skies, the Rhine itself and certainly the outline of the Black Forest will be invisible and the Alsace foothills subjected to a downpour.

In general, however, the weather is fitted adequately around the year's cycle of the vine. There are seldom very hard winter frosts in the vineyards, so few tales of vines 'burnt' and destroyed in this way. True, M. Pierre Huglin has recorded two exceptions: in 1929 and 1956 (the year when the entire Chablis vineyard as well as other regions suffered appalling damage) the temperature dropped to minus 20°C. But usually the cold is no more than healthily so, benefiting the vineyard if it comes at a time when neither young shoots nor buds are at risk, and acting as a type of disinfectant to the soil. The risk of the spring frosts so much dreaded by vine growers, notably the mid-May 'Ice Saints' period (Sophid, Pancratius, Boniface, Servatius, whose feast days occur in the latter part of the month) does not present too great a threat in the Alsace vineyard. Hail, of course, can occur, but again it does not threaten the vines as much here as it can do in other French wine regions.

After Perpignan, Colmar, the centre of the Alsace wine region, enjoys the driest climate in the whole of France. The Alsace vintage usually begins around 20 October and growers benefit from there being few or no autumn rains. The average Alsace rainfall is about 500 mm per annum. From September to November the weather is usually dry, with the mild, often sunny days so favourable to the final ripening to perfection of the grapes. A slight drop in

Niedermorschwihr amid its vineyards – note the way in which these are angled to get maximum benefit from the sun

temperature at night after the pressing keeps the fresh must well under the control of the makers. This golden autumnal weather is conducive also to the leaving of some grapes on the vines until they may be picked after the ordinary harvest for the *vendange tardive* wines and, sometimes, to the formation of the 'noble rot' (*botrytis cinerea*) as the mists begin to rise from the warmed earth when the temperature goes down. This noble rot or *pourriture noble* – the expression in French – develops by means of a particular fungus forming on the grapes, which concentrates the juice inside each berry and causes the skins to shrivel. It must not be confused with ordinary rot – *pourriture grise* (grey rot) – which merely is ordinary rot and wholly undesirable. In Alsace the maturing of the grapes is a gradual process without any of the violent changes

Spiders' webs garlanding the vines in the early morning

in temperature, sudden storms and intensely hot weather that can, in some wine regions, either stop the fermentation in mid-vintage or ripen the grapes by almost scorching them, so that the juice is not always sufficient and the ultimate wine is hard, stiff, very slow to come round to agreeable drinking.

The vine likes the sun – at certain times. But it benefits most by warmth rather than excessive heat. The careful and strictly controlled use of chaptalisation (the adding of sugar to assist the working of the wine yeasts) is administered only by the sugar being dissolved in must, not water, on such occasions when it is necessary to bring the wine satisfactorily through the process of fermentation. It should be noted that there is a traditional difference between French and German practices. Control of the temperature in the fermentation vats is, likewise, a matter that is routine, even in the most traditional cellars in Alsace these days. But the crises that beset the growers and makers of many other classic vineyards are not too prevalent in this one. There are, of course, vintages of Alsace wines that are outstanding, vintages that are very good, good, and those that are highly acceptable if the wines can be marketed and drunk while fairly young. But, thanks to the natural advantages of this vineyard, there are, in recent times, few vintages that have been rained out, devastated by frost, destroyed by hail, or that have never fully ripened.

Ingersheim, with a heavy frost on the vines. This need not do harm providing the vegetation is not damaged

The micro-climates of Alsace are such that, even within a single village, wines of totally different styles may be made as the result of two or more quite different sorts of weather. Those who have never seen rain falling on one side of a road and not on the other find it hard to imagine – but in many wine regions it is not an unusual sight; one section of a vineyard may be affected by rain, frost or hail, while the section adjacent to it is completely untouched; the grapes from one or two rows of vines may be of outstanding quality, those in the next rows slightly less good. The angle at which the sun strikes the vines is of great importance, also when it does so: as most people know, when they are getting a tan, it is the morning sun that causes the skin to burn! On vineyards, the first sun of the day dries any night dew and gets the grapes thoroughly warm; later in the day the effect of the rays is not as efficacious. If warmed in the morning, grapes will remain so and it is the gentle, steady warmth they find more beneficial than sudden heat. The sun strikes the vineyards from the east for a large portion of the day – even more for such vineyards as enjoy a south-east aspect – and the more severe west winds blowing across France are checked by the ridge of the Vosges. Perhaps the vine grower is like any other farmer (and, in Alsace, he may well raise crops other than vines) and never wholly satisfied with weather conditions. But in Alsace there are, as far as the vineyard owners are concerned, probably fewer causes of complaint than elsewhere.

Strasbourg, La Petite France district. Renaissance houses on the banks of the canal

2

The History of the Alsace Vineyard

Alsace is rich in legends and a pleasant one relates to the presence of a large club on the arms of the city of Colmar. Hercules, it is said, during his various 'labours' or mighty feats of heroism and strength, came from Spain with the herd of red oxen taken from the triple-bodied monster, Geryon. He passed through Gaul, where he abolished human sacrifice and, crossing the Vosges, arrived in Alsace where Bacchus had already taught the locals how to make wine. Hot and weary, Hercules stopped at an inn for a drink – and drank deep, after which he fell asleep, waking only when the sun was low and his oxen had spread out over the plain. Rushing after them, he forgot his club, but the innkeeper put it away carefully, in case the hero should one day return for it. Treasured for centuries, it finally became a feature in the arms of Colmar.

The region has probably been inhabited for at least a million years. The prehistoric men who lived there ate the local fruits, berries, fished in the lakes and rivers and hunted the huge number of animals, traces of which have been found: lions, rhinos, hippos, bears, mammoths, many types of stag, aurochs and wild horses. These provided both food and clothing. But it was not until about 3500 BC that man began to make clearings in the forests and, with primitive instruments, cultivate the soil for the plantations of the grain crops then being introduced from the Middle East and the Mediterranean. There is unlikely to have been any cultivation of the vine at this date, however, although wild vines did grow in the foothills of the Vosges and there have been discoveries of fossilised grape pips dating from about 400,000 BC. It is possible that one of these vines, *vitis teutonica,* is an ancestor of *vitis vinifera,* the wine vine of today, and another has been proved to be *vitis silvestris,* a strain still found in the United States; this grew in the Bas-Rhin region, in the Forest of Sermersheim, south of Benfeld, until quite recent times.

The Romans developed viticulture to an advanced stage in many parts of Italy and their Empire – the wine ration was important for the legions, not only as a source of food and as a warming, cheering beverage, but as a disinfectant to any doubtful water supply; it was also a digestive, sedative, dressing for wounds and a tonic. However they did not enter Alsace until some time after the conquest of Gaul in 1217 BC. The region was then inhabited by a tribe called the Sequani who seem to have been peaceful peasants. They began to be harassed by the Aedui, a tribe in the south-west, where Burgundy is today and, so as to repel these attacks, the Sequani sent for help to the German chieftain, Ariovistus. He dealt effectively with the Aedui, but, like many in similar situations, decided to profit by the opportunity of settling in this attractive region. The Sequani this time appealed to Julius Caesar, who, advancing up the Rhône Valley and crossing the Jura Mountains, defeated the German tribes, driving them back across the Rhine after the Battle of Cernay in 58 BC. Caesar was immediately aware of the natural riches of Alsace, which he described as 'optimus totius Galliae' (the best of all Gaul) and the region enjoyed the benefit of a long period of peace under Roman rule. Argentoratum (Strasbourg) became the administrative centre; it was built on the River Ill, not the Rhine, because the latter tended to flood frequently and sometimes even altered its course.

The Romans brought peace and many of the practices of civilisation to Alsace and introduced a huge range of foodstuffs: Alsace author Lucien Sittler in *L'Agriculture et la Viticulture en Alsace* mentions that it was the Romans who first planted cabbages here, also celery, radishes, cucumbers, parsley, anis, cumin and various other spices and herbs, plus cherries, apricots, peaches, plums, chestnuts, almonds and the vine. Little is known about these first plantings of vines, but Roman settlers had developed the knowledge of viticulture to a considerable extent and, by the first century AD at least, Columella, who was born in southern Spain, wrote, in *De Re Rustica,* about all aspects of the vine and laying out a vineyard – so there were sources of information from comparatively early times.

By the second century AD vines were certainly planted on the foothills of the Vosges. There have been finds of pruning knives and viticultural equipment in the Palatinate, which, if one looks at the map, is seen as virtually another extension of the Alsace *Route du Vin.* The Roman villas established in Alsace were those of retired soldiers and civil servants. As with those discovered in other regions of the Roman Empire, their vineyards were only part of the system that made such establishments virtually self-sufficient; the work was done by slaves – although obviously the masters supervised the running of their properties. Freedmen and even Germans who had come across the Rhine took up residence. Pliny the Elder had affirmed that vines had been grown by the Sequani but whether they knew how to use the fruit for wine making is not certain; what is definite is that decorative motifs on remains of wall paintings show grapes.

Much is made in wine history of the Emperor Domitian's edict in AD 91 that all vines in Gaul should be uprooted. Some historians think that this was to avoid over-production, protect Italian wine and make sure that farmers did not plant vines in preference to the grains that were needed to feed – and keep quiet – the peoples under Roman rule. But the peasant is notably resistant to edicts that come from afar and may not be immediately or rigorously enforced; owners of villas and their surrounding estates might have been able to plead that they grew vines solely for their own domestic requirements; those in authority on the spot, who could benefit from the local wine, could have been tactfully blind to the continuation of the vine. In fact it is likely that the edict only applied to the plains where corn could be planted. It could not grow on the thinly soiled hillsides so vineyards were allowed – and even encouraged there. In any event, Alsace was a military area, important as a boundary province and perhaps the edict was not enforced here at all. Certainly, by the time that Emperor Probus (AD 276-82) revoked Domitian's decree, vineyards appear to have been well established; they probably followed Roman methods, being trained up trellises and this system continued in the north of Alsace until World War II.

By the middle of the fourth century, raiders from across the Rhine increasingly attacked the rich province and, although they were defeated at the Battle of Strasbourg by Emperor Julian in 357 and again in 378 by the joint-Emperor Gratian at Horbourg, the Roman Empire itself was partitioned in 395 and, gradually, the keepers of the peace left the province so that by the fifth century the Roman garrisons had abandoned the region. The Alemani came to conquer and, increasingly, settled in the area but they were themselves conquered by the Frankish King Clovis in 496. Christianity, introduced in the fourth century, increased in its influence and in the sixth century St Arbogast – whose shrine in the Forêt de Haguenau may still be seen – established it as the dominant religion. The church needed regular supplies of wine for religious use, also for the diet of the clergy and from this time many abbeys and convents were founded. The monastic orders contributed greatly to the cultural and educational life of the region. In addition to acting as cultivators of the soil, providing medical and geriatric care and providing hostels for travellers, the religious and lay brothers worked the vineyards but also employed a considerable number of people from outside the monastery, often paying them in food and wine. The Bishopric of Strasbourg was the biggest vineyard proprietor and there were many others of widely extending influence and great wealth.

In the eighth century Abbot Adam (whose tag is invariably 'the first Alsace man of letters') exclaimed in delight that 'Happy Alsace is blessed by Bacchus!' At this time there were 120 wine villages but in the next century there were 170. The pilgrims, especially the religious, not only brought news of discoveries and new methods for making better wine and improving conditions in the vineyards, but also acted as publicity officers for the local wine. A Swiss monk compared the Sigolsheim wine to the famous Falernian of Italy. Ermold Nigellus a homesick-sounding poet, exiled from Aquitaine, wrote a long poem in Latin describing Alsace and its inhabitants 'speaking a barbarous tongue' (German) and refers to 'vines covering the hills'. He also refers to the region by its present name, although this came into general use only in the seventh century, when it was briefly (640-740) a duchy.

The first mention of a form of the name 'Alsace' occurs about this time, in 610. The word 'Alesia' is thought to derive from 'Alisa', but some authorities suppose it to be a combination of the Latin 'Ali', meaning 'strangers', and 'Säss', which is old German for a resident. So the two together imply 'residents from outside the area'. Before this, inhabitants of the region were either referred to as 'Franks', to differentiate them from the Germans, or else were known as those who lived in the 'Pays de l'Ill', this river then dominating the area more than the Rhine. There may even be the possibility that these residents in the Pays de l'Ill were referred to as 'Illsäss'–hence, Alsace. But the matter is unlikely to be settled definitely one way or another.

The fact that many of the mother houses of the religious establishments were situated in other countries encouraged the export trade in wine. Many luxury items were brought from one country to another for the glory and enrichment of the big foundations and when Charles the Great, Charlemagne, became Emperor of the Holy Roman Empire in 800 his piety was propitious to the development of many of the activities of the church. Travelling and communication spread knowledge, as both religious and lay pilgrims enjoyed at least nominal protection throughout the regions through which they journeyed.

Charlemagne was definitely wine-minded. It is known that he made certain regulations in Burgundy and, in Germany, noting how some slopes escaped snow, he encouraged the planting of vines there. Unfortunately records have not survived regarding his influence on wine in Alsace, but in the ninth century one of the local bishops persuaded King Louis the Pious of France to allow all wine to travel duty-free – and a considerable export trade sprang up as the result of such cargoes being able to pass the various tax points along the Rhine and even further afield. This is when Italy, Germany in the north and east and even England began to drink 'Ossey' or, sometimes, 'Aussey', both red and white. The enormous cellars of the religious houses were certainly built to contain stocks that would have more than sufficed local demand: 'If the Rhine could not carry away the surplus of the vintage to the Friesians', commented Ermold Nigellus (the Aquitaine poet quoted earlier), 'the people of Alsace would absolutely drown in the richness of their production!' Another tale of the time runs about a Bishop of Strasbourg who, on Easter Day, found himself obliged to make a public confession before Mass to the effect that, having undertaken a comparative tasting of some of the local wines, he was suddenly compelled – by the wine, naturally – to make a pass at his housekeeper. . . .

The reputation of Alsace wine may well have been responsible for many ecclesiastical preferments, a well-timed gift to the Pope or perhaps a cardinal, proving profitable to the donor. And when, in 1048, the son of Hugh, Count of

The Eguisheim vineyard, with the 'three castles on one hill' above. Note the posts used for winching up and tightening the wires along which the vines are trained when the fruit weighs them down

Eguisheim, became Pope Leo IX, the region enjoyed both peace and prosperity. Pope Leo travelled widely in both France and Germany, consecrating numerous churches in Alsace and did much to check the slackness of religious observances and the abuses of those who held high office in the church. But in spite of this, succeeding years saw a rise in the power of the local nobility, who were to challenge the domination of the church. The Hohenstaufen emperors came to power in 1100 and this family name dates from the building of Haut-Koenigsbourg, which was first named 'Staufen' – rocky plateau – which became

'Estufin'. The Hohenstaufen capital was Haguenau, north of Strasbourg, which gave them easy control over their holdings. Other powerful families dominated their particular lands and built their castles. Both bishops and nobles were not only cultivators of vineyards – if necessary, they took up arms to protect them. Sometimes the prince-bishops fought the nobles, sometimes the mother houses of the religious establishments sent troops to combat any attempts to take over their holdings. Although Alsace was vulnerable to invaders, the population was too small to provide both an organised defence force as well as enough peasants and labour to work the land for the production of crops.

Towns, or rather cities, of substance began to be built: Haguenau, Colmar, Wissembourg, Sélestat, Ribeauvillé, Thann, Guebwiller, Molsheim, Saverne and many others. Here, during the period of comparative peace and prosperity, there was to arise a merchant class who indulged in sumptuous feasting that had previously been little known.

The great Alsace historian and man of letters, Monseigneur Médard Barth (1886-1976) illustrates the expansion of the vineyard between 800 and 1400. He calculated that, by 800, there were 109 wine villages in Alsace; by 900 there were 167, then, by 1400, 430. Interestingly, vines were planted in many regions that are now remote from the vineyards of today, particularly to the north of Strasbourg. It must not be forgotten that wine is a food as well as a drink and, certainly at this period, it was almost a necessity of life.

Then began the great expansion of trade in wine to foreign customers. About 1191 Bishop Geoffrey of Viterbo, chaplain to Emperor Frederick Barbarossa, wrote of Alsace that he knew of no other area in the world where there were so many vines, producing wine that was sent away as far as England and Denmark. The rivers acted as highways for much of this trade and when one looks at the shallow, sometimes slow-flowing currents of today, it is necessary to remind oneself of the chain of communications that they provided throughout Europe in former times, the Rhine linking the southern regions to the north coasts and the Baltic, and the Danube carrying cargoes from the east.

In England, King Edward III (1312-77) decreed that 'Rhenish wine', which then came mainly from Alsace, should not be kept in the same taverns as wine from Gascony, for the Vintners' Company had the rights of control over the wines of Bordeaux (with which Gascony was then included as being under the English crown), whereas the Steelyard was responsible for wines from the Rhine. In his *Chronicles*, Froissart (1333-1400) speaks of wines of Gascony, Aussey (? Alsace) and the Rhine being drunk in England. But all authorities are not of the same mind as regards this reference: André Simon (1877-1970), founder of the Wine & Food Society and a respected gastronomic writer, says in his *History of the Wine Trade in England* (1906), that he rejects the associations of 'Osey' with sorrel (*oseille*) made by one writer, also that of another who links 'Alesia, *vulgo Auxois*, with the article l'Aussois and l'Osoy'. He goes on to state that this 'corruption of Auxerre, or, as it is written in the old French, "Aucoirre" is 'easily disposed of', as the names are found cited together and in opposition to each other. He quotes a *fabliau* 'Le Sot Chevalier' (The Drunken Knight) in which the poet says he doesn't know whether a particular wine came from 'Auxerre or Aussai'. André Simon is convinced the 'Osoye or Oseye' 'was a Peninsular wine' and cites various references in which 'Osoye' is linked with Spain much as we might nowadays say 'Spain and Portugal'. But André Simon also mentions a reference in 'Le Domesday de Gippewys' in *The Black Book of the Admiralty,* where 'chescun tonel ou pipe de vin, vinegre, cicer, esyl' are included. It is doubtless a matter that will cause scholars to work over old texts for many years to come.

The big *entrepôts* for the exports of Alsace wine were Frankfurt and Cologne and the merchants there were preferred by the Alsace producers to the Swiss, who were not good payers. German wine merchants also bought from Alsace, having a large area of distribution, including Lubeck and London, where they had enjoyed official recognition for three centuries. The opening of the St Gotthard Pass in 1220 enabled an enormous volume of traffic to pass, including wine; the big 'fairs', then held in mid-winter, when people were less tied to agricultural pursuits, encouraged the meeting of many tradespeople and much dealing. But the Alsace wine business was already organised. Growers formed corporations in the villages and records were kept: the vintage of 1232 was as early as June 24, in 1337, 1339 and 1364 there were plagues of grasshoppers.

In 1361 the Emperor Charles IV granted the right of free shipment on the Rhine to the merchants of Colmar and in consequence the Ladhof, the town's port on the River Ill, became extremely important: other merchants had to pay a tax, called the 'weingeld' on all wine that was shipped there. The town collected this and records dating from the end of the fourteenth century show that it brought in more than the total of all the other taxes contributing to its revenue at that time.

The developing wine trade had a whole series of officials, appointed by the various municipalities. For example, in Colmar the most important were the *gourmets,* who had to be present at every transaction involving wine. For their services they were paid a flat fee, half of this coming from the person selling, half from the purchaser. Basically, they had four tasks: first, they set up all the dealings in wine and fixed the prices. Second, they oversaw the quality of all wines and had the power to inflict punishment for fraudulent practices. Third, they collected the wine taxes for the town. Fourth, they were forbidden to trade in wine on their own account and were not allowed to leave the town to buy wine for their customers.

Then there were the coopers, responsible for racking the wine and for repairing wine casks. They also had to inform the *gourmets* if they thought that there was anything the matter with any of the wines they had to handle.

The wine porters saw to the loading of customers' wagons with wines from growers' cellars and the unloading of wine into the cellars of the buyer. They had to taste each wine and, if it was unsatisfactory, they were obliged to refuse to handle it. In addition, they had to check that casks were of the correct size.

The wine loaders were solely responsible for the loading of wagons going to foreign markets that could not be reached by boat. In practice, this particularly referred to the south German duchies and to parts of Switzerland. As the rôle of the wine loaders was similar to that of the wine porters, there were several disputes as to where one job ended and the other began – there is a familiar ring about accounts of this sort! – and at the end of the eighteenth century the local magistrates once again had to draw up a set of clear definitions of the separate duties of each body of workers.

Finally, there were the tighteners – *tendeurs*. Their main function was to see that the wagons were correctly loaded and secured with ropes. As all these men were employees of the town, relying on the fees they received for their income, it may be seen that business was good, in order to justify the considerable sums involved.

In fact wine became big business. In 1431 there was such a glut of it that the growers, running out of casks or any receptacles in which to store it, had to pour much away, though at Thann surplus wine was used to mix the mortar for building. An empty cask would pay, or be exchanged, for a full one, sometimes even three of old wine being given for an empty barrel. Wine could not, of course, be kept for very long without deteriorating, as air in the cask, quite apart from any infections, would cause it to break up or become sour within about a year of its vintage. It is not recorded what remedial action, if any, was taken in the winter of 1407-8, when the weather was so severe that the Rhine froze over and the wine in many cellars also became ice. But to anyone coming to the region the country must have seemed wondrously abundant in wine.

The part played by the local inns is of particular importance – today, anyone seeing the buildings of those that have survived from medieval times will be impressed by their size and solidity; they were very much founded on wine, even if it wasn't mixed into the actual building materials!

Regulations controlling the inns were surprisingly strict, necessarily so because, although a high proportion of the annual production of wine did go for export, far more was drunk on the spot. Colmar, Turckheim, Sélestat and Obernai were at this time imperial cities, responsible only to the Emperor of the Holy Roman Empire; in fact this meant that each was virtually a small republic, able to make its own laws and levy its own taxes. Strasbourg was a free city, paying no taxes to the Emperor; Ribeauvillé, Dambach, Guebwiller and about forty other towns were 'seigneurial cities', paying taxes both to their immediate masters as well as to the Emperor.

Many of the regulations applying to inns were similar to those of our own time: specific opening hours, defined profit margins and prohibition as to the

Colmar. Fifteenth- and sixteenth-century houses and arcades carefully preserved and still in use

harbouring of girls of evil repute. But some controls seem strange. For example, the innkeepers were the only people who had the right to pay for goods or services in wine, be the wine in cask, bowl or bottle – although the type of bottle used at this period was more in the nature of what would now be known as a carafe. This was important in an area where it had been usual, for centuries, to pay for goods and services 'in kind' within the agricultural communities. Nor were the innkeepers permitted to keep a wine of inferior quality for staff consumption – this had to be the same as that on sale to customers. Each inn employed criers, who went about the town announcing when a new cask of wine was going to be broached – the new wine was, of course, better than one that might have been exposed to the atmosphere for some while. These criers might only be employed by one inn at a time and were forbidden to shout their news in front of rival establishments, for the sake of keeping the peace. If, however, somebody asked a crier the whereabouts of the best wine – which the man was bound to know – then it was allowed to whisper the information into the inquirer's ear.

Within the inns the wine was, of course, drawn from the cask as required. Only one specified quality might be served and sold at one time – nobody was going to risk running out of the most popular wines, which might occur if several casks were broached and, once open, left to deteriorate. Pewter drinking vessels were used, at least until the fifteenth century, when bottles and glasses begin to be mentioned. It is possible to get an idea of how much was drunk, because the records of the 'Wagkeller', the most aristocratic type of club existing at this time, records an average consumption of slightly more than a litre a head at the regular Sunday lunches. (In fact, for anyone accustomed to wine drinking, this is not excessive at a meal that would certainly have lasted for many hours.)

The innkeepers formed their own guild, the *Winlute,* probably in the four-teenth century and in 1462, they bought a building known as 'The Giant' in Colmar; as a result, their association became known generally by this name. In 1518 the guild formed by the coopers decided to amalgamate with that of the innkeepers, thereby increasing the membership from thirty-three to sixty-seven. But this guild, together with all similar guilds and trade associations, was abolished in the French Revolution at the end of the eighteenth century.

The wine growers also had their own guild or association, one of the most important and influential. By 1554, 222 were members of this guild, out of a total of 955 liverymen in Colmar; the Master, elected each year by the members, was an ex-officio member of the town council. This association was definitely powerful: in 1427 someone who described the growers as 'spiteful chatterboxes' was banished to the other side of the Black Forest. The growers had another important rôle; they appointed *bangardes,* who were watchmen, to patrol the gardens and vineyards of the town, so as to protect these plantations against damage both by straying cattle and actual theft. Two men who stole grapes in

1661 were sentenced to be thrown into the town moat, while the *bangardes* received a reward for catching the thieves.

The vintners, as might be expected, owned vineyards, as did the other guilds, and these holdings were in what were then the suburbs of Colmar. However, both the tailors' and cobblers' guilds had even more extensive vineyards.

The reputation of Alsace wines remained high. Montaigne, who visited the region in 1584, noted 'the beautiful and extensive plain, bordered on the left by slopes covered with vines'. Ecclesiastics, nobility and even the smallholders were all apparently set on a course leading to prosperity via their vines and wines.

Yet, from the beginning of the sixteenth century, export sales began to decline. There were several reasons for this. In 1439 and 1444-5 plundering bands of Armagnacs had invaded; there was a great freeze in 1480, followed, when the thaw came, by a terrible flooding of the Rhine, villages being swept away, men and beasts drowned. In 1487-8 there was a frost lasting from early November until April, with consequent destruction of many vines. The 1539 vintage was gigantic – but one vintage alone was not enough to compensate for the earlier damage and depredations. Nor did the policy of those controlling the wine trade always assist, long-term, its expansion in export markets.

The power of the Emperor was declining and, in order to become stronger and to obtain more land, the local nobility needed money. Imposing customs duties seemed a logical step and, at one period, between Strasbourg and Cologne there were sixty-two points where dues were collected. This of course put up the ultimate price of the wine to the eventual buyer. Meanwhile, other wine regions were extending their export business and providing competition. The importance of Strasbourg as a centre of the wine trade declined when it became obligatory for all the wine of the Alsace region to pass through this town – and pay a duty; in addition, a proportion of the wine so shipped had to be sold to the town for the use of the inhabitants, and at a price fixed by the town – a price that often showed no profit for the owners. This short-sighted policy resulted in the creation of new wine markets on the Rhine at Mainz and Worms, both of them more convenient for the traditional buyers coming from Frankfurt and Cologne.

Yet exports still penetrated foreign markets. In his *Weltbuch* of 1534, Sébastien Franck wrote: 'You would be amazed at the fertility and the heavenly endowment of this country, which not only provides nourishment for its own population, but enables almost the entire world to drink its wine... Among those delighting in its wine are the Bavarians, the Swabians, the Dutch, England, Spain and other nations.' In 1576 Nicholas de Bollwiller mentions the despatch of wine to England and in one of the early text-books on wine, *De naturali vinorum hostoria* by Andreas Baccius, which appeared in 1596, the wines of Alsace were cited as having been sent to customers in Switzerland,

Swabia, Bavaria, Lorraine, Imperial Germany '. . . quandoquam etiam in Anglicam' (and sometimes also to England).

The Reformation had an effect on the wine trade that could not have been anticipated. Many monastic foundations began to lose interest in making quality wines, so useful for presenting to influential officers of the church and even the Pope. Alsace, it is important to remember, was neither Catholic nor Protestant, each town, even each village taking its religion from the local lord – *cuius regio, cuius religio* (whoever's the boss fixes the religion). Thus Riquewihr, in the territory belonging to the Duke of Würrtemburg, was Protestant, while neighbouring Ribeauvillé, belonging to the Ribeaupierre family, was Catholic.

But the most appalling of all the disasters Alsace was ever to endure occurred with the Thirty Years War (1619-48). The region was overrun by various armies and companies of totally brutal men, intent only on pillage: mercenaries from southern and central Europe, Spaniards, bands of deserters from Lorraine and the French forces passed and repassed in the formerly peaceful countryside. They burned both houses and farm buildings, slew or carried off the animals and the tortures they inflicted on such wretched human beings as they were able to find were horrific.

Because the marauders ranged far and wide, many people abandoned their holdings in the country and took refuge in the towns, especially Strasbourg, where, simply because of being gathered together in numbers within walls that could be defended, they were less at risk. Others went into the depths of the forests, where they lived on roots and wild plants. There could be no question of working the vines in a regular fashion; by 1631 the formerly thriving vineyard area around Ribeauvillé had declined to half its previous extent and, even where the vines could still be tended, the growers lacked food to keep themselves fit for work, seeds to plant and animals to work the land. It was to take over half a century to effect the rehabilitation of the area and, as the population had declined so much, the available work force was inadequate even after the Treaty of Westphalia which put an end to the fighting.

The devastation of war was increased by outbreaks of pestilence, whole villages often being wiped out by plagues. The great famine of 1636 is described in apalling detail in a history of Thann: 'The wretched people fall on dead bodies and devour them . . . some even kill and eat their own children. For a small roll, anyone would give you an entire vinestock, with the grapes ripe on it. Anyone showing he had a proper loaf of bread would be attacked by twenty or thirty people desperate to get hold of it.' More than twenty villages completely disappeared, houses fell down, churches and religious establishments were destroyed, pillaged, the church bells sold; at least one-third and possibly as much as half the entire population, in all classes of society, simply disappeared. In 1643 a Swiss Benedictine noted that, in travelling from Strasbourg to Rouffach, there wasn't a single human being in any village he passed; the population of other villages might be in single figures.

Gradually the vineyards began to be worked once again and wine made, but the drop in the population made improvement difficult. Owners had disappeared, often no one knew to whom land belonged. A policy of encouraging settlers from neighbouring countries was put into operation and, in 1662, a royal decree stated that anyone owning land had to claim title to their property within three months; any land not being cultivated by the end of this time was thereafter to be given to the various immigrants. At this time settlers arrived from Switzerland, the Tyrol, the Vorarlberg, Lorraine and even from Picardy, the often strange-sounding 'foreign' names often remaining to this day in the different regions in which they made their homes. Around 1650 the population of Alsace had dropped to only about 250,000, but by 1750 it was 540,000 and by the end of the century more than 700,000.

Switzerland offered prospects for the reviving export trade in wine but after a mere two years the merchants of Lucerne complained that wine sent to them from Colmar was not of the requisite quality. As a result, a formula was evolved whereby casks were to be officially sealed in Colmar and supplied with documents guaranteeing the quality of their contents. There appear to have been some dishonest brokers and carriers, however, for in the autumn of 1651 a letter sent from Colmar warns the Swiss merchants to beware of adulterated wine and nine years after this there was a further spate of correspondence, concerning wine arriving without the necessary accompanying documents.

Northern export markets were declining. Tolls on the Rhine continued to increase and much of the wine bought by the merchants of Frankfurt was now used for blending with inferior German wines. Strasbourg lost its supremacy in the wine trade and has never regained it: in the century and a half from 1537 the corporation of the city's wine brokers and merchants declined in numbers by almost a half.

The new immigrants, too, were not always able to make such a contribution to the Alsace wine trade as had been hoped for. Many of them, although they came from wine-growing regions, had not been accustomed to producing quality wines; many vineyards were now laid out on the plain. Quality declined. The situation was grave. A decree put on the statute book on 16 March 1731 was entitled 'Decree of the Council of State which forbids the planting of vines in Alsace without permission, which will only be given if the land is not suitable for other plants'. Although this statement is often cited as evidence of a measure aimed at maintaining the quality of the wines, a reading of the preamble shows that this was not primarily so: it was designed to liberate land for planting grain, also to protect such growers who had their vineyards planted on the slopes 'who gain no reward for their labours'.

Yet it is at this uncertain period, after the Thirty Years War, that many of the families now so well known and established in the wine trade first set up in business. In 1639 H.U. Hugel became a freeman of the town of Riquewihr; the Humbrecht family became vine growers in 1658, the Kuehns in 1675;

Balthazard-Georges Dopff, who was born in 1667, was the first of his family to join the wine trade, though he was a master cooper. Specific grape varieties began to be named. Muscat had been recorded in 1523, Kitterlé, Traminer, Clevner in the late sixteenth century, Tokay in 1750. A great deal of red wine was still being made, sometimes – which may surprise the present-day reader – being referred to as *Sang des Turcs* (Turks' blood): the people of Alsace, like many others in wine regions, have very long memories. The ordinary person in the streets of Colmar may not be able to give the date when Baron Lazare de Schwendi and his Alsace mercenaries went to assist the inhabitants of Tokay, defending their town against the Turks, but they will know of his statue, holding up a vinestock (presumed to be a specimen of Tokay brought back from Hungary), showing him in sixteenth-century dress. It is not, in the world of wine, such a long time ago. In the eighteenth century it would have seemed comparatively recent.

In 1766 a decree defined the viticultural area of Alsace and encouraged replantings on the slopes. At the same time it recommended the uprooting of such vine varieties as could not yield quality wine. But although the region of Alsace was not subject to many of the frightful deprivations and social depression as were other French provinces, the time of great unrest was approaching.

The Château des Rohan at Strasbourg, built in 1704 by the Prince-Bishop, according to plans by Robert de Cotte, the royal architect, on the banks of the River Ill

The eighteenth century Château de Saverne, built from the local 'grès rouge'. Former seat of the Prince-Bishops of Strasbourg, it is now a museum

Arthur Young (1741-1820), the English agriculturalist and writer on many aspects of the subject, travelled in France in 1789. He commented that, in Saverne 'I found myself to all appearance virtually in Germany . . . not one person in a hundred has a word of French; the rooms are warmed by stoves; the kitchen hearth is three or four feet high and various other trifles show that you are amongst another people.' He reiterates his astonishment at how different Alsace seemed from the France he had passed through on the other side of the Vosges. On the way to Strasbourg he passed through 'one of the richest scenes of soil and cultivation to be met with in France', although when he arrived he found the place in tumult: 'a detachment of horse, with their trumpets on one side, a party of infantry, with their drums beating on the other, and a great mob hallooing'. Everyone was excited at the news and rumours of the Revolution in Paris. Young went on to Schkestadt (Sélestat) where 'all in this country is German; the inns have one common large room, many tables and cloths already spread, where every company dines; gentry at some, and the poor at others. Cookery also German: *Schnidst* is a dish of bacon and fried pears; has the appearance of a mess for the devil; but I was surprised, on tasting, to find it better than passable.' In spite of recurrent revolutionary demonstrations, Young continued his journey with considerable courage and frequent displays of English *sang-froid* and, when summing up his impressions in *Travels in France* he says that certain regions, in which he includes Alsace, 'are cultivated more like gardens than farms ... These are provinces which even an English farmer might visit with advantage.'

The stirring French National Anthem the 'Marseillaise' was first heard in Strasbourg, as the result of a musical evening and plenty of wine – only Champagne is mentioned in the accounts of the event, but Alsace must also have been served, for the place was the house of the Mayor of Strasbourg, Baron Frédéric de Dietrich. Dietrich had a fine voice, played the violin and his wife the harpsichord; his sons went into the army, one of them leading a volunteer battalion known as the 'Enfants de la Patrie'. To the Dietrich's house came a young soldier-composer, Claude Joseph Rouget de Lisle (1760-1836), born in the Jura, not particularly successful in the army, and no more so in his attempts to compose songs and lyrics for operettas. For the celebrations attending the promulgation of the constitution of Strasbourg, in 1791, Dietrich asked Rouget de Lisle to contribute a song, his 'Hymn to Liberty', which was publicly performed and much applauded. By April 1792 war had been declared in Paris and a recruiting poster appeared on some Strasbourg walls, urging 'To arms, citizens!' Rouget de Lisle attended a gathering – predominantly male and military – at the Dietrichs, where the Mayor said he regretted that, so far, all the soldiers of the new era had to march to was the revolutionary song 'Ça ira!', which is not only a rather quick step for a march but also somewhat banal. Rouget, asked to compose something more effective, said he would try – and the following evening showed the result to the Dietrichs. The Mayor, accompanied by his wife, used his fine tenor to give the first public performance of 'The War Song of the Rhine Army'; it was received with wild applause – few can hear it without feeling their blood stirred – and, the following Sunday, it was played again in public, by the Strasbourg National Guard, for a ceremonial entry of a battalion of volunteers from the Saône-et-Loire. The song flamed through the ranks of all who heard it, even a Prussian referring to their French opponents singing 'that terrible song'. The song did not get its name 'The Marseillaise' until a battalion from Marseilles entered Paris, singing it. The ever-unlucky Rouget de Lisle heard it when, still not able to make his mark in any of the worlds he wished to conquer, the people of Paris began to sing it after the Legislative Assembly had summoned volunteers to the capital. It brought him no luck – he was imprisoned for being a royalist and ended his days living on friends' charity – and Mayor Dietrich went to the guillotine.

Alsace has a strong line of military men – Kléber (Strasbourg), Lefebvre (Rouffach), Rapp (Colmar), Kellerman (Strasbourg), Ney ('Bravest of the brave' from Sarrelouis) – whose names are commemorated on many streets, squares and public places. So it is not surprising that, from this province, French armies went off on various ventures into Europe in the Napoleonic wars. The region became at this time a vast military encampment as far as the towns and cities were concerned – and the farmers saw that there was much profit to be made from supplying the needs of the troops. At the beginning of the nineteenth century the area under vines increased by one-third but, as the military man would swill down virtually anything, these plantings consisted mainly of inferior vines, with the Burger predominating.

The French Revolution had an important overall and long-term effect on viticulture in Alsace. The property of the nobility and the church foundations came onto the market and the fragmentation of ownership of bits of vineyards increased. The large viticultural domaine disappeared and the peasant proprietor became newly important – whether or not he knew what to do with his recently acquired holding. When the sales of the once big estates started in December 1790 the religious authorities, who still exercised some influence, albeit often from afar, forbade Catholics to bid; this meant that much of the land the church had held passed into the hands of Protestants, Jews (who always enjoyed freedom of both worship and the right to trade in the region – hence so many 'à la Juive' recipes in the cookery books), and the atheist or agnostic middle-class bourgeoisie from the towns. Because of the famous *Code Napoléon,* which regulates the way in which property in France must be left within the family of the testator, the splitting up of the holdings became extremely complicated – and the way in which the vineyards could be run was inevitably wasteful as regards effort and such equipment as might be employed. In 1852 the prosecutor of the Court of Appeal in Colmar could say (with feeling) 'Alsace is rich in the fertility of its soil, but it is poor because its properties are so split-up'.

Another result of the Revolution was a decree that abolished all trade associations, including the guilds of Strasbourg and Colmar. Freedom was given to 'each person to carry on such business or pursue such profession, art or craft as he thinks fit'. All very well – until people found that they had to manage on their own, for good or ill. It was one of the high-sounding theories that does not always stand up in practice.

But for agriculture the nineteenth century started in Alsace as a period of great expansion, the area under grain and potatoes rapidly increasing. The vineyard area increased too: 24,000 hectares in 1808, 30,000 hectares in 1828. The greater part of these increased plantations were, however, still on the flatter vineyards of the plain. The first plantation of hops by Derindinger, the Haguenau brewer, was made in 1805 and the production of beer in Alsace subsequently became enormous: Strasbourg was soon one of the great brewing cities of the world, rivalling Munich, Pilsen and Burton-on-Trent.

Unfortunately, viticulture did not really progress. In 1821 the French government imposed a high rate of customs duty both on importations of cattle and of wine and, in 1826, the German states retaliated, thereby virtually closing their gates to any possible imports from Alsace. In 1850 the Swiss followed suit, accentuating the problems of the Alsace growers. In less than thirty years the price of their wine fell by more than 80 per cent. At the same time, the situation was aggravated by the extended plantations of vines throughout Germany – particularly across the Rhine in Baden.

The Swiss also increased their production of wine. Some of the Alsace growers had ideas as to how sales of their wines might be increased, including the suggestion for setting up a wine market in Colmar, and for various promotional efforts to be carried out in Belgium, Holland and France in particular, where the wines of Alsace were not much known. Unfortunately nothing came of these notions.

Although the wine makers had enjoyed prosperity during wars – for soldiers always require something to drink – they had perhaps concentrated too much on quantity rather than quality; in about 1850 Dr J.L. Stoltz stated that the grape 'petit meilleux ou Knipperlé' accounted for four-fifths of the total crop. At the same time there was a drift to the towns and cities, where, with the rise of industry, jobs were available for many who had previously remained on the land.

The Traminer, first mentioned in 1551, the 'Rissling' (not to be confused with the other name for the Knipperlé, Petit Raeuschling), the Kleber or Clevner and a few other varieties were now augmented. The Sylvaner was brought from Austria, plantations of Riesling were increased and the red wines of the region were popular – Dr J. Guyot, who evolved the method of pruning and training that bears his name in the middle of the century, mentioned a number of these. There seem to have been many good vintages at the beginning of the century, including the 'Comet year' of 1811, in which fine wines were made in many regions of Europe; in Alsace it was recorded as the 'vintage of the century', an example of how excitement and the writing up of a vintage is nothing new. There were, of course, also indifferent or poor vintages, spring frosts, damage by various pests. But far worse plagues were to come: in the 1850s–60s oïdium (powdery mildew) struck the French vineyards and did fearful damage before it was discovered how spraying with a sulphur solution could protect the vines. In the late 1860s, the aphis *phylloxera vastatrix* began to destroy the roots in almost all wine regions of Europe. Once it gets into the soil it is virtually impossible to get rid of, unless the area is flooded. Alsace began to be afflicted in 1876 and it was only after many different remedies had been tried and failed that the grafting of native vines onto aphis-resistant American rootstocks enabled the vineyards to continue. They did not truly revive until towards the end of the nineteenth century.

When, after the Franco-Prussian War (1870-1) Alsace and some of Lorraine became part of Germany – remaining under this rule for nearly half a century – many thought that, as far as wine was concerned, this annexation might be an

Haut-Koenigsbourg, with a
breath-taking panorama over
the plain and the Rhine

advantage. The Germans required more wine than they could make, they liked the general style of Alsace wines and their well-organised wine trade might, it was hoped, be of assistance to the small growers of Alsace. Unfortunately the absence of an established commercial wine trade organisation in Alsace and no big estates or famous properties to create publicity was a serious handicap; as Joseph Dreyer says: 'Furthermore, the clash of personalities between the Alsatians and the Germans was irreconcilable. Each of the new partners found the others' wine of inferior quality and did not hesitate to say so – with the difference, however, that the German was the buyer and the Alsatian the seller.' And although Alsace wine was probably no worse than that of Germany at the time, it was not well known among the potential consumers in the conquering country.

As well as the oïdium and phylloxera plagues, the grubs of cochylis and eudemis afflicted the vineyards. As a result, at the end of the century, they caused the average production to fall as low as 6.2 hectolitres per hectare. To get an idea of the magnitude of this disaster, the production of Alsace vineyards in 1973 was well over a hundred hectolitres per hectare.

Confronted with so many difficulties and threatened with the possible total destruction of their vineyards by phylloxera many growers wanted to follow the wise example of growers in Bordeaux, Burgundy and other wine regions, by replacing the damaged and dying vines with vines that had been grafted onto aphis-resistant American rootstocks. Others, understandably, sought to solve the problem by trying to find vines that would yield the maximum amount of wine for the minimum overheads; this group was supported by the Germans, who had, at this period, prohibited the planting of grafted vines. This solution was supported by Chrétien Oberlin, the very great Alsace ampelographer, whose name is perpetuated by the wine institute in Colmar; his contribution to Alsace viniculture and viticulture is outstanding. He was born in 1831 in Beblenheim. After many difficulties he established an oenological station at Rouffach in 1893 and gave to this institution his own collection of more than 500 different varieties of vines on which he had been working for many years. The Colmar wine institute, named after him, was set up by him in 1897.

It is usually difficult to convince any farmer of the advisability of making sudden and radical changes in his methods; even any modification of 'what was done in my grandfather's day' is usually only achieved with an effort. Sometimes, in the history of phylloxera and the attempts to cope with it, wine growers seem to have been prepared to try everything short of witchcraft. Some farmers obviously gave up and either sold their land – to the subsequent profit of those who were able to buy up holdings cheaply at this time of disaster, such as occurred in the history of Schlumberger – or else they would only grudgingly attempt to replant with grafted vines when they had already come to the verge of ruin. Some, of course, were able to keep going because they were farming crops other than vines.

A British traveller who explored the Vosges in the early 1890s goes into considerable detail about the vast quantities of wine the ordinary Alsace inhabitant required: 'To see a double litre placed upon the table before a thirsty man is nothing unususal . . . their consumption of wine, which stands per head – man, woman and child – at the largish figure of one hectolitre per annum, that is, about ninety quarts – and lands the population in this economical paradox that, although the largest wine-producing country in Germany, Alsace actually does not produce enough wine to cover its own wants, but is driven to import . . . The Germans say that all this bibulousness is the consequence of past incorporation with France. You might as soon carry coals to Newcastle as try to sell Alsatian wine to the French. And you could not formerly export it into Germany, because there was the impassable customs barrier. So the people were compelled to drink the wine, simply to get rid of it . . . labourers, servants, sempstresses, all alike were given wine . . . as part of their wages. Two litres a day for a maid, I am told, is nothing uncommon. And for men, seven to eight litres a day.' He tells a tale of a man from Ammerschwihr who related that, at harvest time, the workers consumed twelve litres a day (in addition to spirits) and took another litre to bed, 'in order not to be dry in the night'! The daily ration of wine issued to vineyard workers at vintage time or, indeed, to the permanent staff of a wine establishment is an accepted convention and it is still followed in many wine areas today.

The same writer describes the sort of wine the workers drank as sour and often being 'in a state of revived fermentation' – somewhat fizzy, which he says occurs during the first three or four years of the wine's life in June or July, when the vines flower. In a visit to M. Oberlin, the traveller writes charmingly about being taken round the vine 'nursery', being shown the methods of training and pruning and being informed about the 'watchers' employed in each wine village to look out for any signs of phylloxera: 'The Prussian Government after their wont have taken very prompt and effective measures for dealing with the foe. The organisation of anything resembling a police-force is to them a congenial task. And their phylloxera police is quite as well manipulated as that which needlessly molests innocent travellers.' When anything suspicious was reported: 'M. Oberlin, entrusted with the honorary inspectorate-general, conscientiously himself repairs to the spot, if that be possible.' If the presence of phylloxera were confirmed, the entire parish was 'proscribed', the vines pulled up, although the vineyard owner was given monetary compensation.

At M. Oberlin's 'hospitable table' there was a progressive tasting, much as may occur today, including a 'syrupy "ladies wine", the *vin paille,* for making which the grapes are kept on straw, carefully turned from time to time, till March, and then pressed. I observed a peculiar practice around Colmar, where people like drinking their wine pure. They buy the produce of a vineyard on the vines, gather it by their own men, and have it pressed in their own houses with hired presses, which make the rounds.'

(This fashion for 'buying at source' has its counterpart in the 'cellar door sales' of today, but the additional and slightly show-off buying 'sur souche' (literally 'on the vinestock'– i.e. on spec, before the crop is picked) is in present times a practice restricted to the shipper; nor does he now make use of his own labour and the service of ambulant presses. One can imagine, however, the snobbism of someone in the nineteenth century offering guests 'a little wine made by the personnel from a likely vineyard I picked out last summer–I've usually found that plot yields sound grapes'.) At this time, it should be remembered, the average household would fetch wines up from the cellar direct from the cask for most domestic consumption; only the finest wines would be bottled and reserved for special occasions. Thanks to its favourable situation and the formerly abundant production, Alsace does not appear to have been actually deprived of wine during the various plagues, even though quality certainly suffered.

At the time of this traveller's visit Oberlin had about a thousand vines, from all over the world. By crossing, he was trying to produce 'a plant which shall be phylloxera-proof . . . The mischief is that their (American) grapes all taste "foxy" – that is, they have a flavour of black currants. The Canadian varieties are . . . the least objectionable . . . Another problem is, to produce a wine red by nature and requiring no whortleberries or chemicals to colour it. There is a vine which produces naturally red juice – the *teinturier* – of neutral taste . . . And so M. Oberlin goes on experimenting, and raising hybrids after hybrids.' The visitor had a somewhat naïve idea about wine and vines, but was accurate in what he obviously noted down on the spot and his account shows the amazing progress of wine making and vine growing within what is little more than a lifetime, for there are still those in Alsace, notably the authority M. Fernand Ortlieb, who remember knowing Oberlin quite well in their childhood. Chrétien Oberlin died in 1916.

Dr Kalisch, the German principal of the Viticultural Research Centre in Colmar, advised against the cultivation of hybrids, but the hybridists prevailed – those aiming at quantity overcame the lovers of quality, not for the first time. Indeed, when growers returned to put their vineyards in order after the end of World War I, it seemed as if the hybridists had been right, because these vines had survived the war years of inattention, whereas the traditional vines were nearly all destroyed by disease. It was not until the overall outstanding vintage of 1921 that the failings of the hybrids were shown up, for their producers could not sell wines made from them on a French market already glutted with mediocre wines from grafted vines, while those who had kept to the traditional varieties then made a wine generally recognised as excellent.

Although Alsace became part of France after World War I, the problems were again enormous: an American writing about the region during the war, called Alsace-Lorraine 'The Land of Unshed Tears'. This lover of Alsace was not very wine-wise, for he seems to confuse Alsace with Moselle on one page and to praise the bouquet of the white wines which 'The great Liebig' affirmed was due to 'the free acid', also he states that many other qualities arise from 'the percentage of tartar pressings', and that 'another great advantage is the almost total absence of brandy, an ingredient invariably found in the wines of Spain and Sicily'.

This reference to 'brandied wines' may puzzle many of today's drinkers, but there are two possible explanations of the writer's error. In this last reference, he may be thinking solely of sherry and Marsala, both of them what Britons refer to as 'fortified wines' – wines made 'stronger' in alcoholic content by the addition of brandy. (The term is unfamiliar in France and EEC countries, where other phrases are in use for these sorts of wines.) Or there may be a reasonable misunderstanding about the alcoholic strength of the wines of Spain and Sicily which, in many instances, do attain high alcoholic strength quite naturally, simply by reason of the generally warmer climate of the vineyards; such wines, to the unaccustomed, might be more immediately registered as 'strong', whereas the traveller would have found the Alsace wines less taxing to drink in quantity.

The reference to 'tartar pressings' is interesting to anyone who has been able to inspect the inside of an old Alsace cask or segment of a cask and seen the huge accumulations of incrustations of tartrates glittering like crystals on the wood.

There are, however, some obviously affectionate descriptions: wine, says the American traveller, is referred to by the peasants as 'the soup of September' and he quotes a saying that at vintage time 'The Virgin unwinds her distaff and spreads the golden threads upon Alsace'. There is also an account of a night scene during a vintage, somewhere near Colmar, with men straining to push at 'the capstan beam which controls the screw of the press' and 'strangely-shaped vessels of wood named "tandelins" ' used to carry the must down to the cellars. The place visited had miles of cellars in the 'tufa' of the hillsides, full of 'great casks of still and sparkling wines'. Perhaps most pertinent is an account of a village fête at Eguisheim before 1914, where the police alone were empowered to permit the festivities to begin – but only when they were satisfied that no French tricolour, even on a bon-bon or wrapper for a cake, was on view and that the German flag was hoisted to fly above all others.

I have never been able to trace the whereabouts of these miles of cellars in the hillsides, but perhaps the visitor had been given a series of samples of wine to taste and received an exaggerated idea of the size of a subterranean cellar. The world 'tufa' today is usually found in relation to the slopes on the banks of the Loire, where vineyards are cultivated on the top and many cellars extend underneath them, in galleries of some length. But the night pressing is significant. Before the temperature of the fermentation vats could be controlled and any sharp rise inhibited the working of the wine yeasts, it was true that wine makers in various regions often chose to do the pressing at night, when the cooler atmosphere was more conducive to making a satisfactory wine – and workers, sustained by wine, could continue the arduous task more willingly and for longer than during the day. There were several long hot vintage seasons before 1914. Nowadays, not only do many wine makers in various regions continue to work non-stop in their wineries, but they also pick the grapes at night in the cooler hours. In Alsace, however, although long hours are expected during the vintage, the freshness of the nights and the dews makes night harvesting unnecessary, although picking can certainly go on as long as anyone can see the grapes.

The decreasing profitability of the vineyards and the increasing cost of replanting, plus the attractions of city life in such expanding centres as Mulhouse, caused a decline in the area under vines, though the fall was nothing like as serious as, for example, in Burgundy. In 1883 there were 26,400 hectares under vines in Alsace; in 1895 22,340 hectares; in 1898 only 18,700. In Colmar, for example, the area declined from 607 hectares in 1893 to 355 in 1903.

Several writers have stated that the circumstance of Alsace having been under German rule for forty-seven years caused the region to produce only inferior quality wine and that, because of this, it thereafter took a long time for Alsace wines to become known and appreciated on world markets. This is unfair. As has been seen, the vineyards were largely planted with inferior varieties, up to three-quarters in Burger, and a large proportion in Chasselas (in the Haut-Rhin) and Sylvaner (in the Bas-Rhin). What must be acknowledged is that it was under German rule that the wine trade in Alsace began definitely to organise itself.

By the late nineteenth century Colmar seems to have become the undisputed capital of the Alsace wine trade and to have taken the initiative in many ventures. In 1869 the Société d'Horticulture et de Viticulture de Colmar was founded; this published a series of treatises on viticultural matters. In 1884 the town set up a mobile smoke-making device, which could be moved round the local vineyards to combat the danger of frost wherever it might be present; public demonstrations of this at the beginning of May 1885 were witnessed by experts from all over France, Germany and as far away as Hungary. At the same time, Chrétien Oberlin was carrying out the researches into new vine varieties as previously mentioned and, perhaps more important, was proposing that vines should henceforth be trained on wires, not as trellises as they had been since the earliest times. Trellised vines look picturesque and there are delightful pictures of them in examples of art from the ancient Egyptians, through the Middle Ages to recent times – some remained in Alsace until after World War II. But although they can be useful when other market garden crops are also to be cultivated in the vineyard – as happens in Madeira today – trellising is not always suitable for vine cultivation as it is now understood. Grafted vines often have a shorter life and, for maximum productivity, training on wires and pruning according to various methods (the 'taille Guyot' or 'double Guyot' is often used in Alsace) are convenient. When a tractor is involved the amount of space between the rows of vines in which it can operate is also a consideration. Trellising is mostly outmoded in the vineyards of the latter part of the twentieth century. In 1895 the Colmar wine market was finally established and, despite the small number of growers who offered their wines there at the outset, it soon gained a reputation for the quality of the goods on sale.

In 1909 the Société de Viticulture pour l'Alsace-Lorraine was created, but this never really got off the ground. More successful was the Elsässiche Weinbauverband, which made positive efforts to raise the quality of Alsace wines. At the beginning of the twentieth century the first two co-operative cellars were formed, at Eguisheim and Dambach-la-Ville; their initial rôle was solely to stock the surplus wine of their members and it was not until later that they began to market wine themselves. In 1906, under the direction of Dr Hecker, the first of the many Alsace wine fairs – 'Expositions de Vins' – took place at Barr. Over one hundred wines from Barr and six neighbouring villages were on show and, before being offered to the general public, these were submitted to a jury consisting of wine producers from other parts of Alsace.

Yet another development in the period under German rule was the sale of wine in bottle. The pioneer of this was Julien Dopff of Riquewihr (also famous for his work on sparkling wines); he demonstrated the merits of conserving wine in this way by sending a consignment from Bremen to Australia and back, after which the wine was shown at the Strasbourg Exhibition in 1913, where it won the major award in its class inscribed 'for a particularly fortunate success'. Though this indicated what was bound to happen in the future, World War I intervened and Dopff 'Au Moulin' remained almost the only company to offer wines in bottle until the early 1920s.

It may surprise many to know how unusual sales of wines bottled by the producer were in the early part of this century. This particularly applies to the British Isles, where shippers and merchants, mostly independents, although the great brewery and retail chains were developing, prided themselves on the standard of bottling they achieved. There was no snobbery about 'bottled where it was made': the great French restaurants often did their own bottling of fine wines and so did many export customers. With white wines, long-term maturation in bottle was not often of importance and not only might the customer have more resources – and time – for bottling than the producer, he might be of the opinion that wine shipped in bulk would be more resistant to any hazards of travel and, should it be in any way defective when it arrived in his premises, he could quickly draw on the knowledge of informed technicians, so as to put it right. The grower and the wine maker produced the wine; they might follow its progress to the point of sale, as many conscientious individuals did, but they might not – and the export customer might handle the wine as he thought fit, which could, sometimes, result in the export bottling being dissimilar to the same wine bottled on the spot.

While it is true to say that the years Alsace spent as part of the German Empire were not prosperous ones for the trade in its wines, it is incorrect to state that the Germans caused this to be so. In fact, Alsace produced 40 per cent of the total crop in what was then Germany and it would take many years for a market to reorganise itself in such a fashion as to absorb such a quantity of wine which was different in style from that to which it was accustomed. Although certain amounts of wine could be utilised for blending, there remained a large quantity of frankly inferior wine, surplus to requirements. The Germans might be criticised because they encouraged the replanting of hybrid vines, instead of the traditional varieties, but this is a judgment easy to make now, when we know the results. It was not only in Germany that the hybrid was considered to be the answer to the many diseases of the vine at that period. There is an interesting sequel to this because, during World War II, when Alsace again came under German rule, the overall reconstruction of the vineyard area of Wissembourg is due to the fact that the Germans then insisted on the grubbing up of all the hybrid vines that still remained there.

During the first German period, the Alsace growers began gradually to establish themselves as producers of quality wines; they were determined to launch these on the market, including export markets, once hostilities ceased. In 1918, however, they found themselves in a difficult position: they were, once again, part of France, the largest wine-producing country in the world and they had to compete openly and without any form of protection with the cheap wines of the Midi and French North Africa. Alsace wines were little known in France itself – and they were very different from the wines known traditionally as pleasing the French palate.

There is – and at this time there was – no group of wines comparable to those in Alsace produced by any of the other French wine regions – Bordeaux, Burgundy, the Loire, the Rhône, and the increasingly important southern areas. Drinkers, especially those in wine-producing countries or regions, are notoriously conservative; they go on drinking what they know. For everyday they drink a local wine or a branded wine. For special occasions a more special wine, but one that guests may have heard tell of, is what is bought – and, it should not be forgotten by Anglo-Saxons, the concept of the 'wine merchant' is only a recent one in France; the special advice about wines available to customers in the British Isles who have 'my' wine merchant, just as they might have 'my' tailor, bootmaker, or more recently, broker, bookmaker, hair-dresser or travel agent, is something that came very late to France. Here, wine was bought from the grocer or from one of the few retailers, such as the Nicolas establishments, or else the customer had some contact with the grower. But the Vosges are high mountains and a considerable barrier. French customers, apart from the buyers of the big hotels and restaurants and, certainly, the brasseries which began to flourish in Paris and the north of France and didn't only sell beer, went down the road to buy wine. Alsace – a sort of 'vin du Rhin' many must have said. I have met many wine-aware Frenchmen who have never tasted any Alsace wine, even today. They are content with what they already know.

It was necessary for the members of the trade to make up their minds whether to produce vast quantities of wine for the mass market, or to make small amounts of fine wine. With the encouragement of the Station de Recherches Oenologiques and the Institut Viticole de Colmar, the growers' association made the important decision in 1925 to concentrate on planting the grape varieties categorised as 'noble' and, at the same time, issued a condemnation of the planting of hybrids.

As a result of this, the area under vines decreased considerably: in 1920 there were 19,220 hectares, in 1932 17,700 hectares, and in 1955 (after World War II) 11,444 hectares. This policy of producing quality wines is one that is still followed but, in the period of economic depression in the early 1930s, it took courage to pursue it. Mechanisation was transforming the vineyard scene, even the use of a bicycle enabling workers to travel easily between the small plots made life easier, but the drift to the towns and more apparently rewarding and attractive work continued.

The effects of World War II on Alsace were far more terrible than those of World War I in human terms, although in the first war far more lives were lost. In the second German occupation the strictest controls were exercised over the unfortunate people, who were forbidden to speak their Alsace language (incomprehensible to anyone from outside) and the families of those of military service age who had managed to get into the unoccupied zone of France were threatened if those absent did not return – then to be sent to serve on the Russian front, or, if slightly luckier, in Italy.

Fritz Hallgarten, in *Alsace, its Wine Gardens, Cellars and Cuisine* (3rd edition 1978), makes the point that, whereas the German annexation of Alsace in 1870 'obliged Alsatian children to attend German-speaking primary schools for decades', during World War II the occupiers 'forbade everything French, including French language and instruction, even as a foreign language'. Fritz cites Jean Giraudoux, the French diplomat, novelist and playwright (1882-1944) who said: 'One must do homage to the Alsatian dialect. Only through it could the Alsatian resist the Germans.' And he notes that 'Like Frenchmen, the Alsatians insist on putting the accent on the last syllable (of words), which . . . led to one of their best witticisms: when the Nazis spoke of "siegen" (to conquer), the Alsatians always repeated "Sie gehn" (they will depart)!'

In the final stages of the war, the Germans retreated up the Rhine, shock troops often fiercely contesting their withdrawal; many of the wine villages were fortunately off the main routes of the fighting, but anyone seeing pictures of what Ammerschwihr was like before 1939, a charming, picturesque little place, will also register with horror the mass of ruins, with a single tower just about standing, to which the town was reduced. The painstaking reconstruction after such devastation is another piece of evidence of the remarkable and enduring character of the inhabitants of Alsace. Yet their insistence on their being Alsace, in a tactful manner, is exemplified by another episode recounted by Fritz Hallgarten in *Alsace, its Wine Gardens, Cellars and Cuisine* (3rd edition, 1978) when his broker reminded him that, after the liberation in 1944, the Mayor of Strasbourg had posters in English put up all over the town addressed to the American troops: 'Allied soldiers, do not forget you are here in a French town, though you may hear a German language.'

Of the total area under vines in 1955, there were 3,791 hectares producing *vins ordinaires,* without any *appellation;* by 1974 this figure had fallen to 959 hectares and it is expected to fall still further. But although the number of vines and the areas under vines are less than they were, as a result of improved methods of cultivation and production – each vine being in better health and,

Ammerschwihr, the 'Tour des Fripons' (Rogues' Tower), one of the very few remaining buildings of the former old town

therefore, yielding more – the quantity of wine has slightly increased: in the 1920s the average crop was about 750,000 hectolitres, but over the years 1970-74 it had risen to 870,000 hectolitres and the vintages of 1982 and 1983 have bumped up the totals dramatically.

Will the vineyards that have disappeared and that may be seen as shadowy lines along the hillsides, ever be replanted? It is difficult to say. Current forecasts anticipate an overall increase of about 10 per cent in the total area over the period of the 1970s, but outside problems may slow down this increase. Another point of view is put by Christian Wolff: 'Can one talk of the vanished vineyards of Alsace? The real answer is no, but the retreat is very apparent in the plain, in the valleys and is taking place in front of our eyes in the hinterland of Strasbourg. The future shows no likelihood of a regrowth of the vineyard in these marginal areas, where the area most fit for survival covers the land between Obernai and Wasselonne. As for the kernel, the true vineyard, there is no threat of a reduction. But history teaches us to take care: the climate, political circumstances, the economic situation can all combine to have an effect on the extent of a vineyard, either in a favourable or unfavourable direction.'

In promoting the wines of Alsace, both in France and abroad, two sorts of action were necessary: first, quality had to be improved and to have some form of official guarantee, then promotional and publicity campaigns had to be undertaken, to introduce Alsace wines to the potential consumer.

The banning of hybrid vines in 1925 was only the first of several decisions taken to improve the quality of the grapes used for making wine. In 1932 a whole series of German large-cropping varieties were banned and in 1945 the Burger or Elbling were banned as well; this grape variety had for a long while been the mainstay of Alsace viticulture. A period of twenty years was allowed for phasing it out. In the meantime two individual vineyard names had been protected as a result of action taken in the courts by local growers: these were the Kaefferkopf at Ammerschwihr in 1932 and the Sonnenglanz at Beblenheim in 1935. This was to have far-reaching consequences when, in the present day, specific site names began to be proposed for many other wines in a further effort to promote top quality Alsace wines.

It was in 1935 that the laws of *appellation contrôlée* were first introduced in France, a series of earlier decrees aimed at protecting the consumer as regards the precise origin of wines having been started with the so-called 'Capus Law' in 1909. It should never be forgotten that, although there are many other controls built in to the *appellation contrôlée* regulations – vines, pruning, alcoholic content and so on – the full expression is *appellation d'origine contrôlée,* the definition and delimitation of the exact area where the grapes may be grown and the wine made. It was realised, however, that special laws would have to be made for the Alsace wines, because of the very different traditions prevailing there as compared with those in other wine regions of France; it was too soon, at this time, for the system of controls to be worked out in satisfactory detail, but the growers did draw up guidelines for the eventual regulations in 1945 and in 1962 Alsace became part of the great *appellation d'origine contrôlée* wine family – last of the major French wine regions to do so.

In the 1950s and 1960s strenuous efforts were made to promote the wines on export markets, but there were still hesitations and prejudices. In 1923 André L. Simon, founder of what is now The International Wine & Food Society, had commented that there were four million gallons of Alsace available for export but, in his subsequent wine dictionary, published ten years later, he does not allocate a separate entry to Alsace, although Ammerschwihr, Riquewihr and Ribeauvillé are mentioned as wine-producing villages. In the education courses run in London for students of the wine trade in the late 1950s, the teaching was that only the very finest Alsace wines would ever be shipped in bottle as the majority were bought in bulk. Most of those lecturing to the trade thought it unlikely that this situation would change.

In an effort to upgrade the image of Alsace wines from *vins de comptoir* (sold by the glass over the bar counter) to those drunk by the bottle at home or in restaurants, the sale of both Riesling and Gewurztraminer in litre bottles was prohibited in 1971. In the following year, 1972, another decree laid down that Alsace wines had to be bottled in either the Haut-Rhin or the Bas-Rhin *départments.* This was an attempt to counteract the adulteration which was taking place, particularly in Germany, but the result once again hit the bar trade hard–for this had accounted for a large proportion of sales, particularly in Paris, where the local merchants had been accustomed to doing their own bottling as has been mentioned. The decree also caused a great deal of concern in other regions, notably among the shippers of Beaune, who for many generations had bottled wines coming from other areas, including those of the Beaujolais, Côtes du Rhône and Chablis. In Britain, of course, the additional expense incurred by shipping wine in bottle put up the overall price.

However well intentioned these decrees were, they were not totally successful. The exceptionally large vintage of 1973 left a lot of stock on the growers' hands so, in September 1974, the bottling of Rieslings and Gewurztraminers in litre bottles was again permitted–though, for the Gewurztraminer, theoretically only until the beginning of 1978.

Because Alsace was the last major wine region in France to submit to *appellation contrôlée,* perhaps the regulations were better adapted to the local circumstances than anywhere else in France–those making them had learned by seeing what happened elsewhere. But since then there seems to have been an excess of eagerness to change the regulations to suit what may well be merely transitory circumstances and there is currently a strong movement to abolish the compulsory bottling of Alsace wines in Alsace. (Additional information on the wine laws will be found on p. 113ff.)

As far as the U.K. market is concerned, there are several references to the quality of the wines; author H. Warner Allen (1881-1968) refers to a visit to Colmar in 1918, when he tasted some excellent wines; when he went back a few years later, however, he found the growers pessimistic about their prospects in Britain–and he spoke good French so would have appreciated what they said. For a long while Alsace wines were shipped both to Britain and the United States as 'French Rhine wines', which must inevitably have caused confusion in the minds of many consumers. As a result, they came to be compared–often unfavourably–with German wines, although the style of wine that Alsace tries to produce is completely different. This notion of Alsace wines being a sort of 'poor relation' of the aristocrats of Germany persists– Alsace is even sometimes written about as 'essentially German' and a few years ago the assistant editor of one important Sunday paper in Britain wrote an account of a holiday there, not only making this statement but giving the impression that everything about Alsace is wholly and naturally Germanic– wines, food, people; in reply to the protests written by lovers of Alsace who knew better, this writer returned irritable and uninformed answers.

It was only after World War II that Alsace wines began to enjoy a real success in the U.K., outstanding efforts being made by certain shippers, particularly Hugel; indeed, it is probably true to say that, for many British wine drinkers, the world 'Alsace' is synonymous with Hugel, even though they and their representatives abroad are wholehearted in urging the U.K. to drink Alsace in general and try the wines of other houses. In the U.S. progress has been less, although some companies, for example Willm, have shipped Alsace there since the 1930s; Alsace wines account for less than one per cent of French wines imported by the U.S. and they seldom make headlines in the publicised tastings. Possibly the German population in the U.S. is firm about remaining loyal to the wines of the country of their origin.

West Germany, however, takes vast amounts of Alsace-odd, when one considers that the wines were hardly appreciated when they were produced in a former 'German' region; perhaps the German palate is accustoming itself to the more urbane and drier taste of Alsace? There are also the drinkers among the foreign troops stationed in West Germany, whose awareness of Alsace-easy for them to reach via the Palatinate-appears to be increasing. In addition, the official export totals cannot include the enormous quantities of wine bought by the Germans who swarm across the Rhine to buy bottles from their favourite grower or co-operative cellar; one, from Karlsruhe, seen loading ten cases of Alsace into the boot of his Mercedes, was asked why he preferred Alsace wines and replied that it was prescribed by his doctor. . . .'Our wines are natural', say the people of Alsace, 'not made in the laboratory', they often wickedly add. It is certainly true that, in recent years the creation of 'trocken' and 'halb trocken' wines in Germany indicates the tendency to 'drink dry' and, indeed, it is not easy to place the finer German wines in the context of a meal, whereas Alsace wines are, in this respect certainly, versatile.

Belgium comes after West Germany in the export markets, then Britain, Switzerland and the U.S. But it should be borne in mind that the export of Alsace wines only represents about 10-12 per cent of the total production; this figure may appear small and indeed it is tiny when compared to the equivalent statistics of the exports from other French wine regions, but it is significant that, between 1969 and 1972, exports of Alsace more than doubled. The effort represented by this sort of achievement is impressive.

The home market for Alsace wines seems healthy. The average drinker nowadays is young and it is good for the trade that Alsace wines are well represented in supermarkets, where customers select for themselves, without any fear of seeming ignorant of wine. Slightly more than one bottle in three of white *appellation contrôlée* wine drunk in the average French home now comes from Alsace. This is even more remarkable when one considers the competitors-the white wines of Bordeaux, Burgundy, the Loire and a host of lesser-known names. But the French housewife, like her sisters across the Channel, caters for a different mode of life today and the wines of Alsace accord with both the foods she serves most frequently and the way in which she entertains.

Rebuilt Bennwihr, with a panorama across the Rhine to the Black Forest

So the outlook for Alsace wines seems good. Useful and effective methods of propaganda include the Centre d'Information de Vin d'Alsace, recently re-established in a well-designed building on the outskirts of Colmar, able to cope with conferences and large-scale tastings, as well as providing detailed background and statistics for both the specialist and lay enthusiast, and the Confrérie Saint Etienne, now with its headquarters in the Château de Kientzheim, which is described in Chapter 10. Regular tastings in export markets, backed by particularly attractive advertising, reinforce the cumulative effect of the decision, taken after World War I, to concentrate on producing quality wines. This was a definite turning point. Although Alsace had never enjoyed the reputation of, say, Bordeaux or Burgundy, it had been recognised, by those who knew wine, of being capable of making good wines. Now, after sixty years, the policies adopted at a time of great stress and crisis, are beginning to establish Alsace wines among the world's 'greats'.

3

The Grapes, Wines and Vines

The Main Grape Varieties

The quality of the wines of any region depends upon a number of factors, including the soil, the weather and the grape varieties used. Over the centuries, each area has found the grapes best suited to itself. For example, the 1982 edition of Cocks & Feret (the 'bible of Bordeaux' in which the majority of the properties are listed) mentions exactly the same grape varieties as the 1922 edition; in Burgundy the Pinot, the Chardonnay and the Gamay have been planted for centuries. On the other hand, new species are being developed and used in Germany. In both France and Germany, however, it is generally the geographical area of production that tends to predominate on labels. In Alsace it is the grape variety that is all-important. (For more detailed legal particulars see Chapter 6.)

It is difficult to get an exact idea of the proportion of Alsace wines sold under a grape name but, considering the production figures for the past few vintages, it appears that well over 80 per cent of the wines have been produced from varieties likely to be sold unblended, the remainder being made from lesser varieties or from parcels of vines where an assortment of different varieties have been planted and are continuing to grow together.

For these blended wines there are three main options open: they can be sold under a brand name, under a geographical name, or under the title 'Edelzwicker'. In any event, the label will bear the *appellation contrôlée* either of 'Alsace' or 'Vin d'Alsace'. Until recently, the term Edelzwicker could only be applied to wines blended from the better varieties – sometimes referred to as 'noble' (*edel*); the more ordinary wines were simply called 'Zwicker'. The latter term, however, has now been abandoned and any blended wine from permitted grape varieties can today be called Edelzwicker.

With regard to the geographical term that may appear on a label, this is generally clearly indicative of the wine's origin: Côtes d'Eguisheim, for example, is the house wine of 'Le Caveau', the local restaurant that belongs to the growers in that village. Brand names usually involve the word 'Alsace', such as the 'Charme d'Alsace' of Ammerschwihr shippers Kuehn, or indicate the wine's suitability for some special purpose, such as Léon Beyer's 'Spécial Fruits de Mer'.

In *Le Vignoble et les Vins d'Alsace* (1932), R. Brunet says: 'The grapes which give the great white wines of Alsace are the Traminer, the Gewurztraminer, the Sylvaner, the Riesling, the Pinot Blanc and the Tokay. Those which give white wines for ordinary consumption are the Pinot Gris, the White Chasselas, the Rosé Chasselas, the Knipperlé, the Burger and the Trollinger.' But it will be seen that much has changed in the half century since that was written.

To start with, there are a number of grapes grown just for making ordinary wine without any *appellation*. The least important include the Abondant, the Seyval Blanc (which has been quite widely planted in today's English vineyard), the Landal and the Maréchal Foch. These have never been allowed to make *appellation contrôlée* wine in Alsace. Next, there are a number of grape species that were allowed to be used for *appellation contrôlée* wine until 31 December 1979, though they did not appear on labels. These are the Knipperlé, the Goldriesling, the Pinot Meunier, the Chardonnay and the Müller-Thurgau. These vines have generally been planted in small vineyard holdings belonging to older growers and, usually, any remaining vines which have not been grubbed up are by now very old. Of these varieties, perhaps the Müller-Thurgau is the most surprising among those to be banned and there are many experts, including Monsieur Fernand-Paul Ortleib of Beblenheim, who consider that the decision may have been premature. As this grape ripens early, it has been planted on some poorly exposed slopes in Alsace, particularly at Turckheim. The fact that it is being increasingly planted in Germany demonstrates that it must be one of the more successful 'newer' varieties (although it was first evolved a century ago in Germany). The Goldriesling, or Riesling Doré, is the result of a cross between the Riesling and a variety of Muscat; it is very early ripening and has traditionally been used for the production of *vin bourru* or new wine, which is drunk in the wine bars of Riquewihr accompanied by warm bread and a bowl of freshly gathered walnuts. If you come across it, beware – for it is deceptively powerful. The Pinot Meunier was planted in the extreme south of Alsace for making rosé wine, but has been discounted for some time.

Today the ordinary wine of Alsace is produced by the Chasselas, Sylvaner and Clevner grapes. The Pinot Noir, the odd man out, the black grape, makes the red and rosé wines. The Pinot Gris or Tokay d'Alsace is another grape variety much discussed as to origin and current nomenclature.

CHASSELAS

This is a variety that is steadily disappearing. In 1969 there were just over a thousand hectares planted and it accounted for more than one-tenth of the total production of the whole of Alsace. Now there are just over four hundred hectares and it is responsible for 3.3 per cent of the total crop; most of the vines are well over twenty-five years old and no extension of planting in Chasselas is permitted today. In France this variety is generally thought of as a table grape and is widely cultivated in the Midi for this purpose. As a wine, it is probably better known as 'Fendant' because this is its name in the wines it makes in Savoie and in parts of Switzerland. Its history in Alsace – where its local name is 'Flambeau d'Alsace' – is a long one, for it is mentioned in documents of more than two centuries ago. According to Pierre Galet (*A Practical Ampelography*, trans. by Lucie T. Morton, 1979), the Chasselas is of unknown origin, but likely to have been a variety brought from the east of Switzerland by the Romans. In *Guide to the Wines of Germany* (1978) Hans Siegel says that it is thought to have originated either in Turkey or even ancient Egypt, where it seems to have been mentioned as early as 2800 BC. It seems to have been introduced to French vineyards in the sixteenth century. It was certainly widely planted in the past: in 1874 ampelographer Pulliat, in classifying the main *V. vinifera* grapes, did so in five groups, according to the order in which they ripen, by comparison with the Chasselas. The full name is Chasselas Doré, but it has a number of synonyms: sometimes it is called after the various places where it is grown, but its other names include Golden Chasselas in the U.S. (although this is sometimes used in error for what is in fact the Palomino grape), Fendant in Switzerland and, even, Royal Muscadine in England. In Germany it is called the Gutedel. There are a number of types of Chasselas that are grown only in small quantities, of which those with the suffixes musqué, rose, violet and cioutat are cited by Galet. Len Evans' *Complete Book of Australian Wine* (third edition 1978) gives the name 'sweetwater', which I admit I have not come across, although he says it is often used when the grapes are sold for the table in Australia. The European drinker will meet the Chasselas in the Loire, where it makes the white wines of Pouilly-sur-Loire that are everyday quality not entitled to use the local name for the Sauvignon grape, Blanc Fumé, which makes the finer wines. At its best here, however, it can make a very fresh, slightly 'green' wine, uncomplicated and dryish. It does not surprise me to read that in Australia some wine makers apparently consider it a good grape to use when making sparkling wine by the Champagne process. In Germany there are plantations in Baden where it makes rather ordinary wines.

Chasselas is the ideal base wine for Edelzwicker, as it is fairly neutral in taste (see pages 59 and 81), low in acidity and very flattering in style. Both bunches and the individual grapes are very large and the grapes come in two colours – a yellowy-green and a faint pink. The yield is high.

Traditionally, Chasselas is a speciality of the Haut-Rhin, nearly all the plantings being in the heart of the quality vineyard area between Wintzenheim and Ribeauvillé. Although the word 'Chasselas' cannot appear on a label, it is possible to find pure Chasselas wines if you know where to look: given its name, this must be true of Hugel's Flambeau d'Alsace and it is certainly so as regards the Côtes d'Ammerschwihr of the local growers Sick-Dreyer.

SYLVANER

While the Chasselas is the speciality of the Haut-Rhin, the Sylvaner is that of the Bas-Rhin, where it is responsible for almost half the total production. For long it has been the most widely planted variety in Alsace though, with efforts being made to increase the overall quality of the wine, it has recently been in retreat. The area planted in Sylvaner has remained around the 2000 hectare mark for the past fifteen years, but, as a proportion of the total, this now represents slightly more than 21 per cent rather than the former figure of nearly 30 per cent. The Sylvaner is also widely planted in Germany, although it is of Austrian origin and did not arrive in Alsace until the beginning of the nineteenth century. Galet in *A Practical Ampelography* gives other names for it such as: Franken Riesling, Oesterreicher, Schwabler, Gruber, and, in Hungary, Szilvani zöld, also Selenzhiz. In some countries, such as New Zealand, a wine may bear the name 'Riesling/Sylvaner', which in fact is the name of the cross that is probably better known today as the Müller-Thurgau.

The region of Germany where the Sylvaner (or Silvaner) probably gives of its best is Franconia; here it is even sometimes referred to as the 'Franken Riesling', although, as is stated in *The Wines of Germany*, by Frank Schoonmaker, revised by Peter M.F. Sichel (1983), this is rather a joke name; in the Palatinate it is termed the 'Franken'. The same source observes that 'in the United States, the Silvaner has had the effrontery to call itself simply "Riesling", instead of Franken Riesling, and this absurd misnomer has received, alas, official sanction, so that in order to get a true Riesling wine from California, the consumer now has to ask for "Johannisberg Riesling".' Franconian Silvaners can be very fine-drawn, delicate wines, some of them, in the 'stein' wine category, getting into the higher categories when made by the famous estates. The greenish grapes are formed in tight bunches and ripen some two weeks after the Chasselas. The yield is high, the wine is low in alcohol and with an agreeable acidity. A local drinking song suggests that it is the ideal wine to drink when you are thirsty – a jug at a time. The Confrérie Saint Etienne (see Chapter 10) describe it as the *vin passepartout* – all-purpose wine.

While no one would claim that the Chasselas produces great wines, the Sylvaner, on the best slopes, can do so. It is perhaps at its best on the Zotzenberg, a north-facing vineyard in Mittelbergheim. Local growers, such as Boeckel and Seltz, can make truly extraordinary wines which make a mockery of the suggestion that *grand cru* wines should never be made from the Sylvaner. More common, however, is the jug wine made from this grape, served in the bars and restaurants of Strasbourg, perhaps slightly lacking in bouquet, but soft and agreeable.

PINOT BLANC/PINOT AUXERROIS/CLEVNER

Clevner (sometimes casually spelled Klevner) is the Alsace name for a variety of grapes of the Pinot family. Most commonly it is either the Pinot Blanc, which appears occasionally in Burgundy, or the Pinot Auxerrois, which has come from Lorraine. Clevner can also be made from the Pinot Gris, or the Pinot Noir vinified as a white wine – that is, without allowing the pigments in the skins of the black grapes to tint the 'must' or freshly pressed juice.

Clevner takes its name from the town of Chiavenna, just north of Lake Como in Italy and it has been known by this name in Alsace since at least the middle of the sixteenth century, when it is mentioned by Jerome Bock (or Tragus, as he preferred to be known in the literary world) in his *Kräuterbuch* (Herbal), which was first published at Strasbourg in 1551. At that time he mentions it as being planted near Wissembourg, in the extreme north of Alsace and it is interesting that the most successful wine of the Cave Co-operative at Cleebourg, some six kilometres from Wissembourg, is their Pinot Auxerrois.

The Clevner has been one of the most popular varieties in Alsace over the past few years. There are many reasons for this. First, it can replace the Chasselas as the base wine in an Edelzwicker; second, it can be planted on generally unfavourable soil, often the deep, rich earth of the plain, and still thrive happily; third, it provides the ideal base wine for that rising star in the local firmament – 'Crémant d'Alsace', the sparkling wine. The supple, soft wine it makes is easy to drink and not difficult to make, although the grapes are particularly sensitive to all forms of fungal infection.

In the early 1970s, permission was given for the Alsace vineyards to be increased by a further thousand hectares; although these areas had been planted with vines in the Middle Ages, Pierre-Marie Doutrelant in his book *Les Bons Vins et les Autres* (1976) describes them as 'better suited to the growing of the cabbage than the grape'. Nonetheless, the Pinot appears to have adapted itself satisfactorily to this land. While it comes from the second division of Alsace grape varieties, it can occasionally have pretensions for promotion: one Pinot Blanc that is often excellent is that produced from the Sonnenglanz vineyard by the Cave Co-operative at Beblenheim. More prosaically, a drinking song says it is the ideal wine to drink on coming home from work. It is also an ideal wine bar wine, for the name of the grape means something to most people and the simplicity of the wine is likely to offend few.

This grape has been planted in small quantities in California, and has been the subject of experiments in South Africa, but Hans Siegel in *Guide to the Wines of Germany* (1978) comments that it 'is very successful in certain areas where many traditional German grapes do not really thrive'.

KLEVNER DE HEILIGENSTEIN

Something of an oddity in a small way in the Bas-Rhin is the Klevner de Heiligenstein – the 'k' of the German spelling is always used for this. The only thing it has in common with the Clevner is that it too came from Chiavenna. It was introduced to the village of Heiligenstein by the local priest in the middle of the eighteenth century and has flourished there ever since – though 'flourished' is perhaps too optimistic a word, as the plantings now represent less than five hectares.

The grape is the Savagnin Rosé, closely related to the Traminer and giving a full-flavoured wine. Although relationships are often difficult to work out in the grape world, it seems likely that this one is the same variety that produces the long-lived *vins jaunes* (yellow wines) of Château Chalon and of Arbois, in the Jura region of France. The statue to the priest, Erhard Wantz, in front of the *mairie,* is inscribed 'Instruction leads to progress'. Perhaps sadly, his instruction in the use of this grape variety has not progressed far–though one of the few producers of the wine today is a Monsieur Charles Wantz of Barr; perhaps he is a distant relative or descendant from Erhard's family, proud of maintaining his ancestor's teaching!

PINOT NOIR

Of all the grape varieties of Alsace, the most 'discuté' as the French say, is the Pinot Noir. It is a world-famous grape and it is thought to be the variety shown in many of the wall paintings and illuminated manuscripts of early French history. It is even possible, according to D.P.Pongrácz, in *Practical Viticulture* (1978), that the vines may have been brought to Gaul by Greek settlers, who founded Marseilles in 600 BC. Other names for it include Blauer Spätburgunder (planted in 1318 in Salem in Germany and in Affental in Baden in 1330). According to Galet in *A Practical Ampelography* it is referred to in Germany as the Schwarz Klevner (and, he says, also in Alsace), Noirien, Morillon, Auvernat Noir, Vert Doré, Savagnin Noir, Cortaillod (in Switzerland) and, in Germany-speaking regions, Burgunder, de Bleur and Blauer Klevner. The Pinot Noir is planted in many vineyards, including in Austria, Hungary, Roumania, the U.S.S.R., California, New Zealand, Australia and South Africa. It seems, however, not to give of its best in very warm vineyards and, as Galet says 'The special character of its wine is lost in hot, dry conditions'. The Pinot Noir ripens early as a rule, but risks harm from spring frosts.

Only as recently as 1970 T.A.Layton wrote in *Wine and People of Alsace* that it was 'hardly worth the printer's ink to mention that some woebegone growers try to make a red wine with the ubiquitous Pinot Noir grape. The wine, which I find terrible, represents less than 0.5 per cent of the total output.' About five years ago Christopher Fielden wrote: 'Although the Alsatians like to describe their Pinot Noir as a red wine, this is mostly wishful thinking, as it is more often a deepish pink. Every shipper says he has one, but he deceives himself.'

Now things have changed. Efforts are being made to make true red wines in the Burgundian style from the grape that makes the great red Burgundies. To extract the full amount of colour, the musts of the new wine are heated–to loosen the pigments in the skins. The wine is aged in small oak casks. Hugel, for example, use casks that have already made wine–these they buy from Château

Mouton Rothschild, one of the great first growths of Pauillac, in the Médoc; one Ammerschwihr grower, when he thinks the vintage merits it, buys casks from a grower in Volnay in Burgundy and has new 'heads' (the ends of the cask) put in so as to increase the tannin that the wine will acquire from cask maturation. How successful these wines will be is not yet certain, but it is definite that, over the past few years, more effort has been put to the improving of the quality of Pinot Noir wines than of any other variety. One measure indicating the increased acceptance of the wine by the authorities, is that it now is part of the tasting presented for the Confrérie Saint Etienne–but only since 1981. In the Confrérie's first booklet about the wines of Alsace they did not even mention it.

Though there are still many who have doubts about making red wine in Alsace, there are very good commercial reasons for doing so. The Germans who pour across the Rhine every weekend in their thousands, to enjoy the fine restaurants of the region look for red wine to drink with their meals; they can find little enough of it in their homeland. So the wines made from the Pinot Noir have been created to satisfy this demand. From the 200 hectares of vines recorded when T.A.Layton was writing in 1970, there are now more than 700. Much bad wine has, admittedly, been produced–but many growers, certainly at the outset of this increased production, had no clear idea as to what they were trying to produce. This is exemplified by the experience of one well-known and respected local dignitary, who, at a blind tasting at a high level, submitted a bottle of Lirac Rosé, from the Rhône Valley (made from quite different vine varieties) and was congratulated by many of his colleagues on the quality of his Pinot!

The cuisine of Alsace also often demands a red wine–so red wine has been made. (Though one cynic has commented that the mark of true hospitality in hospitable Alsace is to be offered a bottle of claret with your lunch.) There are three villages which have a historical reputation for their Pinot Noir: Ottrott, Marlenheim and Saint Hippolyte. It appears that, in former times, the wine of Marlenheim was also vinified as a red wine, but nowadays its *Vorlauf* or first-run wine made from the Pinot Noir is of a lighter shade. Maybe the old traditions will revive with the assistance of new technology.

PINOT GRIS/TOKAY D'ALSACE

A more highly regarded member of the Pinot family–at least in Alsace–is the Pinot Gris. This is called the Ruländer or Grauburgunder in Germany and takes this name from the merchant Ruländ, who first planted it in 1711, when he came to Germany from Burgundy; Pongrácz in *Practical Viticulture* (1978) says that it is 'a spontaneous mutation of Pinot Noir'. Other names for it include Pinot Beurot, Gris Cordelier, Auvernat Gris, Malvoisie, Fromentot. Schoonmaker in *The Wines of Germany* (1978) says that it produces in Germany 'full-bodied, juicy wines in Baden, Rheinpfalz and Württemberg'. In the region it is more commonly known as the Tokay d'Alsace, although there was recently a directive from the civil servants in Brussels to the effect that this name should no longer be used, because the grape has nothing to do with the production of the famous Hungarian wine Tokay, and is in no way related to the Furmint grape mainly used in Tokay. But no matter what the authorities say, the growers of Alsace seem determined to continue using the name 'Tokay' and at the time of writing there appears to be no definite legislation governing the use of the word.

Legend, however, does give the Tokay an East European parentage. It is said that this grape variety was brought from Hungary in the sixteenth century by Baron Lazare de Schwendi, who led the imperial forces that captured the town of Tokay from the Turkish invaders. Schwendi then returned to his estates in the Kaiserstuhl, the centre of present-day German vineyards in Baden, and also to his properties in Kaysersberg in Alsace, where he died in 1584. Although French wine makers had settled in the Tokay region as early as the twelfth century, because of the encouragement of King Bela III of Hungary, the region's reputation for fine wines was not created until the middle of the seventeenth century. Indeed, Bishop Miklos Olah in 1557 describes the wines as being no more than mediocre in quality. Even more surprising is the fact that Tokay, as a grape variety, is not mentioned in Alsace until 1750, when it appears in a description of the Weinbach vineyard in Kientzheim.

Perhaps a more credible story is that this grape was introduced to Alsace by someone returning to Württemberg from Hungary during the first half of the eighteenth century. Anyway, the grape is mentioned as being planted in Riquewihr in 1780 and, as that village then formed part of the Duchy of Württemberg, the route followed appears logical. At about the same time, the Duke Donath Trautsohn, Lord Steward of the imperial houshold, was encouraging Germans to settle in the Tokay region. But, whatever is the truth, Baron Schwendi has not lived in vain: the Pinot Gris of the Colmar establishment Charles Jux bears his name, his former castle in Alsace at Kientzheim is now the headquarters of the Confrérie Saint Etienne renamed the Château de la Confrérie Saint Etienne, with the museum of Alsace wines in part of the buildings.

While the Tokay is more widely planted in Alsace than anywhere else in France, this grape is none other than the Pinot Beurot of Burgundy, the Fromentot of Champagne and the Malvoisie of the Loire Valley. I am informed, however, that in parts of France the Maccabeo grape is also referred to as the Malvoisie. The wine it makes is full-bodied, soft, with a subtle flavour but, because of its alcoholic strength and – for Alsace – comparatively high degree of acidity, it is frequently suggested as the accompaniment to foie gras and meat dishes.

The area planted with Tokay has never been very big and, while there has been a recent increase in plantings to reach the present figure of 550 hectares, the proportion has remained constant at between four and five per cent of the total vineyard area. The yield this grape gives is not high and the vine is sensitive to attack from most directions, although it possesses one big advantage in that it is an early ripening variety.

MUSCAT

For some writers, notably Pierre-Marie Doutrelant in *Les Bons Vins et les Autres* (1976), the Muscat does not rank among the fine grape varieties (*cépages nobles* as they are often categorised) of Alsace. He places it on the same level as the Pinot Noir. A more general view is that of Monsieur Brunet stated in his *Le Vignoble et les Vines d'Alsace* (1932): 'The white and rosé Muscats of Alsace, together with the Muscat Ottonel, give very aromatic wines, which are nevertheless very different from the Muscats of the south of France. As a result of their late ripening and their finicky demand for the right soil, they are generally planted only in the finest sites . . . They give a very elegant wine, with a delicate bouquet. This causes them to be much appreciated in the region, particularly by the women.'

It is interesting that the name Muscat is given to wines coming from rather different grape varieties. The white and rosé Muscats, of which Brunet speaks, are the Muscat de Frontignan, the base of all the great Muscat wines of the Rhône Valley. More popular in Alsace is the Muscat Ottonel, which ripens earlier. This has been developed from a Chasselas seedling, found in Angers in the Loire Valley in 1852. While it has a big yield, it is particularly sensitive to *coulure* (the disease that causes the grape to fall from the vines before they have swollen and ripened). In some years, therefore, such as 1978 and 1980, the crop is small and it is now the least planted of all the fine grape varieties in Alsace. Other names for the Muscat, a huge and world-wide grape variety, include Muscat Canelli, White Frontignan – a name which, as simply 'Frontignan' or 'Frontignac' was well known in England to our ancestors – Muskuti (in Greece), Muscatel Branco (in Portugal), Moscata Blanca (in Italy) where the Moscato grape is the foundation of sparkling Asti, and, in Germany, Weisse Muskateller. The full name for the basic grape is Muscat Blanc à Petits Grains but the use merely of the term 'Muscat' may, as has been indicated, involve various different types. These Muscats must not be confused with Muscadelle, or Muscadet, which are different varieties of grape. To make the matter a little more confusing, there is a Morio-Muskat (a cross of Silvaner and Pinot Blanc) grown in Germany and, in some areas, there is a table grape called Muscat, often the Muscat d'Alexandrie, which is also used for wine making. The Muscat Ottonel has been used successfully for a number of Rumanian and some Greek wines.

One comes across Muscats in many parts of the world – there is a fine dry Muscat wine made in Australia by McWilliams, named 'Lexia', which smells as if it were going to be full and sweetish and then has a surprisingly crisp flavour; the Muscat is also sometimes referred to as the Gordo Blanco in Australia. Many sweet Muscat and fortifed Muscat wines were made in the past, when sugar was not yet cheap and drinkers wanted a rich, full postprandial drink –

hence Málaga. Málaga is mainly made from Pedro Ximenez. In South Africa, the Hanepoot grape, often sold along the roadsides and used mainly as a esteemed table grape although some is made into wine, is also a Muscat.

Another reason for the Alsace Muscat's lack of popularity may be the difficulty of finding a place for it in the context of a meal. (A glass of Muscat is like a mouthful of grapes.) There is a current vogue for serving it as an apéritif, where it has to compete with the host of sugared wines the French seem to delight in, such as the proprietary branded drinks.

Although the Muscat may not be the oldest grape of Alsace, it is at least the earliest one to be mentioned specifically by name: at Wolxheim in 1523 and in the minutes of a meeting of the town council of Colmar for the year 1552. Now it is planted more towards the southern end of the vineyards; its relative importance is twice that in the *département* of the Haut-Rhin as compared with the Bas-Rhin: three times as much is planted in the region of Guebwiller as in the region of Barr – and not a single bottle of Muscat is produced by the Cave Co-operative of Cleebourg, in the north. It is sad that the small cropping Muscat à Petits Grains is being rapidly replaced by the Muscat Ottonel – perhaps it is for this reason that it is slipping in the estimation of such experts as Doutrelant. Whatever its rating, a drinking song suggests that Muscat 'restores youth, strength and ease of mind to the man suffering from sadness and the weight of his years'. To get an impression of another aspect of the Muscat, one can try the sparkling wine Clairette de Die, from the east of France, where the aroma is distinctive and, usually, unmistakeable.

GEWURZTRAMINER

If the Muscat restores strength to the old, it should be taken as an apéritif to the Gewurztraminer, for this is the wine to be drunk when a

> *. . . belle dame douce, clémente*
> *pour me voir vient en ma maison*
> (charming, gentle and generously inclined lady comes to see me at home).

If there is one wine that is immediately recognisable as coming from Alsace, it must be this. Its rich flavour overwhelms that of its – by comparison – lacklustre cousins from the same grape variety made in Germany, Yugoslavia and California. Other names for it are Traminer Musqué, Gentil Rose Aromatique, also, in California, Red Traminer. There are plantings of it in central Europe, where it usually makes agreeable aromatic but rather lightweight wines, also in Australia – Len Evans comments in *Complete Book of Australian Wine* (3rd ed. 1978) on the 'lychee fruit' character. He also makes the pertinent observation that: 'The berries range from deep pink (almost red) to white in colour. Only the pink clones are grown in Alsace, as these are regarded as producing the best-flavoured wines and are invariably the most vigorous and productive vines.' This is why, in looking at colour pictures of grapes, the

Gewurztraminer is often mistaken for a black grape that isn't fully ripe.

The other French vineyard where this grape is of importance is in the Jura – not all that distant from Alsace. Here the Traminer is used for some of the rather unusual local wines, although some authorities do not seem definite that this grape is the same variety as the Savagnin used there.

French wines do not often do well in the popular and publicised comparative tastings carried out in California, but in the spring of 1975 thirty-five wines from this variety were tasted blind and, out of the five wines considered best, four came from Alsace. Number one was from Léon Beyer of Eguisheim and the home-based (California) interloper was from Mirassou – at a higher retail price.

The attractions of the Gewurztraminer are obvious and it is the best wine of all for the beginner in wine, for it has enormous fruit and flavour and, although dry, is full-bodied and low in acidity. As it is such an obvious wine, there is a tendency for some people in Alsace to despise its charms, but, as the late Jean Hugel has written (in '. . . and give it my blessing' published by his own firm): 'This is the great speciality of Alsace, a wine which has the widest appeal all over the world. In no other wine region is Traminer of such quality to be found. It is full, mild and well-rounded and it has a bouquet which appeals to everybody. This wine sells very well in England and in America. A great future lies before it. It might be called "everyman's *grand vin*"! There is no need to be an expert to realise what a good wine this is; but the fruitiness and elegance of the Traminer also appeal to the connoisseur.'

Monsieur Hugel speaks of the 'Traminer'. Is this different from the Gewurztraminer? For long, one found either name on Alsace wine labels and there was much discussion as to the nuances between the styles of the two wines. Whilst it was generally considered that the Traminer was the Gentil Nature Blanc, or Savagnin, and the Gewurztraminer was the Gentil Aromatique or Savagnin Rosé, in law there was no distinction and the two names were interchangeable. Often, the growers sold their more highly flavoured (and highly priced) wines as Gewurztraminer (for 'Gewürz' is the German word for spice) and the more neutral wines as Traminer. Indeed, as T.A.Layton says in *Wine and People of Alsace* (1970), thirty years ago the Traminer was sold almost to the exclusion of the Gewurz, as it is often referred to in wine trade talk. Though the growers of Alsace themselves seem rather confused about the matter, they generally claim that, over the years, a strain with a more exaggerated flavour has developed and almost entirely replaced the older breed. The law makers, however, have solved the problem once and for all. From 1 January 1973 the description 'Traminer' has ceased to exist and the term 'Gewurztraminer' has been the only one permitted.

The term Gewurztraminer is not, however, a new one. Such noted experts as Ortlieb and Lucien Sittler do not really clarify the matter by saying that it was developed by the noted ampelographer Chrétien Oberlin (1831–1916) in Colmar around the turn of the century. This view is sustained by Jean Gachon in

Katzenthal, famous in poetry for its wines since 1560, has been carefully restored after suffering destruction in the battle of the 'Colmar pocket' in World War II

an article in the periodical *L'Alsace*, where he writes: 'But Oberlin was a great innovator, working already on (varietal) selection. It is he who created the Gewurztraminer, the lord of our great wines of Alsace!' Sittler also confusingly says that the botanist Kirschleger came across it in Wissembourg and the neighbouring vineyards of the Palatinate as long ago as 1850. In fact Oberlin, as part of his work, appears to have listed it in 1900 as a new variety, together with such a mixed assortment as the Sauvignon, Malvoisie, Pinot Meunier, Muscat Ottonel and the Muscadelle.

The history of the Traminer is clearer. Four hundred and thirty years ago Jerome Bock said that 'great quantities ripen in the valley of the Adige, at Tramyn, and in Alsace'. Indeed, the Traminer is still widely planted in the Alto Adige, particularly around the village of Termeno, which is the Italian name for Tramyn. In 1770 the name appears in a document about a Colmar family and just ten years later a doctor from Mittelwihr, Frederick William Faudel, published *De Viticultura Richovillana*, which dealt in detail with the vineyards of Ribeauvillé; of great importance is the list of the twenty different grape varieties planted – and among them is the Weissedel or Traminer.

The Gewurztraminer has one great advantage: it will grow almost anywhere. The soil and the exposure of the slope to the sun are not of great importance. Even in years lacking in sun it is capable of producing reasonable wine. On the debit side, however, is its lack of resistance to *pourriture grise* (grey rot), which can mean some years with grossly deficient crops, and also its restricted yield. In good years, the sugar content of the grapes can be extraordinarily high and it is perhaps the variety best suited to the production of *vendange tardive* wines (see p.101ff). Indeed, the wine claiming to have the highest must weight ever recorded in Alsace is a Gewurztraminer of the 1976 vintage from the Guebwiller domaines of Schlumberger: this has 156° Oechsle, which fermented out to 13.5° of alcohol, with a further 7.5° in residual sugar. (The German system referred to as Oechsle is for measuring the amount of sugar in the must. One degree Oechsle represents the number of grams (0.04 oz) by which one litre (1.75 pints) of must is heavier than one litre (1.75 pints) of water; the sugar content is about 25 per cent of this calibration.)

Because of its general appeal as a wine and its wide adaptability as a vine, the Gewurztraminer is now challenging the Sylvaner as the most widely planted grape in Alsace, being responsible for more than one-fifth of the total plantings. Its importance is, however, rather less than it used to be – the peak years were the decade from 1955 onwards. Although the area it occupies is important, the variability of its yield can perhaps best be indicated by some comparative figures for the crop from 1977 to 1982.

Year	Hectares planted	Yield in hectolitres	Hectolitres per hectare	Percentage of total crops
1977	2368	140869	59.49	14.8
1978	2367	90319	38.16	13
1979	2397	214573	89.52	20
1980	2169	17151	67.91	2.9
1981	2433	164679	67.69	18.2
1982	2453	269650	109.93	18.6

With the possible exception of the Muscat, there is no other grape variety in the region capable of showing such widely differing production figures.

While the Gewurztraminer is grown throughout Alsace, it probably reaches its peak as regards quality in the neighbourhood of Wintzenheim in the Haut-Rhin. Here, the Hengst vineyard has an excellent reputation for this wine. Other single vineyards known for their Gewurztraminers include the Kitterlé at Guebwiller (indeed, at one time Kitterlé seems to have been accepted as an alternative name for the grape), the Rangen at Thann, the Kaefferkopf at Ammerschwihr, the Mamburg at Sigolsheim, the Sporen at Riquewihr, the portion of the Osterberg vineyard at Ribeauvillé known as Trottacker and the Zisser at Barr. More individually, the Eichberg at Turckheim is planted solely in Gewurztraminer.

Most companies will also have a particular brand name for their best Gewurztraminer and among the best known must be Les Sorcières of Dopff & Irion, Cuvée des Comtes d'Eguisheim of Léon Beyer, the Cuvée des Seigneurs de Ribeauvillé of Trimbach and the Cuvées Anne and Christine Schlumberger.

Of particular note, too, are the wines of Hugel, especially their *vendanges tardives* and *sélection de grains nobles* qualities (see also p101ff).

One final use for this grape variety to be mentioned here – though it will be dealt with separately (see page 172) – is that its marc, the residue left after the grapes have been pressed, is distilled to make *eau de vie de marc de Gewurztraminer*, a spirit having its own *appellation contrôlée*.

RIESLING

While every grower in Alsace recognises the commercial merits of the Gewurztraminer, most seem to be proudest of their Riesling. As a variety, this is planted widely throughout the viticultural world. In many vineyards where it is grown it is referred to as 'the king' and there are plenty who would rate it as the supreme white wine grape of all. It is quite a hardy variety, but not particularly impressive to look at. Because of the numerous forms in which its name appears on labels – some of the so-called 'Rieslings' have no relation to 'the' Riesling – it is important to know something about it especially as its name appears in vineyards all over the world (including Chile and other South American wine-producing countries).

Professor Doctor Helmut Becker, of the Vine Institute at Geisenheim, thinks that the White Riesling had its origin in the wild vines that still grow in the Rhine Valley; today, the overall name is 'Riesling', but there is even a local name for it in Baden – Klingelberger, probably deriving from the vineyard of the same name near the Castle of Staufenberg in Durbach, where the Riesling was first planted in 1797. In former times, those buying vinestocks would particularise what they required according to the origin of the vines – thus were referred to as either 'Rheinriesling' and 'Moselriesling' so, from such geographical specifications, the terms Rheinriesling and Johannisberger Riesling came into use, the Johannisberg name coming from the place name on the Rhine and being nothing to do with the Swiss white wine made in the Valais region, which also bears the name Johannisberg, and is made from the Müller-Thurgau grape. If the full name is given in Europe, the form is usually Rheinriesling, but Johannisberger Riesling is used in the U.S. This is the original White Riesling.

Until fairly recently there was much debate as to whether the Riesling d'Alsace was the true Rheinriesling, some members of the wine trade supposing it to be one of the huge family of 'other' Rieslings (see below). I was certainly unable to pronounce on this but, after tasting a number of late-picked Alsace wines, I ventured to remark to a member of the trade there that there seemed to be a difference between these and the late pickings of certain wines made from 'Riesling' – as far as their labels were concerned – from other countries, except for Germany; the late-picked Alsace wines were akin to, though not at all identical with, some of those I had tasted from the Rhine and Mosel. Could this indicate that the Riesling d'Alsace, making wines from grapes that had been infected by the 'noble rot' (*botrytis cinerea*), was indeed the Rheinriesling, from

Riquewihr – looking down from the vineyards

The Alsace grapes, showing colour when ripe and shape of bunches

Riesling

Gewurztraminer

Sylvaner

Pinot Blanc

Muscat

Tokay d'Alsace/Pinot Gris

Pinot Noir

The new season's shoots

Contoured vineyards in full leaf

which the finest German late-picked wines in the top categories are made? Yes, I was told – it is definitely the same. (And this was prior to the general recognition of the fact.)

What prompted my thought was that the Rheinriesling is the only grape that, when the *botrytis* acts on it, gives me an impression of 'barley sugar', an intensity and almost viscous texture, plus the curious lingering fragrance of this grape at its ripest. Other 'Rieslings' made from nobly rotten grapes don't convey this: they are full, even fat, usually somewhat liquorous and generally sweet. The Rheinriesling is the aristocrat when it is possible to compare the wines it makes with that of other Rieslings.

There are, however, a multitude of grapes and wines using some form of the name 'Riesling'. It is worth bearing this in mind – and knowing that none of them are planted in Alsace. The most abundantly cultivated is called, in Germany, Welschriesling or Wälschriesling; this appears as Riesling Italico (Italy), Olasz Riesling (Hungary), Riesling Italien or Riesling de Italie (Rumania), Italiansky Riesling (Bulgaria), Laski Riesling, Grassevina, Grasica, Italianski Rizling, Taljanska Grasevina, Biela Sladka Grasica (Yugoslavia), Risling Vlassky (Czechoslovakia) and Risling Italianski (U.S.S.R). This is according to the Deutsche Wein-Information of Mainz.

A further list adds to the confusion. The following have nothing to do with the Rheinriesling and, says Professor Becker, are only a few of the erroneous names: The Frankenriesling is the Green Silvaner; Briesgauer Riesling the Ortlieber (Knipperlé), as is the Kleiner Riesling. The Grauer Riesling is the Ruländer; the Schwarzriesling the Müllerebe; the Budaer Riesling is the Kleinweiss, the Keesmeter Riesling the Weisser Pressburger and Langsteiler; the Banater Riesling is either Zakkelweiss, Kriacza, Kreaca or Creaca. The Goldriesling is a cross of the White Riesling and Muscat Précoce de Courtiller, the Bukettriesling a cross of the Red Riesling and the Muscat St-Laurent; the Firnriesling, the Marienriesling and the Muscat Riesling are crosses of the White Riesling and the Muscat St-Laurent; the Missouri Riesling is an American cross of Riparia and Labrusca. In the U.S. there are also Grey and Emerald Rieslings and an Okanegan Riesling in Canada. Added to this – and most confusing to the drinker who merely sees 'Riesling' on a wine's label – it must be remembered that, in Australia, the Hunter River Riesling is actually the Sémillon and the Clare Riesling is the Crouchen, which is planted in various wine regions in Australia and also in South Africa, where it may simply be labelled 'Riesling'. Fortunately nowadays many growers do make use of the correct terms or evolve their own, such as 'Cape Riesling', but if one is preparing to enjoy and appraise a wine that, reasonably enough is supposed to provide a bouquet, flavour and general style of a Riesling, even if one has reason to believe – often because of the price – it is a Welschriesling and not a Rheinriesling, the total surprise of encountering, say, a Crouchen or a Sémillon is disconcerting, as all these false Rieslings are really quite unlike the Rheinriesling or, even, the Welschriesling.

It is probably not necessary to inform readers that the name of this grape should be pronounced as if the first syllable rhymes with 'geese'–but one still hears the word 'Riceling' uttered by many wine buyers.

As a grape, the Riesling has one particularly useful advantage in such northern-lying vineyards as Alsace and Germany. Although it is very late in reaching full maturity, it will continue to ripen in cool weather conditions. This means that, on the best slopes–those facing east and on either sandy soil or gentle schist–it is sometimes possible to make excellent wines in years when the other varieties are considered to have failed. In Germany the Riesling is regularly used for the production of *spätlese* (late-vintaged) and higher quality wines, but the years when *vendange tardive* (late-vintaged) wines are made in Alsace are rather rare. However, as Pierre Huglin, Director of the Colmar Viticultural Research Station says: 'As long as it is vintaged late, it can give a wine with extraordinary finesse and breeding, matching an elegant bouquet to marvellous fruit. It is certainly the wine preferred by the Alsatians themselves.'

With a yield that is never very large, even though it is a variety that resists most diseases, the Riesling is planted in almost one-fifth of the vineyard area of Alsace. Since 1969 the area under this vine has almost doubled, apparently largely at the expense of the Sylvaner in the Bas-Rhin. Indeed, in the villages of Scherwiller and Châtenois this grape now accounts for well over one-third of the total crop and it is encouraging to see that efforts are beng made to raise the overall standards of wine by planting it.

Though the Riesling is now the great grape of Alsace, it is a comparatively late arrival on the scene. Jerome Bock mentions it in the sixteenth century, but only in connection with the vineyards of Germany and the Mosel Valley. It was in fact for centuries considered to be a foreign variety, as two of its alternative names suggest–the Orleanzer and the Rheingauer. In some legislation for the town of Riquewihr, in 1644, the Riesling is mentioned for the first time as a permitted grape variety.

During the eighteenth century its popularity increased rapidly, but it was thought to be something of a luxury and was largely planted in the 'clos', the walled vineyards belonging mainly to the church and to the aristocracy. Thus it was the main variety in the Pinkenberg, which belonged to the Carthusian monks of Molsheim and, in the inventory of the Weinbach at Kientzheim, dated 1730, seven hundred 'Riesselin' vines are noted. Later in the same century a memorandum written by a member of the Sandherr family of Colmar rates it as 'Rüssling, le meilleur vin' (the best wine). In these times it was often mixed with wines made from other varieties to increase their potential for ageing (in cask at this period).

There are a number of sites renowned for their Rieslings, among which are the Brandluft at Mittelbergheim, the Schoenenberg at Riquewihr, the Schlossberg at Kientzheim and the Mandelberg at Mittelwihr. The one wine which has probably the highest reputation in Alsace, however, is the Clos

Sainte Hune at Ribeauvillé, which belongs to Trimbach; this minute vineyard of just one and a quarter hectares has belonged to the Trimbach family for more than two centuries and its production is a mere eight thousand bottles. This wine typifies the ability of the Riesling to make great wines in what are generally considered to be poor years: such an example is the 1977. I have previously described the wines of this vintage as 'ordinary, without staying power'. The Clos Sainte Hune of 1977 is still (in 1983) big and firm, with a considerable future.

It is interesting to study the effect that different soils and slopes can have on wines made from the Riesling. This can be well illustrated at the Zind-Humbrecht domain in Wintzenheim. There, side by side, can be tasted wines from the Clos Saint Urbain, which is in the Rangen at Thann and has volcanic soil; the Brand at Turckheim, which has granitic soil; the Herrenweg, which is on pebbly, alluvial soil, and the Clos Hauserer, on chalky clay. Each one of the wines demonstrates the Riesling style developed in a way typical of the grape from various sites.

So well is the Riesling partnered by the local gastronomic speciality – *choucroute* (see p.156) – that it is frequently used as an important ingredient in making the dish. (It should be pointed out that even the most chauvinistic German accepts that the *sauerkraut* of his homeland is a mere humble cousin of the Alsace noble dish.) Also, Riesling is the best accompaniment to that delightful clean dish – simple, direct, wholly adequate – a *truite au bleu* (poached trout) from the Vosges. It is the Riesling that inspires the 'deep purple' from local poets:

> Du Riesling dans le verre
> C'est le Ciel sur la Terre

(Riesling in the glass is simply heaven on earth).

More surprisingly, it even seems capable of turning the most ardent lover's thoughts away from sex:

> Quand au ciel s'allument les étoiles
> Et que ma mie me parle d'amour
> M'offrant son âme sans fardes ni voiles,
> Je caresse sa main de velours –
> Et lève au ciel mon large verre
> Où miroite claire mon Riesling,
> Et le réflet des yeux de ma chère
> Alors que cloche sonne dong ding.

> (When the stars begin to shine and my sweetheart snuggles up and says she's mine – without conditions, without restraint – I stroke her hand, and to the gods I lift my glass of Riesling, where, in ample bowl, the wine's limpidity reflects the eyes of her who wonders what comes next . . . and all the time the church bells ring their typical chime.)

André Simon brings us down to earth, when he says that 'Riesling is the noble grape *par excellence* and most of the fine Alsace wines are Riesling wines'.

At the first dinner he arranged for the Wine & Food Society, Alsace wines were featured. Pierre-Marie Doutrelant in *Les Bons Vins et les Autres* (1976) has rather a pessimistic outlook for the future of Alsace wines and imputes dubious motives to the planting policies of the growers. 'They', he says, 'think that in the next few years Alsatian wines are going to split into two categories. On the one side, ordinary Alsace *vins de comptoir* (wine served by the glass in bars), a carafe wine, which will be called Côtes d'Alsace and which will come from the low-lying land where the coarser varieties will be concentrated: the Chasselas, the Pinot Blanc, the Sylvaner; on the other hand, an Alsace-Villages, or a *grand cru* (see p. 155 ff.), born on the slopes and coming from the greatest grapes, the Muscat, the Riesling, the Tokay, the Gewurztramimer and Pinot Noir.' If these are the thoughts of the growers, it seems a great pity, for, given the right circumstances, even the unfortunate Chasselas is capable of making most enjoyable wine. What perhaps is sad is that every grower who sells his wine under his own label continues to try and make the full range of wines from the different varieties, even if his vineyards are not totally suited to them. Each vine has its ideal as regards soil and exposure, but not all can be planted on the slopes and it appears logical that the finer varieties, which have smaller yields and sell at higher prices, should benefit from the best positions.

One further relevant comment on Riesling. It is easy to say that the greatest wines of Alsace come from, say, the Riesling grape. But it should be firmly understood that not *all* Rieslings are or can be great wines. Conversely, as has been mentioned, the Sylvaner, which is generally considered to be a poor relation – if one continues the family analogy – is quite capable of demonstrating riches. Knowledge of the grape varieties and the wines they make certainly does have some value but – and this must be stressed – the name of the grape on the label should only be taken as a part of the other information that may also appear there: the vintage, the vineyard or village name, and, certainly, that of the grower or merchant.

There is no other region in France where the grape variety plays such a dominant rôle in the style of the wine. Perhaps the Alsace concept may be most easily understood if it is related to what might be the experience of a possible potential consumer of California wines, who might be able to buy Chardonnays costing either three dollars or thirty dollars a bottle. He would certainly not expect the same drinking experience from them. In California Gallo (the largest wine establishment in the world) and Heitz (one of the most highly respected likewise) each have their customers and their admirers. So it is in Alsace. Wines that may be made from the same grape varieties are put on the market in a wide range of qualities and at a wide range of prices. The grapes are, therefore, just a part of the picture – an essential part, but by no means the whole portrait of the ultimate wine.

The Wines

Trying to describe a subjective experience - tasting - in terms that will convey meaning to other people is difficult. It is even more so when shades of smells and flavours vary considerably, not only within the wine region concerned, but within the range of the individual establishments making the wine, each possessing their own ideas as to quality. In some of the wine villages there may be several producers literally within a stone's throw of each other (plus the wine co-operative), yet the wines from each house will be as individual as the human beings concerned. So generalisations are hazardous. (In this context, 'co-operative' means a grouping of growers who utilise their joint resources, owning the machinery to make the wine and the storage space, if necessary, marketing the wine and organising publicity for the members. From region to region the detailed arrangements naturally vary.)

It is perhaps possible, however, to provide some indication as to the character of a wine made in Alsace from a particular grape variety, always with the proviso that there are exceptions to every statement. And it is also relevant to stress that grapes grown in Alsace will make wines peculiar to Alsace, even though they may be varieties familiar to consumers all over the world. This is not just a matter of clonal selection (although nowadays makers are well aware of the great difference that can be made by this) nor is it wholly accounted for by methods now in use that can make not only tolerable wine in what would previously have been a disastrous year but also very much finer wines than our ancestors could have enjoyed. The situation and composition of the Alsace vineyard are also markedly influential. Although there are now some wine growers in the vineyards of the world who are of the opinion that soil can be changed if a vineyard or a vine variety requires it and others who think that climatic variations, such as exist in many of the classic vineyards of Europe, can be ameliorated or at least partially regularised, the fact remains that, in a vineyard established for a considerable time in one place, the contribution made by that vineyard and its climate or micro-climate to the ultimate wine is and must be of importance.

It is obvious that, in a vineyard such as that of Alsace, there will be marked differences in the wines if, for example, one village or a particular site suffers or benefits from the weather in a particular year. It is also obvious that wine makers utilise their resources and skills to make wines that their particular customers require; it is poor business, for example, to attempt to make a wine that, albeit fine, will cost so much to produce that few will be able to buy it. As with other fine wines, some of the best of Alsace are simply not 'commercial' at all and never can be.

Some indication of pronounced 'house styles' will be found in the sections dealing with the major producers. Here, the potential characteristics of the wines made from the principal grapes are noted, in the order in which travellers may encounter them on wine lists.

Consumers who formed their impressions of wines made a quarter of a century ago, however, should not now rely on these too much: improved methods of cultivation, vinification and conservation have made significant and, in many instances, considerable changes. Traditions have been adapted, sometimes discarded. 'What was good enough for *grand-père . . .*' isn't necessarily good enough for a younger generation, both of makers and consumers. So it is worth while giving a fresh appraisal, as unbiased as possible, at fairly frequent intervals, of all the wines, in order to keep the palate alert and the mind stimulated by variations and changes.

Sampling young wine from the spigot

The following account of what the wines made by the Alsace grapes are like has been written with the consumer in mind. I have been fortunate enough to know Alsace and its wines for a quarter of a century yet I remain the outsider – the person who goes into the supermarket, the local outlet of a big retail chain, the specialist shop, and pays over the counter for a bottle.

The way in which wines are described is not only difficult, it is a great challenge; those who work in wine will speak one language, those who merely write about wine another. I have always tried, remembering the teaching of several great authorities, to translate the words and phrases that are intelligible to those who know a great deal about wine, into language that may be more easily understood by those who are beginning to know something about it; this is seldom satisfactory when I read over what I have written, but the intention is always to provide even a few clear indications of what may be expected from good examples of certain wines from those who are sympathetically studying them.

RIESLING

This, the great and noble grape of Alsace, should not, it must be re-emphasized, be directly compared with regard to the wines it makes in Alsace with any other wines bearing the name on their labels. Unfortunately many drinkers only drink the labels!

The Riesling d'Alsace makes wines that combine a very elegant, wafting bouquet and direct flavour, a pronounced fruit (unless the vintage has been very unripe), with a balance between the crispness of the acidity and spreading, lengthy flavour. A Riesling of even moderate quality can possess depth and weight; the finer examples are impressive in this way and in the *vendange tardive* wines (see p. 101) the Rieslings are usually massive – albeit discreetly so. A quality Riesling demonstrates the nervous intensity of a fine, dry wine, subtle but, although sometimes not obviously alluring, of great charm and power once the drinker begins to appreciate it. As Jean-Louis Gyss notes, it is the Riesling that, for many, symbolises Alsace: 'Who knows the Riesling, knows Alsace and anyone who loves Alsace loves the Riesling.'

SYLVANER

It used to be said that the best Sylvaners came from the Bas-Rhin, but, like other generalisations of former times, this is no longer a safe statement to make. The Sylvaner normally makes rather lightweight wines, fresh as to bouquet, mouth-filling and lightly 'green' in flavour. The Sylvaner may be characterised by the adjective 'cool', for it is especially good to quaff by way of apéritif, its initial fragrance and agreeable delicate dryness making no serious demands on the drinker, but providing clear-cut pleasure. 'For any time, any occasion serving' say some guides, but I think it should always be remembered that it tends to be fresh and easy drinking, not usually to be studied too seriously, although the

79

1973 Sylvaner of Trimbach I remember as impressive – a wine that remained somewhat of a *soubrette* but played by a star with a particularly charming smile. Indeed, many French writers use the term 'smile' when describing Sylvaner wines. It should not be too closely associated with the wines that this grape makes – often remarkable – in Franconia; the Sylvaners of Alsace are not in this league, but can be highly agreeable.

GEWURZTRAMINER

This, the 'spicy' Traminer, is a variety that makes an immediate impression on any drinker. Its intense, complex bouquet and full, highly developed flavour, with many subtleties of taste (sometimes even leading drinkers to suppose there is a sweetness there on account of the opulent, trailing nuances on the palate) make it perhaps the most immediately popular and the 'when in doubt' choice for the beginner in the Alsace wine scene. (For more about the partnerships of food and wine, see Chapter 9).

There is usually a concentration about the Gewurztraminer that makes it easy to like, at least either for its 'mountain meadow' fragrance or its slight freshness and sturdy flavour. At its best, it is a big fat wine, but always possessing some refinement, some inner tenseness that can be imposing, never lollopy or unbalanced. It can remind some drinkers of vegetation; few people nowadays will be able to recall the smell of a slightly overripe midden or a haystack that is hot and may have a touch of rot in its aroma, but that, to me, is the better type of Gewurztraminer: a little earthy, full of the different smells of summer and the farm, quite definite, firm and lasting long on the palate.

PINOT BLANC/PINOT AUXERROIS/CLEVNER

Sometimes this grape will be referred to as the Klevner, or occasionally even Weiss Burgunder although not in Alsace. Its wines are dry, straightforward, lightly fragrant, with a clean, fresh smell, almost salty (to me), and the taste is four-square, sturdy in style and moderately mouth-filling. It may give the impression of lightness on first tasting, but the wines it makes tend to have a final 'push' at the finish, so that essentially it can be fairly full-bodied and robust. Its use in the sparkling wines is considerable and it is certainly a wine to accompany food, even of the more highly flavoured recipes, when it will not easily be swamped. Possibly one might say that it lacks much delicacy or charm but it can have considerable easy appeal.

PINOT GRIS/TOKAY D'ALSACE

Because of possible confusion with Tokay, the place, and the wine in Hungary attempts are made to stop the use of the term. However, some forms of 'Tokay' persist and, for example, it is permitted to use the word in the form of 'Tocai' in north Italy.

The Pinot Gris is, in my view, a more interesting grape than the Pinot Blanc among the wines of Alsace; it is usually light in fragrance, but slightly flowery – some French writers describe it in general as *capiteux* and, if this term (heady) can be disassociated from any suggestion as to high alcoholic strength, it may be said usually to possess a prettiness and easy-going style, of immediate appeal. In the finer examples, this grape can make wines that are both aromatic and, sometimes, definitely scented. In character, the wines can be fluid, smooth and with a somewhat subtle flavour – generally pleasing.

MUSCAT

This is a grape that makes wines that people either love – or do not like at all. 'Muscat – Muskrat' say those in the second category. The huge family of Muscats are, as has been stated, very obvious, both in the way they smell and the way they taste, whether they are dry or sweet and they display their characteristics at all levels of quality. Muscat wines, of any kind, are those of which it can truly be said that they 'smell of the grape', which very few wines actually do, but a good Muscat bouquet soars out of the glass and assails the nose almost as if the taster had plunged his face into a bunch of ripe grapes and crunched some of them. The fragrance is big, obvious, sometimes wafting languorously, sometimes arriving with a rush and crescendo of perfume. Often people receive the impression that they are going to find the wine sweet on the palate – not necessarily so and it may be partly this that makes some drinkers dislike the Muscats, which are – or should be in Alsace – dry. On the palate these wines do not usually display much complexity or shades of flavour and, although they can linger agreeably, they do not build up to a climax of taste, but maintain a direct, straightforward style.

CHASSELAS

This is somewhat of a workhorse and, today, does not contribute much in the way of notable drinking, but its wines can be fresh, crisp and dry, the flavour quite mouth-filling. The name does not appear on labels.

PINOT NOIR

This world-famous black grape here makes a red and a rosé – but not even those who produce them would claim that they can be more than agreeable, lightly fragrant, neat, slightly fruity drinks. Those that are able to stress the fruitiness can be very pleasant and the touch of velvetiness in the bouquet of good examples has definite appeal. The importance of the fruit is emphasised when the wines are served slightly chilled.

Vineyard Routine

Although disasters, such as frost at the wrong time and hail at almost any time attract public attention, vineyards are only generally in the news at vintage time. Yet this is only the climax of the wine year, when the new wine comes to birth; the preceding eleven months involve different activities, all of which contribute to the ultimate wine. Indeed, some makers would assert that it takes two years to make a vintage, because factors conditioning the style, character and quality of a wine are so closely related over a considerable period. Investment in equipment, a change in methods, an alteration in clonal selection all can have long-term influence. Here some of the wines' background is described.

In all the wine villages there is really only one crop - vines. Although, because of its fertile soil and exceptional climate, Alsace rates high in France for the production of such diverse agricultural products as cabbages, tobacco and apples, below the tree line on the steep, east-facing slopes of the Vosges, the vine is dominant, split up only by the small villages, many of which retain their medieval character, even those that had to be rebuilt after World War II.

Making wine in Alsace is essentially a family affair - though there were five times as many families involved in it fifty years ago. The vineyards are, generally, worked by the owners themselves, helped out by their wives, sons and daughters; only in exceptional cases do such concerns employ others to work their holdings.

Although, as with any other type of farmer, it is difficult to find a grower who will admit to being rich, there is no doubt that, by working hard, one can make a good living from producing wine in Alsace. The fact that the production per hectare is higher than that of any other *appellation contrôlée* wine in France (except Champagne) makes for a healthy income in most years. According to some calculations made at the end of 1974, the amount of time needed to operate one hectare of vines throughout a year totals 1044 man hours: this works out at something under twenty hours a week, including all the secretarial work necessary to satisfy the vast army of French civil servants. It must be borne in mind, however, that one hectare of vines is scarcely in itself a viable proposition and that, according to the same source of calculations made in 1974, if the cost of labour done both by the family and grape pickers imported from elsewhere at vintage time is also taken into account, running a vineyard would have cost something over £3500 a year at that time.

The work of the grower who makes his own wine is concerned with two major activities - the work of the vineyards, and that of the cellar. In both, the real working cycle begins after the vintage in the autumn.

Out in the vines, the first work that has to be done is to protect the vines against the frosts of winter, for it should be borne in mind that the Alsace

Securing the new shoots of the vines to the wires that will support them and contain the foliage

climate is quite severe, with temperatures dropping sharply and low at this time of the year. Although there is little rain, snow and heavy frosts are frequent. Also at this time, vines that have passed their useful life are grubbed up and the soil is deeply ploughed, so that it may be broken up by the frosts.

At the end of the winter, if the weather is not too severe, the first pruning takes place, so does the replacement of the soil that was carried down the hillsides by any storms during the previous summer – this is often a very difficult task, as the slopes may be as steep as one in two. Machines cannot yet solve this problem.

When spring comes, pruning reaches its peak and the women can start tying the vines to the wires that support them. Just to give some idea of the possibly unexpected and unrealised expenses of a vineyard, it is worth knowing that, in each hectare of vineyard, there will be about 36 kilometres of wire in use.

With the first real sun the vegetation begins to show on the vines and the important work at this time is the planting of new vines, which will not produce saleable wine for another three years. Formerly, vines were planted very closely together, which made vineyard working extremely difficult, but nowadays there is normally a gap of between 1.40 m and 1.50 m between the rows of vines and also between each vine and its neighbour. On most ground a tractor can pass between the rows, or straddle them. This gives about 5000 vines to each 2.4 acres (or one hectare). As an alternative to planting the new vines in March, some growers now have modern ideas and allow the young vines to spend a month or two in heated greenhouses, planting them out at the beginning of the summer.

With the advent of May there is also the necessity of protecting the vines from the spring frosts – the mid-May period of the 'Ice Saints'. Although, as most of the vineyards lie on the slopes, they are not susceptible to any great extent, a watch must be kept. Also at this time it is necessary to clip off any additional shoots that might absorb some of the moisture required by the main producing branches.

Throughout the summer there must be treatment of the vines against the fungi that seem to cause problems in vineyards all over the world – mildew and oïdium. As this is the time of greatest growth, the women must tie the shoots to the restraining wires; the rows of vines are also trimmed so that the air can circulate and sun reach the bunches of grapes now beginning to form after the flowering of the vine.

From the end of August – the French holiday month – until the middle of October there is little that can now be done by the grower, for this is the period when the grapes are ripening and their fate is in the hands of the weather. As in Germany, birds can be a serious problem, causing considerable damage to the grapes as they fill out, so the vines are sometimes protected with a type of netting to keep the grapes safe from the greedy beaks.

An Eguisheim street prepares for the vintage, cleaning *hottes* and *bennes*, the latter being the wooden containers that hold grapes during transit from vineyard to winery

The Vintage

Traditionally the vintage in Alsace begins towards the middle of October although – and this is another relic of the days under German rule – the date of the harvest is officially announced and it is an offence to go into the vineyards to pick prior to that date. In other wine regions the formal proclamation of the start of the vintage has usually become a survival from centuries ago; growers or estate owners start vintaging when they think fit and there is considerable variation. Alsace remains old-style – picking when it is decided by the authorities that quality is as it should be because of adequate ripeness. Depending on the crop, the vintage period may spread into the first fortnight in November, sometimes even later for the *vendange tardive* wines.

Because the different vine varieties planted in Alsace ripen at different times, it is normally easy for a grower or a co-operative to arrange that the different grapes be picked in sequence of ripening; traditionally, the earliest variety to ripen is the now rare Goldriesling, which is drunk at vintage time itself without the fermentation being finished – the slightly bubbly wine being enjoyed by those involved in the vintage, as was recorded by a nineteenth-century traveller, quoted on page 47. But if you are not accustomed to the hazards of drinking new and 'unfinished' wine, beware of following the local custom; wine that is still undergoing its fermentation tends to continue fermenting inside the gut of the drinker, with tiresome consequences.

The latest variety to mature is the Riesling and this can take on sweetness even during the cooler or actually cold days of autumn, which is important in years exceptional for late pickings. It is fair to say that, although no one would dispute the merits of such wines when produced by reputable companies, such as Hugel (who pioneered the publicising of them throughout the world), it is a wholly personal matter as to whether one likes them or not. Critics of *vendange tardive* wines point out that for all Alsace wines of any quality, the grapes must be late picked to a certain extent. But should any written description dealing with these special categories of wine suggest that the wines have a certain amount of residual sugar after fermentation, this must be considered as wholly alien to Alsace traditions. 'Residual sugar' which can cause problems to makers in other regions, is any sugar remaining in wine once the process of fermentation, which has been allowed to continue as long as the yeasts will work or are allowed to work, is completed. The wine is, therefore, dry – although even in the very driest wine there is a minute amount of sugar left, certainly not enough for any ordinary taster to notice. Of course, in some instances wines have their fermentation arrested by various means for various purposes, as, for example, is done in the making of port by adding spirit to stop the fermentation, but this does not happen in Alsace. It is possible, I am informed by a British Master of Wine, to filter out the wine yeasts and stop the

At one of the gates of Riquewihr, a *vigneron* carries an *hotte* of wickerwork

fermentation, by removing these, the 'work horses' of wine as they have been described. However, as what he told me on this subject contradicted the statement in the previous sentence, also made to me by a British Master of Wine, obviously I am not going to take sides! It is always possible to set authorities fighting about the technicalities within their own fields – what they assert is not invariably relevant to public understanding or, as here, to lay enjoyment. When the technicians subtract the residual sugars from the total extract, which is a concept based on what would remain if the wine could be boiled down to dryness, then what is left after the residual sugar has been subtracted is 'sugar free extract'; it is this that accounts for the 'body' of the wine.

Making the Wine

Anyone reading about Alsace wines will, after a time, become aware of a gap, an omission in any account of how they are made, for in very few books do the authors actually state what happens stage by stage and how, during the process of vinification, the juice from the crushed grapes is transformed into wine. This may be because many writers on wine are themselves wine makers or at least in the wine trade; they take the processes involved somewhat for granted. So, for the benefit of the reader not moderately familiar with what happens to grapes once they are picked, here is a general but fairly detailed account. It will be appreciated that each establishment making wine will vary the processes followed and, certainly, the installations of the long-established firms and the big co-operatives will be very different from the homely winery in use by some small maker. But the basics are the same.

In many of the individual firms, the place where the wine is made is within the enclosure of what is both the family home (often, now, being encroached on by offices and archives and the computer) and the centre of any other form of husbandry; the stables and carriage or coach houses around the courtyard of some historic firms today serve as bottling departments, tasting and reception rooms, stores for casks, cartons, equipment and files. There are still many wine families who live 'above the shop' or, as it might be more accurate to say, in the middle of it; their courtyards, often blocked by lorries, give onto the area where the press or presses stand and the fermentation vats are ranged, while the cellars, for maturation and conservation, are below ground, sometimes comprising two levels or more. Living-rooms and bedrooms may look out onto a gallery running around the courtyard, or, with windows high up under the roof, enjoy views and vantage observation points over both village and countryside.

Anyone viewing a typical installation of some age will notice a pleasing mixture of ancient and modern equipment. The *hotte*, the deep, triangular container that is strapped to the back – and holds a surprisingly heavy weight of grapes – is in use in many French wine regions, but very noticeably in Alsace; carriers have both arms free to pick or, as often happens, to use to manoeuvre up and down the steeper slopes, or hold a staff on a long tramp. The carrier will take it to a waiting cart and then, without unstrapping it, bend and tip the grapes into the baskets in the cart or on the lorry. These and the *hotte* itself may be plastic these days as they are not only cheaper, lighter but far easier to keep clean than wickerwork. Baskets used for transporting grapes are *bottiches*.

In cellars one may sometimes see a big cask which will be a *pipe* (pronounced 'pip' in Alsacien); this is a container of 600 litres and should not be confused with the *pipe* used for port, which holds 522.48 litres. The Alsace *pipe* is closer to the *Halbstück* of the Rhine (610 litres) or the *Halbfuder* of the Mosel (580 litres), a relic of the time when large casks served both for storage and

Vintaging in the vineyards above Riquewihr. The *hotte* is today made of lightweight plastic.

transport and also for making an impressive effect when fine wine was drawn from such a large vessel for some important occasion.

The modern installations, of course, have been able to be planned and built to accommodate modern equipment; many of those whose premises were damaged or razed to the ground in World War II and whose cellars might have had to shelter people rather than wines during the fighting, cheerfully admit that, starting from scratch, they could often benefit from the advice of contemporary cellar and winery designers. The layout of many of these newer establishments is impressive, because of their size and also the care with which details have been worked out and incorporated: 'practical is beautiful' in this context. But even in the smaller, older concerns no space is wasted, no opportunity neglected to ensure that, during the whole procedure of grapes coming in, being pressed, wine being made and then matured in wood or tanks, with a multitude of movement and treatments along the way, everything should be done as speedily and easily as possible and–most important in dealing with wine–everything should be able to be kept impeccably clean. It is as if the Alsace wine makers have made a virtue from the necessity of, in former and troubled times, having to contain their operations within fairly small spaces and make the most of each inch. It is remarkable how cellars often centuries old are still in use, adapted to present-day efficiency, the passage of fork-lift trucks, the siting of steel bins for bottled wines, the installation of modern bottling, labelling and packing lines; like an iceberg, the above-ground part of a winery that the ordinary visitor sees may be only a part of the entire establishment.

Anyone used to the sometimes picturesque but often primitive appearance of many of the wine installations in both Burgundy and Bordeaux will have an agreeable surprise on seeing the almost clinical cleanliness of most of the press houses of Alsace, even at the busy time of the vintage. Mould on the walls of old

Modern presses–note the chains inside–with pipes that can feed in the grapes and pump away the debris, after the juice has run out through the slatted sides as the presses revolve

cellars, of course, is not 'dirt', indeed, it is sometimes referred to as 'the cellarmaster's flower', because its presence can contribute to the preservation of wines and aid their maturation, especially while they are in cask. Mould, draped over bins and formed like padding on walls, is in fact perfectly clean to the touch even when it looks black.

The Alsace wine maker is a purist. An example of this is the fact that the late Jean Hugel insisted that, so as to avoid the slightest risk of any contamination during the tricky stage of starting to make the wine, even the screws inside his wine presses should be of stainless steel, consequently able to be cleaned as thoroughly as any part of the equipment of a modern operating theatre. True, the period of vinification for white wines tends to be fraught with more difficulties than when making reds, but the fairly high alcoholic degree of most Alsace wines and the circumstance of them all being 'fully fermented', with no potentially troublesome sugar remaining, does mean that there is here no need for the hyper-sterility of many a German press house and cellar. But no chances are taken, premises are cleaned and kept clean and equipment and people likewise.

The vintage, as has been said, usually starts in October. Earlier vintages have been known, but this is the most customary date. It lasts for about four weeks although any *vendange tardive* wines may be picked much later.

The grapes ripen at different rates, the Sylvaner tending to be first after any Goldriesling; this enables pressing and fermentation to be spaced out, with the Riesling and Gewurztraminer grapes generally being picked towards the end of the vintage. Much depends, of course, on the relative ripeness of the grapes on different sites, but the varieties are picked and processed separately, although in the past there are accounts of several varieties being flung into the press at the same time, which might well occur when somebody had only a small holding and wished to make all his wine within a short period.

This processing of all the different grape varieties at one time is what evolved in Burgundy as the 'Passe-Tout-Grains' wine, when the Pinot Noir and Gamay are picked and made into wine together. In Alsace today this is not done and any blending of the wines from different grape varieties, as for Edelzwicker, takes place later. As well as the increased knowledge of today's wine makers, so that different grape varieties can be left until exactly ripe, the grower's impression can be confirmed by reading an instrument that will register the sugar content of a drop of grape juice prior to picking, so that the must weight can be established. It would be extremely difficult to cope with huge quantities of grapes all arriving at the wine-making establishment at the same time. Grapes left in the baskets or containers in which they have been tipped after picking can begin to 'press themselves' by the sheer weight and, after a time, fermentation may start, which is wholly undesirable. Each day it is decided what variety is to be picked, from each particular plot.

Mechanical harvesters have not yet appeared in Alsace, although many

Alongside a press, the final contents of a *benne* are emptied of grapes and debris

European vineyards have begun to use them; for large, flattish areas there are obvious advantages, in spite of the high initial cost of the machines and the necessity for using skilled operators to avoid damage to the vines. To be able to wait until grapes are fully ripe and then, within hours instead of possibly days –always with an eye on the sky for a change in the weather–to be able to rush the fruit to the winery can, certainly, enable quality to be improved for what might, in former times, have been rather 'ordinary' wines.

The steep or steepish slopes that produce the fine wines of Alsace would not be able to take such mechanical harvesters as are yet produced, but the vineyards on the plain could; this, of course, would cut overall labour costs and enable vintagers picking by hand to be concentrated where their work is required. My Alsace friends tell me that the subject has been discussed and that the Alsace growers are willing to allow experimentation to continue; Guy Dopff, as President of the C.I.V.A., says: 'We shall wait and reserve judgement. We do not say that machines should or should not be used–as yet.' Once again, the Alsace temperament demonstrates its breadth of vision and its good sense.

Pressing

Something else that tends to be taken for granted is the press – the device that starts the process whereby grapes yield their juice that becomes wine. They must be squeezed or crushed, but the days of stamping on them or the use of heavy rounded gigantic wooden beams to operate a screw are long past. The exact control of the pressure and the necessity for keeping anything involved with pressing scrupulously clean involves a variety of sensitive equipment. Several sorts of press may be used by a single firm and there would appear to be various kinds working throughout Alsace. It is even possible that a small-scale grower, making wine solely for family purposes, may still utilise an antique wooden press. It is, after all, only in use for four weeks in the year. But in general the grapes are broken up by being gently squeezed in a horizontal press, with chains looped on the sides, to break up the 'cake' of fruit. Two plates, one at each end of the Swiss-roll-shaped cylinder, then gradually advance, so that the juice runs off through the slats in the sides of the slowly revolving press. Another type of press contains a bag that slowly inflates, squeezing the grapes against the sides of the press and allowing the juice to run off. The first type, most in use, is generally referred to as a 'Vaslin' after a well-known manufacturer, the second as a 'Willmes'. My friend Mrs Aileen Trew, who is not only a Master of Wine but has taught those going in for this difficult examination, has lent me her notes on the pressing in Alsace, which read: 'The grapes are . . . bruised between two rollers, so that they can be more easily transported (i.e. by pump) into the horizontal press'. The rollers are like a small mangle propped over a recipient. 'Vaslin presses', adds Mrs Trew, 'are generally used, but some of the quality wine producers use the more gentle Willmes press. Formerly the juice was left to fall clear by gravity for a couple of days (*débourbage*), but nowadays the centrifuge is very widely used. It "cleans" the juice by separating any particles of grapeskins, stalks or leaves. After passing through the centrifuge some liquid SO_2 (sulphur dioxide) is added to the juice in order to inhibit the wild yeasts and to slow the start of the fermentation . . . The fermentation commences three to four days after the addition of SO_2 and by strict temperature control it is kept slow and cool. In a tumultuous fermentation the aroma and bouquet of the wine would be lost. Fermentation lasts three to four weeks and the wine is then racked (off the dead yeast cells) into a clean vat.'

The big co-operatives will have several parallel rows of presses, each able to handle a large quantity of fruit; in such large press houses the grapes may be first unloaded into hoppers, which can move along rails to discharge their loads into the presses to which they are directed, after which the juice is taken by pipeline into the fermentation vat or cask.

Mrs Trew's mention of the use of sulphur dioxide as a disinfectant, preventing the work of the wild yeasts, which may start the fermentation but

93

An old press in the Musée d'Unterlinden in Colmar

are seldom strong enough to carry it through and complete the process, will be familiar to most students of wine. Putting the must—the unfermented grape juice before it becomes wine—through a centrifuge not only draws off solids and impurities that might later cause trouble in the wine, but also extracts the maximum amount of juice.

Fermentation

Fermentation may take place in tanks or vats or, still, in huge wood casks. It is perhaps worth stressing that, although 'old looks beautiful', and many of the giant wooden vats have been doing their job satisfactorily for a long time, the use of stainless steel, enamel or other contemporary materials for vats can have advantages at this stage of wine making. It is possible to keep such modern vessels scrupulously clean and free from any potential infection and, of course, steel is easier to maintain than wood, which requires the skill of the experienced cooper – tending to be a rarer and rarer person these days. Modern vats also take up less space than casks.

It is not always immediately realised by visitors to wine installations that wine seldom remains long in the vessel in which it has undergone fermentation – or, even if it does, it will be moved out at one stage or another, or else the lees and deposit will be pumped off. Newly made wine is usually run off from the fermentation vat into other containers – tanks or casks of various sizes. During fermentation the container does not, most authorities think, contribute much to the ultimate wine; it is afterwards that the vessel in which the wine

Antique casks still in use but, at the back, modern vats, taking less space. Note the tiled floor and gutters to facilitate hosing down at frequent intervals. The 'door' to both casks and vats is still tiny – yet this is how men get in to clean the inside

'grows up' or matures can play its part. It is not, however, often worth while these days to have wooden casks specially made for this stage of the wine's development, except for the very finest wines; thanks to the assistance of the laboratory and if the wine has been correctly appraised and made at the outset, it can be brought to its prime in a tank and kept in this condition. Technicians see that the wine is correctly constituted and balanced, especially, with white wines, as regards the acidity; they observe that the wine yeasts are working satisfactorily or, if they are not, that they are assisted to do so. This is why the 'cleansing' (*débourbage*) of the new wine or must is important; the process allows any elements in the liquid to settle. The wine is especially vulnerable at this stage of its life, but much depends on what it is proposed to make and what the basic materials are: in certain vintages the wine may happily resist infection and appear mainly to look after itself, in others it often requires protection and help.

Cask head, featuring a
mermaid around the spigot

Casks

Cooperage is, however, still an art in Alsace. Many cellars can display a great variety of both fermentation and maturation casks, some huge, holding up to 100 hectolitres. In Hugel's cellars there is a giant cask of this kind, made in 1715 and still in regular use – the firm's claim that this is the oldest 'working' cask in the world has so far remained unchallenged. There are various sizes in use for maturation, some casks being elongated ovals, such as are often seen in Germany; their shape makes it possible to fit more of them into a rather cramped cellar. Small casks often hold a limited quantity of very fine wine. It is difficult for visitors to imagine how such old vats and casks are cleaned and maintained by men who go into them through the little arched 'door' in the head

The late M. Jean Hugel in front of the Sainte Cathérine cask in Hugel's Riquewihr cellars. Built in 1715, it has been in continuous use for wine ever since – the oldest in the world of its kind

or at the side, but until a cellar hand gets too fat in he will go, one arm and shoulder first, then his head, then the rest of him, his feet and legs supported and given a helpful push by a colleague.

The casks gain a beautiful patina with age. Inside, the huge deposits of tartrates, several inches thick (as can be shown in Hugel's cellars by examining a section of a dismantled cask) indicate the contribution wood can make to the maturation of wine. One maker of great repute relates how his father would always 'finish' any wine that had undergone certain difficulties in a particular favourite cask. The improvement was always noted. I am, however, informed by members of the wine trade that 'this skin of tartrate crystals is scraped away from the wood so that there can be contact between the wine and the wood'. These commentators point out that tartrate deposits will form in any vat or container, whatever it is made of. I can only report what several wine makers have told me in Alsace where the reaction of wine and container – wood, steel, cement or what have you – is demonstrated through displaying the tartrate deposits to visitors.

Many of the casks and vats are decorated with carvings, especially around the spigot. The tradition of these carvings goes back a long way: the Hospice Civile in Strasbourg has three casks with patterns and designs on their heads of which the youngest is four and a half centuries old. Sometimes important national or regional events are commemorated on casks or the occasion when the head of the firm got married or his children were born. There are recurrent biblical themes: Joshua and Caleb returning from the Promised Land with a huge bunch of grapes, Noah suffering from the after-effects of having discovered how to make wine. Bunches of grapes – emblem of Christ 'the true vine' – St Urbain, patron of many wine makers, the Virgin and Child, the 'monogram' of Jesus (I.H.S.) may all be seen; coats of arms, both religious and civil, intricately decorated cross pieces with initials and various signs and symbols often complete the main scene or design, frequently in high relief. The carvers were often themselves owners of vineyards and makers of wine and, as well as making the full-sized casks and vats, they would put together and decorate little casks, either for use at table or on a buffet, for drawing off wine down in the cellar or for carrying on journeys, or to the fields, all miniature versions of the cellar casks. As the power of the church declined, secular and pagan subjects became popular: Bacchus and Silenus, often straddling the spigots, dolphins, lions, sirens, horses, fishes and figures representing countries all appear; scenes of peasant celebrations are also shown. Sometimes a cooper would make a cask of deliberately fantastic shape and decoration, to demonstrate his skill. There are two in the museum in Strasbourg of interlaced ovals, mounted on extremely elaborate stands. These were probably intended only for very special wine on very special occasions, not for routine cellar use. Before bottles were in common use such casks would dispense wine at large gatherings.

Treatment and Malolactic Fermentation

Both ancient and modern equipment that may be seen in an Alsace cellar are likely to be still in use – anything kept purely for historic or decorative reasons will be in the reception room or any museum of the establishment. The makers do not shun progress, but they retain their traditions and their independence of outlook. They are united, however, in their aim to conserve both the body and natural taste of the fruit that makes the wines. Pierre Seltz, a grower in Mittelbergheim, who was sufficiently outward-looking to go and study the production of wine at the world-famous department of the University of California, familiarly referred to as 'Davis', says: 'I have sought to know as much as I can so that I can return as closely as possible to nature'. Or, as the late Jean Hugel would say: 'A wine that has been well treated has not been treated at all'.

Because of this overall policy, Alsace wine, as mentioned elsewhere, is treated as little as possible before being bottled. Usually only one racking (the process whereby the wine is taken off the lees in cask or vat and transferred to another vessel) is required after the fermentation is complete. How long that fermentation lasts depends largely on the individual wine but, generally, the wine will have fermented out (all the sugars in the juice having been converted to alcohol by the fermentation process) by the early spring after the vintage. However, there are exceptions. Hugel tell of a Gewurztraminer 'Beerenauslese' (as it was then called) that they made in 1947 – a hot summer – which continued fermenting until August 1948!

The general procedure in Alsace is to avoid – by careful preparation and treatment – the malolactic fermentation, the stage at which the malic acid in the wine is converted into lactic acid and carbon dioxide (CO_2). This need not much concern the drinker but some makers prefer either to get the 'malo' over early, even, if possible, along with the first stages of the ordinary fermentation, or else to suppress it, because they wish to preserve the freshness resulting from this retention of the malic acid – if that is the type of wine they aim to make. But the decision must rest with the individual wine maker and the various wines involved. In *Le Vin d'Alsace* J. Victor Dietrich states that allowing the malolactic fermentation to take place is in order for the red wines, but he is cautious about the possible advantages of allowing it with the white wines, some of which may gain in fruit and charm if it takes place, while certain grape varieties may, on the other hand, lose their particular appeal. He states that between fifteen and twenty per cent of Alsace wines do undergo their malolactic fermentation.

From talking to many makers, it would seem that, although some definitely suppress the 'malo', others do not invariably do so and, if it should start, they do not interfere with its progress. Because of the great individuality of the wines between region and region, site and site, maker and maker and, of course, vintage and vintage, processes involved in wine making vary within the scope of what is known, what is possible, what is available and, of course, what is permitted. The same applies to all the handling of the wines. But it is fair to say that, although the Alsace oenologists are highly qualified and experienced and not at all chauvinistic or resistant to change, it is remarkable how many of the Alsace wines are still made without recourse to more than the most basic procedures, plus, naturally, improved methods of hygiene and handling, such as have been previously mentioned.

Bottling

Bottling takes place at any time from six to eighteen months after the vintage though, with demand for wine increasing and also a tendency to drink wines while they are young, the former is nowadays more likely than the latter. The weather is influential in selecting the time for bottling, also, naturally, the characteristics of the wines and the vintage must be taken into account. In a modern cellar, however, it is quite possible to maintain wine in a state of suspended animation, so that it does not suffer by delays prior to bottling.

Most makers yearn for a really up-to-date bottling plant. Indeed, when showing off a recently acquired one to a visitor, they may seem to spend rather a long time enjoying looking at it. (But this is something common to all wine makers of the world–the drinker tends to be more interested in what is in the bottle rather than the mechanism that gets it there.) Filtration takes place before bottling, except in the establishments of a few very reactionary makers who feel that this process takes away something, however infinitesimal, of the wine's character: the public insistence on 'star bright' wines, however, usually prevails and some U.S. customers continue to complain that the wines are not yet filtered sufficiently to get all the 'bits' (usually tartrates) out of them, harmless though these are.

It is significant, though, that few bottles of Alsace wines are returned as 'defective' to the makers, although certainly some are less good than others. And the makers claim that, in many instances, it is just this absence of too much 'chemistry' in handling their wines that makes it possible to drink a fair amount of Alsace without ill effects. One maker was definite that the appeal to those who cross the Rhine from Germany to load up their cars with Alsace is because it is easier to drink more bottles of Alsace at a sitting than the wines of the neighbouring country!

4

Some Special Wines

The Alsace wine maker is adventurous and inclined to experiment when he sees some likelihood of attracting more customers. By varying the style of his wines, it is possible for him to offer either a novelty or else something a little different from competitors' products. As early as the thirteenth century a *vinum nobile* was sought after (it seems to have been a superior type of Edelzwicker) and in the seventeenth century vast numbers of merchants from Baden, Württemburg and innkeepers from Munich came to buy *vin noble*. Wines bearing site names, such as Rangen and Brand, were esteemed and fetched high prices.

So the post-World War II evolution of certain special wines was not revolutionary, though possibly inevitable. Increased technical knowledge and the ability to control making wines at each stage of their production encouraged growers to attempt to perfect the sorts of wines that, hitherto, were the result of favourable circumstances and a happy but chancy coincidence of various factors. In studying the sorts of wines attracting both publicity and money, the Alsace growers were conscious of the increased production of the late-picked wines of Germany where, increasingly, even 'Eiswein' was made in some regions from grapes that had to be actually coated with ice when they arrived at the press; such wines, previously usually made as something of a last hope in otherwise unsatisfactory years when vineyard owners at least thought it worth their while to make some use of grapes still hanging on the vines, began to be much publicised and, in the saleroom, to run up the bidding.

The use of German descriptive terms, such as 'Spätlese' (late picked), 'Auslese' (specially selected bunches) and even the categories of 'Beerenauslese' (specially individually selected grapes) and 'Kabinett' (implying special reserve), began to be put on Alsace labels when a grower felt that the bottle was out of the ordinary as regards quality. Hugel, especially involved with such unusual wines, put the words 'Réserve exceptionnelle' on the labels of some of the bottles they considered particularly fine. It is unlikely that these wines, produced in small quantities at the best of times, attracted much attention from all but the most interested customers outside the region, but the authorities were at once aware of their potential importance and, in 1976, forbade the use of any German words and expressions on Alsace labels, thereby establishing an individuality of character for certain special wines.

It is slightly ironic, however, that in the regulations governing the wines, the Oechsle scale – a German system for measuring the amount of sugar in the must (the fermented grape juice) – is used. In very general terms, when a sweet or sweetish wine is the aim of the maker, the higher the degree Oechsle the better; however, if a not so sweet wine is to be made, a lower degree of Oechsle is acceptable. This applies of course to truly dryish or definitely dry wines. In many New World vineyard regions, however, the system of 'Brix' is used and it has been defined by Alexis Lichine as 'a hydrometer scale used to measure the approximate sugar content of grape juice, sweet wines and sugar solutions. The scale is calibrated to indicate percentage by weight of sucrose when it is immersed in sucrose solutions. The Brix hydrometer is usually calibrated at 17.5°C or 20°C. The sugar in the must will – if the subsequent wine is correctly handled and kept – result in a certain specific quality being attained; this is why, these days, wine makers go out and take samples of the juice in individual grapes before the vintage – they are assessing the potential capabilities of the wine that may be made from these grapes. Of course, they may not wish to make wines of a certain style, quality and price – but it is up to them to know what they are doing with the material available before they utilise it.

For those who find all scientific terms difficult to grasp, it may be easier to understand the Brix hydrometer if it is translated into Baumé degrees. This is a French system, measuring the sugar content in wine, one degree (1°) Baumé being approximately equal to 0.6 oz (18 grammes) of sugar to each litre of wine. A somewhat luscious table wine may have 3-5° Baumé, a rather dry wine about 1° Baumé. (With fortified wines the degree may be higher.) But it should be stressed, especially in this context, that one producer's 'dry' – or one maker's 'Auslese' in Germany – may be someone else's 'medium dry', or, even, 'verging on sweet'. This is what makes generalisations about wines, even those subject to fairly strict controls, difficult; one firm's 'dry' may, quite legitimately, be someone else's 'medium'. The maker determines the style and the basic character of the wine.

Until April 1983 those wines that were entitled to be called *vendange tardive* (late vintaged) were obliged to attain 108° Oechsle or 24.5 Brix and a natural minimum alcohol potential (14.3 per cent for Tokay and Gewurztraminer). Those described as *sélection de grains nobles* (wines made with specially selected grapes of the 'noble' varieties) were obliged to attain 126° Oechsle or 29 Brix and a natural minimum alcohol potential (16.4 per cent for Tokay and Gewurztraminer). But a law governing these wines came into force on 1 April, 1983. See Appendix VIII for details of this.

For any *vendange tardive* wine, the Riesling, Pinot Gris, Gewurztraminer and Muscat d'Alsace are permitted. The grapes go in whole bunches into the horizontal press. But there are many opinions about when and how they are picked: in the 'long hot summer' of 1976, the Hengst vineyard as vintaged and made by Jos. Meyer of Wintzenheim made their *vendange tardive* Riesling from grapes picked on 28 November. The clay-chalk soil contributes to a briskness in the ultimate wine. The Cuvée Christine Schlumberger, 1976 Gewurztraminer, displayed a light, almost 'quaffable' style, but the astonishing Cuvée Anne Schlumberger (picked on 7 and 8 November, attaining 13.5° Gay Lussac – percentage of alcohol by volume – and an amazing 156° Oechsle) was an amber wine, intense, lingering, aromatic rather than fragrant, wholly imposing. The 1976 Hengst Riesling of Zind Humbrecht (127° Oechsle) is another extremely concentrated wine, but finished dryer than perhaps initial impressions of smell and opening flavours might indicate. This is true, although the wine is quite different in character, of the 1976 Riesling *vendange tardive* as made by Hugel, which possesses an inner crisp, almost zippy style and, again, is dryer than is immediately anticipated.

Possibly because of the increased popularity and number of *vendange tardive* wines made, dates for picking are now often much later than would have been previously risked: Schlumberger picked their 1981 on 6 December, when there was actually snow on the vineyard. There are also very different styles within this category of wine – indeed, the concepts and aims of the various makes is emphasised notably, even more so with the *sélections de grains nobles*, although these wines, for obvious reasons, are not made as often as the *vendanges tardives*. One respected maker feels that the degree of alcohol should not be too high, ideally not in excess of 12.7-12.8 Gay Lussac, as this results in well-balanced wines, without too much residual sugar. Others do not find this a detraction.

What should be remembered is that some growers either cannot or do not wish to make wines of this kind; commercial considerations are obviously important but also there is the matter of the vineyard or vineyards; the Muré establishment, for example, who produce excellent wines from the Clos St. Landelin at Rouffach, don't make *vendange tardive* wines at all, because, it has been found, the grapes grown on this particular site invariably ripen early and cannot be left. Sometimes grapes from other plots are combined with others, the 1971 *vendange tardive* Muscat of Meyer, for example, was made with grapes from both Ribeauvillé and Wintzenheim and displays all the qualities of a thoroughly ripe wine with a touch of the 'noble rot' (*botrytis cinerea*).

In very general terms, wines made from late-harvested grapes seem to come from soils that are light, rather than very rich (the Hengst wines, for example, are from vines planted in clay-chalk soil), so that the vines anyway possess the ability to convey brisk, almost vivacious qualities to the wines. Nor should the site be very flat or low-lying, because aeration is important, if as the *botrytis* develops, it is not to be accompanied also by the ordinary grey rot. Hugel's *sélection de grains nobles* wines come solely from two vineyards at Riquewihr, the Sporen and the Schoenenberg, which have been praised for centuries. Hugel were at one time the only major firm producing this particular category of wine but 1983 added others.

When and alongside what are these wines to be drunk? They must not be thought of as primarily sweet. Some are–according to the style of the maker–but it would possibly be more correct to generalise about them as being weighty, intense and overall more 'important'. They should never be relegated generally to the category of 'sweet wines' for serving with a sweet dish. The late Jean Hugel considered that such rare and choice wines should be sampled in a leisurely way, in sympathetic company and, definitely, outside the context of a meal; thus, they can be registered and remembered with pleasure and the respect they deserve. Nor, he adds, should they ever be tasted with the slightest reference to their price.

However, Jean Hugel did admit that wines in this special category, made from the Gewurztraminer, can be impressive partners for 'the mellifluous flavours of the *pâtisserie*, and enhance ice-cream and sorbets, in short, anything that does not include chocolate, which annihilates the flavour and bouquet of any wine.' Of course, much also depends on what the dishes and the wines preceding any important conclusion have done to the drinker's palate.

Some have found that–again with the appropriate company and plenty of time to sip rather than quaff–it is possible to offer a *vendange tardive* wine before a meal, possibly omitting any subsequent wine with the first course, which would have to be a dish with which wine needs not to be served, or a form of 'palate changer', such as a soup or consommé. The weight and depth of these wines does mean that any that follow them must either be quite different, from a different region possibly, or that they must be even weightier and more important than the wine preceding them.

Otherwise and in case anyone wishes to experiment, it is perhaps worth noting the possible general styles of the different grape varieties: the Muscat, in these special categories, develops great opulence and allure, whereas the Gewurztraminer seems often to fine down, intensify and become extremely complex. The Pinot Gris gains in weight, but spreads its style, so that it becomes ample and, even if you are appraising it outside the context of a meal, this full, demanding character seems to require some form of 'blotting-paper' or food to accompany it. The Riesling, as might be expected, develops in nobility and authority and, in most late-picked examples, achieves a wonderful 'smiling' bouquet that lures the drinker, plus a depth of fruit and tautness of construction that make it imposing without ever being overwhelming.

Mr Pearce   (Angleterre)

3 x 1   R. rés 85   43,80
                    ——————
                    131, 40 F

5

The Sparkling Wines

Twenty-five years ago sparkling wines were a rarity in Alsace. Even as recently as the mid- and late 1970s production was a mere million bottles. In 1983 more than five million came onto the market–and this figure does not include the sparkling wines made by the less complicated and less expensive method known as 'sealed vat' or *cuve close*. They cannot be termed 'Alsace' like the *crémants*. Today *nos crémants,* as the proud recommender of the wines in a restaurant may refer to them, are increasing business and, in fact, fill a rôle in the wine scene that gives pleasure to many. If you do not select a Muscat as apéritif, why not a *crémant*?

The term, however, requires some explanation in this context. The word 'crémant' means 'creaming'–foaming; but, in Champagne and other regions where sparkling wines are made, such as the Loire Valley, the term signifies a wine that sparkles but slightly less so than one that is fully 'mousseux' (fizzy). The difference is not always easy to spot, unless it's possible to compare two glasses side by side, but, in essentials, the wine that is fully sparkling (*mousseux*) will have a pressure of approximately 5.6 atmospheres behind its cork, that of a *crémant* between 3.5 and 4.5 atmospheres. This involves some further explanation, to make the 'push' behind the cork of a sparkling wine understandable, Patrick Forbes' masterly book *Champagne, the Wine, the Land and the People* (1967) must be quoted: 'One atmosphere is the equivalent of 15 lb per square inch', the expression referring to the compression, because 'air compressed to half its volume quadruples its force'. This is easy to understand if the unscientific reader remembers what happens when they squeeze out the air from their mouth when blowing up a balloon–the air is compressed into the balloon's space and, if the grip on the balloon's neck is released, the air already compressed in it rushes out with some force into the surrounding air. The force behind the cork of a fully sparkling wine is, as one Champagne establishment explains it, the same as the force that would rush out if one released the valve in the tyre of a London bus–something akin to a bullet.

Now, EEC regulations (not to be confused with those that apply only in France) define a wine that has more than one atmosphere and not more than two behind its cork as *pétillant* (subdued mini-sparkle-liveliness without exuberant fizz). The EEC says that, if a wine has more than three atmospheres behind its cork, then legally it is a sparkling wine. It would, however, be quite difficult to differentiate between a wine of 2.5 atmospheres and one of three - unless one knew. Taste and the laboratory are not always doing the same job - the one appraises a wine as the potential pleasure to the drinker, the other provides the analysis of what the wine is and what it contains.

As if this were not sufficiently complicated, it has to be stated, for U.K. readers, that British regulations insist that if a bottle is sealed with a mushroom cork (the type used for fully sparkling wines, including, of course, Champagne), if this is wired down and if the bottle is 'dressed' or in any way labelled to look as if it contains sparkling wine, then H.M. Customs and Excise consider that the wine *is* fully sparkling - and, therefore, it pays the duty exacted on fully sparkling wine. In some instances, producers of Coteaux Champenois (the still wine of the Champagne region, sometimes formerly referred to as Champagne *nature*) have used a mushroom cork, clipped onto the neck of the bottle to ensure that the traditional and natural vivacity of the region's still wine will be kept within bounds - and the wine has had to pay fully sparkling duty. The same has occurred with *pétillant* wines from the Loire, similarly stoppered and presented, but often having only a slight sparkle. The buyer of such wines in the U.K. must put up with the price.

In Alsace, however, the term 'crémant' does not mean that a 'Crémant d'Alsace' is less than fully sparkling. The *crémants* here are fully sparkling wines, with approximately 5.6 atmospheres behind the cork of each bottle.

The name 'crémant' has been adopted fairly recently. The Alsace makers sought a descriptive term in the period after World War II. In 1976 a decree authorised the use of the term 'crémant' which, as it had not been previously defined but was only understood to possess a certain significance in relation to certain specific wines, was considered to be 'in the public domain' - in other words, a term that might be used in another context without any misleading or erroneous implications. So, henceforth, the sparkling wines of Alsace have been known as *crémants* although - and this is an important condition - the word is restricted in Alsace to those wines only made according to the Champagne method and that have been granted the *appellation contrôlée*, signifying their origin as that of Alsace. The producers of *cuve close* or sealed vat method sparkling wines are not permitted to be referred to as 'Crémants d'Alsace' and they are not able to bear the *appellation contrôlée*. Some pleasant sparkling wines are made by this sealed vat method, but they are not Crémants d'Alsace.

Pioneer of the quality sparkling wines of Alsace was Julien Dopff (1875-1972). Already a respected wine maker, he enjoyed a lifelong friendship with the Heidsieck family of Reims; it was therefore natural for him to be familiar with and interested in the production of sparkling wine and, eventually, he decided that it was both possible and commercially interesting to make these in Alsace. This was a creative notion because, it should be remembered, the Germans, unwilling to allow serious competition with their own wines from Alsace, discouraged quality wine making in the region and concentrated on buying large amounts of medium grade wines, many of them intended for use in blends – sometimes with those of Yugoslavia, or for the production of German sparkling wines; even then the consumption of sparkling wine in Germany was high.

Julien Dopff observed the Champagne method demonstrated at the Paris Exhibition of 1900 and made definite, albeit slow progress with his own wines. It is possible, though, that they might have remained largely a local speciality had not the world demand for sparkling wines risen markedly in the 1960s and 1970s.

Changing patterns of social drinking have also contributed to the demand: an apéritif in the form of a sparkling wine makes it possible to avoid offering a range of other drinks. The 'party spirit' swiftly created by a fizzy drink is well known. The tonic effect of a sparkler along with the suggestion of gaiety and instant pleasure is highly acceptable. The swing away from the habit of many people – especially in wine regions – taking their preprandial drink in a café on their way home has been conducive to making a glass of sparkling wine an appreciated, often slightly luxurious and chic drink before a meal. Indeed, the 1982 sales of *crémants* show an increase of 350 per cent over the 1981 total.

Today, there are more than a hundred firms making Crémants d'Alsace, some of them having been formerly reluctant to do so but, viewing the market and the popularity of the sparklers, joining the current trend. Each house, it should be stressed, follows its own style – that of Dopff 'Au Moulin', is somewhat austere, a little reserved; but, because it is not worth while subjecting indifferent wines to the process whereby the sparkle of the second fermentation is retained within them, most provide pleasant drinking.

The huge, modern co-operative at Eguisheim utilises 'gyropallettes', frames that will take 450 bottles each and, within fifteen days, will both rotate and incline them progressively, necks down, so that the deposit inevitable in the bottle is directed onto the wine's first cork. At Ammerschwihr – where the wines' acidity makes them specially suitable for transforming into sparklers – the independent family firm of Sick-Dreyer has not yet (in 1983) released their first *crémant*, made in 1981, because they consider that the wine requires marked bottle age before being put on the market. They are using silver capsules for their *crémant*, following the earlier tradition whereby all *Sekt* (German sparkling wine) had similar capsules in the nineteenth century and they have even designed a special glass for *crémant*; it has a foot with a *knop* or knob of the green glass traditional for the stems of many Alsace wine glasses, and this is topped by a clear glass bowl, narrow at the base and opening to a slightly 'open tulip' shape towards the rim. Usually, *crémants* are served in the type of elongated tulip glass familiar in most catering establishments.

The main grapes used for *crémants* are the Pinot Blanc, Sylvaner and Riesling, although sometimes certain others are allowed to be used, including the Pinot Noir; the Tokay or Pinot Gris is not generally considered suitable and some producers are not much in favour of the Riesling, although it would seem that, adroitly incorporated, a little of this grape can bestow individuality and quality. Dopff 'Au Moulin' do make use of the Tokay in addition to the Pinot Blanc because, Pierre Dopff thinks, it adds additional charm and fragrance to the upstanding character of the Pinot Blanc. The Pinot Blanc is the most important of the varieties.

Grapes for the production of *crémants* can come from wherever the maker chooses to buy them, but producers must declare their intention of making a sparkling wine well in advance. The vintage for grapes intended for *crémants* usually takes place about fifteen days before the ordinary picking starts, so that the grapes are not too ripe and will possess sufficient acidity; when the wine has been made, it is officially tasted before undergoing any of the procedures whereby it is to be made sparkling. Only if it is approved can it be subsequently described as 'Crémant d'Alsace', any wines that are rejected may only subsequently be sold as 'vin blanc', without the *appellation contrôlée*.

The stages of the Champagne process cannot – for reasons of space – be given in detail here, but essentially it is the base wine that makes a good sparkler and by this is meant a certain robustness of style, a good balance of acidity and fruit and a clear-cut, well-defined character overall.

Particular care must be taken of the grapes in the initial stages. (The makers like to stress that, although they follow the Champagne method, they are both personally and officially concerned with far more detailed care – a point that it might be undiplomatic to argue.) The grapes go into the press in whole bunches for *crémants*, so the use of the *fouloir-égrappoir* (crusher-cum-destalker) is not involved. The actual pressing of these bunches will, of course, include the stems and stalks in addition to the fruit pulp and grapeskins, thereby adding 'backbone' to the ultimate wine.

The actual pressing is also controlled. It is not as hard as in Champagne. In Alsace 180 kilos of grapes may only yield 100 litres of juice or 'must'; in Champagne 150 kilos yield 100 litres. This, say the Alsace makers, ensures that in their wines only the juice of the initial, light pressings is included in the *cuvée* (vatting or ultimate blend) and this is superior in quality to any final hard pressings that might be utilised to increase the amount of juice.

In brief, the wine as first made is still and, after the first fermentation soon after the vintage, has died down, it remains in the vat during the cooler weather, throughout the winter; the wine yeasts cease to work when the temperature drops. Then, in the spring, the yeasts start to activate the wine as the warmer weather comes but, before this, the wine goes into the bottle in which it will spend the rest of its life, the first cork is put in and the bottles are removed to the cellar. Here, after some further maturation – if possible and if demand is not too importunate – they then undergo the process known as 'remuage', being upended in frames and both shaken and rotated, either by hand or machine, so that the deposit in the wine is directed downwards to lodge on the first cork. This operation is a delicate one, for the 'bits' in suspension in the wine – which of course cannot be filtered now that it is in bottle – tend to be both of the dusty, light type and also of a sludgy, slightly sticky sort, both of which have to be directed onto the cork; then, when the wine is required for release, this first cork is removed and any 'dosage', the sweetening by means of cane sugar dissolved in wine, is incorporated as the bottle is topped up. The second cork goes in and the bottle is 'dressed' with capsule, label and any strip or back labels. Ideally, it should then receive a further period of maturation, to assist the wine to settle down – but this is not always possible.

In general, for *crémants* the disgorging and insertion of the second cork usually takes place about nine months after the first *prise de mousse* or acquiring of the sparkle when the wine first goes into bottle. The *dosage* can vary, but is never much – there is no such thing as a sweet Crémant d'Alsace and 0.5 per cent is an approximate figure. In general, too, *crémants* are not intended for laying down but for immediate enjoyment when they come onto the market.

As with all sparkling wines, Crémants d'Alsace should be served cool but not iced – too much chilling robs the drinker of the pleasure of the bouquet and this, in any Alsace wine, is one of the notable charms. More information about 'what with what' is given in Chapter 9, but Monsieur Pierre Dopff often recommends a *crémant* to accompany a meal, not merely as an apéritif; the slight assertiveness and crisp style of a sparkling wine of this type balances many of the rich, often creamy recipes of Alsace; the light fruitiness of a well-made *crémant* can combine agreeably with both fish and meat dishes – the use of a sparkling wine with an unctuous sauce is always possible. A sparkling wine, too, is unlikely to be overwhelmed by anything very sweet or *piquant* – the extra 'push' of the bubbles enables the drinker to retain an impression of its flavour, even when eating something that might overwhelm a rather delicate still wine.

The famous Renaissance well in Boersch, the tiny town that combines medieval and eighteenth-century buildings

6

The Alsace Wine Trade

Allthough the dominant factors in the production of any wine are and must remain the climate, the soil and the grape varieties, man has an important part to play. This is as true in Alsace as anywhere else in the wine world. Alsace is a country of small vineyard properties: of the 9000 or so growers, more than 40 per cent have less than a quarter of a hectare of vines, almost 80 per cent have less than a hectare. At the other extreme, there are thirty-six growers owning ten or more hectares.

It is fair to point out that many of the small growers do in fact produce wine solely for their own family requirements. But the circumstance that white wines are often difficult to vinify and also the fact that many producers hardly grow enough grapes to justify the outlay of money on expensive and complicated machinery and equipment, only in use for a few weeks in the year, means that in Alsace the co-operative system is very highly developed.

The Co-operatives

Although the initial idea of co-operation dates back to 1900, when, at the instigation of the local bankers, cellars were set up in Eguisheim and Dambach-la-Ville to stock surplus quantities of wine that could not be accommodated in the homes of the growers, it was not really until after World War II that cellars were created specifically to cope with both the vinification of the wine as the grapes were picked, and, subsequently, with the storage and distribution of the wine in bulk or in bottle. The villages of Bennwihr and Sigolsheim, which had suffered greatly in the war, thought that it would be logical to spend the money paid in reparations in constructing modern central cellars to be utilised by all the local growers, rather than to attempt to rebuild the individual facilities of all those in the area. About the same time, the growers in the vineyard of Cleebourg, well separated from all the others and having benefited – after having been turned out of their holdings completely for a time – from the complete replanting on which the Germans insisted, constructed their own co-operative cellar, modest at the outset, but well designed and with all the growers in the region belonging to it. From 1950 onwards co-operative cellars were built throughout the Alsace vineyard; these now number seventeen–twelve in the Haut-Rhin, three in the Bas-Rhin, plus the Co-operative Divinal at Obernai and the Covidal cellars in Beblenheim, which serve solely as stores for the stocks of bulk wines.

In the minds of many people, the word 'co-operative' seems to evoke wines of low quality, but this is not true for many, indeed, for the majority of Alsace cellars, as the numbers of medals they gain at both national and international wine fairs can bear witness. Although it is possibly invidious to single out particular establishments, the co-operative cellars of Eguisheim, Beblenheim and Westhalten have reputations matching those of the top and most respected *négociants* (shippers).

The Growers

The local authorities split the growers into seven different categories:

1 *Manipulants totaux* These are growers who bottle all the wine they themselves make and sell it directly to the consumer. According to the 1973 statistics, they account for 4.8 per cent of the total number of growers, but for 17.4 per cent of the total area under vines.

2 *Manipulants partiels* This is the largest group–those who bottle and sell a proportion of their crop themselves, while the balance is sold in bulk to the *négociants*. They represent 30.2 per cent of the growers and account for 34.5 per cent of the area. It is interesting to note that between 1969 and 1983 these figures have almost doubled.

3 *Vendeurs en vrac* These are the growers who vinify the wine themselves but who do not bottle and sell in bulk to the *négociant*. As a group they are in decline, now accounting for only 6.6 per cent of the total number of the growers and for 6.4 per cent of the vineyards. There is no doubt that their decline has been hastened by the banning of the sale of wine in bulk outside Alsace itself, also by the increasing desire of the individual grower to sell wine under his own label, thereby making more profit and gaining some gratification in the promulgation of his name.

4 *Vendeurs raisins* These are mainly smaller growers, who sell their grapes to a *négociant* at vintage time; he will then undertake the vinification and bottling. Often, indeed, the grapes are actually picked by the teams working for these *négociants* or shippers and it is common to find that, although they may only themselves possess a limited holding or domaine, they often, by this means, control a considerable area under vines. Again, though, as a group they are in slow decline and now represent 23.4 per cent of the total number of growers, accounting for no more than 11.6 per cent of the total extent of vineyards.

Rodern, with Haut Koenigsberg on the mountain above

Above: Vintage, with a plastic *hotte,* wooden *bennes* and a modern lorry

Below: Designed by Hansi, Hugel's sign in Riquewihr shows a vintage party – a man bearing an *hotte,* a woman and a man with small casks and a boy with a giant pretzel – bearing a gigantic bunch of grapes. A snail climbs the front of the sign

5 *Members of co-operatives* The importance of the co-operative cellars is borne out by the fact that the numbers in this movement are increasing, now representing 25.1 per cent of the total, 26 per cent of the vineyard area. Through the co-operative, members get advice on the grape varieties to plant and they are relieved of the necessity of worrying about the sale of their wines, as this duty is taken on by the commercial side of the cellars.

6 *Négociants (Producer/shippers)* While some shippers do not own any vineyards themselves, many of them do have a medium-sized domaine of between eight and twelve hectares to guarantee them a certain source of supply for a proportion of their annual requirements. However, as part of the total scene, they are not an important group, as they number only about 0.6 per cent of the total number of growers, controlling only 3.3 per cent of the vineyards. The rôle of the *négociant*, then, is primarily on the commercial side, although he can, as has been explained, vinify much more than the actual production from his own vineyards.

7 *Family consumption* This group is really outside the scope of this book and consists of a large number of people who own vines and make wine not for commerce at all, but only their personal requirements. Nearly all their vineyards are planted with the lesser grape varieties and the area they own accounts for a mere 0.8 per cent while they are 9.3 per cent in numbers.

The Alsace Wine Law

The concept of having wines sold under the name of the region from which they come is not a new one – wines are mentioned by name in both the Bible and in the work of several writers of classical times – but it was not until the twentieth century that the French began to protect the standing of wines of specific regions. By the law of 1 August 1905, certain vineyard areas were given boundaries, although these were often based more on geography than history. What this law failed to take into account were the geological differences within these defined areas, the grape varieties used and the methods of cultivation; a site a mile or even a few hundred yards in distance from another may make wines – but these, even though they can both be sold under the name of the region, may not be even approximately both of the same quality. So it was that, in the early part of this century, much fraud was perpetrated by local merchants, exploiting vineyard names; eventually this led to a great deal of unrest and dissatisfaction and, in 1911, to the Champagne riots, when the Champenois objected, violently, to wines brought in from other regions being made into wines sold as 'Champagne' in the Champagne area and, thereby, lowering the quality and reputation of Champagne.

As has already been seen in the history of Alsace, laws referring to the making and selling of wine were widespread during the Middle Ages but, for the most part, these only applied locally. As has been mentioned, in 1731 a royal decree forbade 'the planting of vines in Alsace without permission, which will only be given if the land should be unsuitable for other crops'. During the first half of the twentieth century major efforts were made to improve the quality of the wines by restricting the grape varieties that might be used; the idea was to effect a transition from Alsace being an area making masses of base wine for the German market into a region and producer of top quality wines. In 1925 the Association of Alsace Wine Growers forbade the use of hybrid grape varieties; in 1932 the planting of the Trollinger, the Putschera and the Lamber were prohibited and in 1945 so was the Burger or Elbling, which had been one of the commonest varieties in the region.

Indeed, it is from 1945 that the current wine laws of Alsace have grown up. In that year the local growers produced an order for the definition of *appellation contrôlée* in the region. As this gives an idea of what their thoughts were at this time–immediately after World War II–it may be worth quoting some of the preamble to the order.

> The status of the wines of Alsace greatly preoccupied the growers of the region during the years leading up to the war of 1939; the Alsace vineyards deserved to extend their markets, both within and outside France, because of the excellent quality of the produce.
>
> The reason for any delay in the introduction of this order has been because of the difficulty in simply applying to Alsace viticulture rules adopted for the protection of *appellations d'origine* in the rest of the national territory.
>
> Since the return to France in 1919 of the three *départements* of the Haut-Rhin, the Bas-Rhin and the Moselle, it seemed necessary to continue applying the principles of Article 3 of the local law of April 7th, 1909, as this legislation confirmed local practice.

These specific local practices had been largely to do with the controls applied to wines made in the German fashion: for example, sugar could be added to fermented wine, either of the latest or previous vintages, from the time of the vintage up to the end of December.

Among the various points in the order of 1945, the most important were that 'Vin d'Alsace' had to come from vineyards on the slopes or directly adjacent to the slopes in communes in the Haut-Rhin and Bas-Rhin traditionally planted in vines.

The permitted grape varieties were now to be: *Cépages nobles* Traminer, Riesling, Pinot, Tokay, Clevner, Muscat, Sylvaner and their sub-species; *Cépages courants* Knipperlé, Chasselas, Goldriesling.

The wine had to have a minimum natural strength of 8° (in terms of percentage of alcohol by volume). Each year the local authorities would decide whether chaptalisation would be permitted; in any event, the maximum to be allowed would be the addition of 2.5°.

Each year the local authorities would announce the opening date of the vintage; anyone picking before that date would lose the right to describe his wines as 'Alsace'. (This is an interesting survival of what was the custom in other regions from very early times – the grower would not be allowed to pick too early, because although he might thereby gain a start in dealing with making the wine and, later, be able to start selling his wines in advance of his competitors, wine made in this way could be of poor quality through insufficiently ripe grapes, thereby risking a general reaction against the wines of the entire region. In many French vineyards today there is a *Ban* or proclamation of the vintage accompanied by a somewhat picturesque ceremony although now the decision when the Bordelais or Burgundians start picking their grapes is a matter for individual firms and growers to decide.)

Wines made from *cépages courants,* either mixed or not with those of *cépages nobles*, were to be described as Zwicker. If they were made from a blend of *cépages nobles* only, they were to be known as Edelzwicker.

Any wine sold under the name of a grape variety must be made 100 per cent from that variety.

The expressions *grand vin* and *grand cru* were only to be applied to wines with a minimum of 11° of natural alcohol.

It is upon this order that all legislation for the wines of Alsace is based. It must be stressed that, at this time (1945) the wines of Alsace did not have the status of *appellation contrôlée* anyway. This was not granted until the decree of 3 October 1962. It is also interesting to note two aspects of the order that are specifically German – as has been said elsewhere, although the occupation of Alsace by Germany was much resented, there were some good elements and traditions that resulted.

First, although sugaring of wine – as opposed to the must – was still permitted, wines made involving this sugaring could only be sold in Alsace and Lorraine and not on export markets – and even this right was to disappear in 1964. Alsace was determined that its wines should be as natural as possible. Then, there is the official announcement of the date when the vintage might begin: in Alsace this *Ban des Vendanges* is still a matter of law.

Subsequent changes to the legislation have generally been aimed at improving guarantees as to the quality and authenticity of the wine – in addition to increasing the potential revenue of the growers. In relation to the improvement of quality, the most important alteration came into force, with immediate effect, on 5 July 1972, from which date all Alsace wines had to be bottled within the region of production – the two *départements* of the Haut-Rhin and Bas-Rhin. As a result, Alsace is, even now, the only area in France producing still wines where this bottling obligatorily takes place. While the growers said that this law came into force as a result of demand from their customers, there is little doubt that it lost for them a fair proportion of their market overnight. Up to that time, many Parisian wholesalers had bottled the wines of Alsace, then sold as *vins de comptoir* (wines sold by glass or carafe) in the bars of the capital. A year earlier it had been decided that neither Riesling nor Gewurztraminer could be sold in litre bottles and a substantial number of important outlets for wines of lesser quality disappeared for good.

The Alsace point of view was expressed in the magazine *Les Vins D'Alsace* as being that: 'Almost all Alsace wine already left the region in bottle, therefore it [the new law] did little but confirm legally a situation that already existed, which meant that there was little chance of losing much of the market . . . Moreover, the consumer is undeniably in favour of Alsace wine being bottled in the area of production, as it gives him an undeniable guarantee of authenticity and quality.'

Whatever the consumer may have thought about guarantees of quality–and, sadly, there is plenty of poor quality Alsace wine still around–the growers in regions such as Muscadet must have shouted for joy: their wines immediately took the place in bars of the wines of Alsace that local merchants became less willing to sell. Indeed, the ban on sales of litres of Riesling must have had some local repercussions, as this was soon rescinded. Could the exceptionally large vintage of 1973 have made the growers change their minds? They *had* to sell their wine–somewhere, somehow!

With regard to the grape varieties used, there has been a steady move towards the suppression of the lesser varieties. In 1971 a law was passed which foresaw the phasing out of a number of both traditional and less traditional species of vine. These included local types, such as the Knipperlé and the Goldriesling, as well as vines successful in other regions, such as the Müller-Thurgau, the Chardonnay and the Pinot Meunier. The Chasselas appears to be holding its ground, albeit in the face of official disapproval.

The Question of 'Grand Cru'

It is perhaps in relation to the use and definition of the expression 'grand cru' that there has been the longest-running search to find legislation that is both satisfactory and acceptable to all concerned. Because the situation is not yet resolved, it is only possible to indicate the problems and possible solution, but the matter is certainly one that will crop up in any discussions about the finer Alsace wines.

For centuries there has been, in Alsace, a tradition of naming the individual vineyard slopes and some have had, not unexpectedly, better reputations than others. In 1643 the writer Merian described the Schoenenberg vineyard of

Riquewihr as producing the most 'noble wine of the slopes'. There is the well-known verse:

> At Thann the Rangen
> At Guebwiller the Wannen
> At Turckheim the Brand
> The best wines in the land.
> But the Sporen of Riquewihr
> Conquers all, and has no peer

But fame and popularity exacted their usual penalties: often the vineyard names were abused and became little more than generic terms for the wines of the area in which the famous vineyard was sited. As a result, local growers took steps in the courts to protect the use of certain vineyard names, for obviously it was important that some definition about these should be registered in the interests both of producers and consumers. In February 1932 regulations concerning the production of the Kaefferkopf at Ammerschwihr were drawn up and, three years later, in 1935, the Sonnenglanz at Beblenheim was defined by a decision of the Colmar tribunal. (It should, of course, be remembered that these sites were not and are not the property of single owners, and in no way resemble 'estates'; they may be sub-divided to a considerable extent and, in addition, may be planted with several of the permitted vine varieties.)

The order dated 2 November, 1945, however, made no mention of specific sites when it spoke of *grands crus*. In the same way, the decree of 30 June 1971, stated that, in order to be called 'grand cru' a wine had to be made from the Gewurztraminer, Muscat, Riesling, Pinot Gris or Pinot Noir, and it had to attain a minimum natural strength – 10° for the Riesling and Muscat, 11° for the other grape varieties. Such a system suited the *négociants*, for it enabled them to make *grand cru* wines by blending together the better quality wines from all over the region, and, also important in business, they could offer these to customers in reasonable quantities. Anything of supposed superior quality is, in normal trading, likely to attract a queue of buyers, if the price is right, and it is not unusual for demand greatly to exceed supply.

On the other hand, the growers were keener on maintaining the strictures applying both to the grapes and to the minimum strength of the wines, while being able to attach the description *grand cru* to the produce of individual, named vineyards. This would enable them to sell some of their wines at premium prices. It is perhaps pertinent also to comment that, whereas many consumers in the mass market for wines, including those of Alsace, outside France might not realise that the 'Riesling' of Firm A could be different in style from the 'Riesling' of Firm B, even if the two wines were in the same price range, it was easy for shippers in export markets to appreciate the advantage of being able to offer a wine bearing a specific and, perhaps, evocative and attractive name. Firms had already understood this when launching their blends and brands (such as Hugel's Flambeau d'Alsace), but there is at least an implied, even definite snob appeal exerted by a wine with a name such as the (imaginary) 'Riesling Silberberg' or 'Gewurztraminer Koenigenkrone'. If the consumer in the export market can pronounce the name, so much the better! The very grape names, much more the names of some makers of Alsace wines, worry those foreign customers who are shy of trying to get their tongues round words that look 'difficult', so that there is something to be said for the wish, on the part of the growers, to sort out their own image on export markets and promote the names of certain sites associated traditionally with quality wines.

A draft for the new definition of the term 'grand cru' was drawn up in June, 1975, together with a list of ninety-four vineyards considered worthy of being categorised as such. But eight years later and at the time of writing the law has still not been passed.

The reasons for this delay have been many. There are four main causes. First, applications to register the names had to come from the owners – in many instances numerous owners – of each of the vineyards so specified. It will surprise no one to learn that in many negotiations there have been difficulties in reaching agreement.

Then, the proposed legislation definitely excluded any possibility of a *grand cru* wine being made from the Sylvaner, even though this grape, in such particular sites as the Zotzenberg at Mittelbergheim, can make exceptional wines.

Third, the court decision protecting the Kaefferkopf of Ammerschwihr allowed the use, based on old traditions, of the Clevner grape: why should this valuable right be forfeited?

Finally, opposition has come from the merchants who have shown little interest in the possibility of being able to offer wines from a multiplicity of individual vineyards in small quantities; profits are not made on the 'fine and rare' wines, however good, but with the everyday qualities, sold in large quantities. So merchants have tended to look on this new proposal relating to vineyards as being of direct financial benefit to growers – who would have to be paid by the merchants – and, generally, against the merchants' interests.

As a result of this varied opposition, the initial list of *grand cru* vineyards has been considerably shortened. At present, it should consist of the following, with, perhaps, other names to be added in due course:

Village	*Vineyard*
Bas-Rhin	
Andlau	Kastelberg, Moenchberg, Wibelsberg
Barr	Kirchberg
Bergbieten	Alterberg
Eichoffen	Moenchberg

Village	*Vineyard*
Haut-Rhin	
Beblenheim	Sonnenglanz
Bergheim	Altenberg, Kantzlerberg
Bergholtz	Spiegel
Eguisheim	Eichberg
Gueberschwihr	Goldert
Guebwiller	Kessler, Kitterlé, Saering, Spiegel
Hattstatt	Hatschbourg
Hunawihr	Rosacker
Kaysersberg	Schlossberg
Katzenthal	Sommerberg
Kientzheim	Schlossberg
Niedermorschwihr	Sommerberg
Ribeauvillé	Geisberg, Kirschberg
Rodern	Gloeckelberg
St Hippolyte	Gloeckelberg
Thann	Rangen
Turckheim	Brand
Vieux-Thann	Rangen
Voegtlinshoffen	Hatschbourg
Wintzenheim	Hengst
Wuenheim	Ollwiller

Among the notable and sometimes historic names that do not appear in this list are: the Mamburg at Sigolsheim, the Mandelberg at Mittelwihr, Zisser at Barr, Sporen and Schoenenberg at Riquewihr, the Osterberg at Ribeauvillé and the Kaefferkopf at Ammerschwihr. In almost all these vineyards it is merchants (who may, of course, also be shippers as well) who have been and are the major owners and who, therefore, are generally opposed to the new legislation.

What will happen to such old-established and popular names as Sporen? At present, nothing seems totally clear, but it does appear likely that vineyards not categorised as *grand cru* will have in future to be labelled with the name of the village as well as that of the vineyard. For example, and with reference to the preceding paragraph, there might be: 'Riquewihr Sporen; Appellation Alsace Contrôlée', whereas *grand cru* vineyards will be labelled merely with the name of the vineyard as: 'Rangen; Appellation Alsace Grand Cru Contrôlée'.

Will this make much difference as far as marketing the wines is concerned? It is difficult to say, but, whereas many consumers have little idea as to the implications of the details of a wine's label, others definitely have; will they, even sub-conciously, feel that a wine from a specific vineyard that they have known and appreciated as being high in quality is somehow demoted by not being able to include the term *grand cru* on its label? (It is still quite common for drinkers of red Bordeaux to suppose that, somehow, a classed growth of the Médoc in the *troisième cru* section is vaguely 'not quite so good' as a wine in the 'deuxième', although acquaintance with the history and the implications of the classification of these wines would dismiss the supposition.) The consumer tends to be conservative and, once a liking for a particular wine has been established, any wrench away from the familiar nomenclature can risk a querying of the quality and value of the wine–however unfairly. There is also the fact, seldom appreciated by the ordinary consumer, that, whereas a wine can be wholly entitled to a certain label according to legislation, this legislation and the relevant pieces of paper that enable it to bear certain terms cannot, ever, *guarantee* either the finest quality or, indeed, that the drinker will like it! Only the maker and grower can establish the quality, only the experience of the drinker can enable him or her to sort out whether a wine is good as regards quality but not to the personal taste of the drinker, or whether it is both appreciated and enjoyed.

Another aspect of Alsace wine laws that has incurred criticism is the amount of wine that may be produced each year. It might be supposed that a sudden and unexpectedly large vintage would be a subject for rejoicing–but the subject is complicated. Laws cannot be held in abeyance during the vintage and the *appellation contrôlée* regulations establish controls as to how much wine may be made in a particular area: the reason behind this is that exploitation of a vineyard would lead to a decline in quality and, of course, risk local depression if sub-standard wines were left unsold. As in other regions of France, the permitted *rendement* or yield varies from vintage to vintage but, in Alsace, the standard base is 100 hectolitres to the hectare, which may be averaged out over the total holding of the owner. Thus, if the owner has some vines on the slopes which only produce 50 hectolitres per hectare, he may produce 150 hectolitres to every equivalent hectare of vines in his holdings on the plain. In addition, he may make an additional 20 per cent, on approval of samples submitted to the authorities.

This Alsace figure is the largest production figure approved for any vineyard region in France (although that for Champagne is similar) and it is a relic of German control, where high yields per hectare are commonplace. It is probably true that, particularly for white wine, the size of the yield is not likely to affect the overall quality, but it can result in a collapse in prices and difficulties in maintaining a stable market.

The problems that these large yields can cause is well illustrated by the 1982 vintage–admittedly large, as were most yields in French vineyards in this year. The average yield of all the *appellation contrôlée* vineyards was, in 1982, 120.53 hectolitres per hectare–remember, the standard is 100 hectolitres per hectare! So, in 1982, the local authorities had to block half the crop in growers' cellars, in order to maintain prices. It is relevant to note also that a severe note has been sent round to the growers, reminding them about the law on pruning, which should prevent excessive yields. The 1983 crop was also large, although not quite as copious as in 1982.

For *grand cru* vineyards, the base maximum yield per hectare is fixed at seventy hectolitres but, as most of these vineyards are on slopes that are often quite steep where copious yields cannot be expected, this does not seem to be a very restrictive figure.

The growers of Alsace have had two great advantages when their wine laws have been formulated and come into being. Being the last of the major French wine regions to introduce *appellation contrôlée*, they have been able to avoid many of the pitfalls that have beset the Burgundians and the Bordelais. In addition, the traditions of two nationalities have given them undoubted advantages. Sadly, though, there has been what, to the outsider, seems an ambivalent attitude to wine legislation. On the one hand, as in the case of Riesling being bottled into litres, it might be thought that it was necessary to try out a law to see if it could work within a year or two and, if not, abandon it; on the other hand, as with the *grand cru* law, so many vested interests have been allowed to become involved and to have their say that the result, at present, seems to be verging on anarchy.

It cannot be the subject of this book to discuss whether wine laws should be designed to protect the grower, the merchant or the consumer, but, unfortunately, the interests of the last, the drinker of wine, often seem to be subordinated to those of the others.

The Alsace Bottle

The *Flûte d'Alsace* is today the only bottle that may be used for the quality wines of Alsace. It is elongated, as if it had been pulled upwards and, because of its height, it often presents problems to the wine trade when mixed cartons of wine have to be packed: Alsace bottles tend to stand up higher than others in the case.

The base is flat – no need for an indented punt to catch deposit, as with red wines in other regions – and the colour is a dark green, somewhat similar to that of a laurel or bay leaf.

The bottle was first given official recognition in 1930, when its shape, size and content – 717 ml. or 72 cl. holding 700 ml. of wine or thereabouts – was established. The post World War I enthusiasm for the wines of the region newly restored to France caused some producers in other wine regions to adopt the same type of bottle; it certainly pleases the eye of the experienced and is easy to handle. Therefore, in 1959, the Alsace authorities decided that it must be more rigidly defined and it was decreed that the *flûte d'Alsace* or, as it may also be called, *bouteille du vin du Rhin* must be of a particular size and that only certain

121

Green-stemmed Alsace glasses and the Alsace *flûte* bottle, against a panorama of vines

specified wine regions other than Alsace may bottle their wines in a container of this shape and form. There is an obvious advantage in a shape that is easily recognised on the shelf of supermarket or restaurant. For the United States and Canada, however, a slightly larger bottle must be used – 767 ml., holding about 750 ml. of wine: the 75 cl. size. This is because, rather oddly, these countries, have not yet 'gone metric'.

Drinkers are not often aware that there is detailed control exercised over the shape, sizes and colour of the glass used for bottles of quality wines in the various regions, but in fact they are subject to regulations; some slight variations are permitted, but not many. Alsace wines are now always bottled in green glass. The *eaux-de-vie* of the region are put into bottles of the same shape as the *flûte* but of clear glass.

The other regions permitted by law to use a bottle similar to the *flûte* are: Cassis, Château Grillet, the red and pink Côtes de Provence wines, Crépy, Jurançon, Rosé de Béarn and Tavel Rosé. Some similar-seeming bottles are in use, but examination will reveal that they are not identical: some have the rings or ridges round the neck, which makes them *véroniques* (I have never been able to discover why) and the bottle used in Germany is actually slightly shorter than the *flûte d'Alsace*. Even if a very old wine is found, dating from before the bottling of quality Alsace in the region, it will usually be in the elongated *flûte* bottle. There is, however, one slight disadvantage to the use of this graceful container: it tends to stick up from any ice bucket or cooler, so that the wine inside tends to be tepid when first poured, as only about two-thirds of the bottle can, usually, be satisfactorily chilled. (There are tall 'hock' buckets in existence, but they tend to be somewhat rare.) The remedy for this is to reverse the bottle in the ice bucket, so that it is upside down while being cooled; of course, the wine inside turns round when the bottle is again put right side up, but it can be poured through a section of the neck that will be adequately cold. This makes a surprising difference. It can be done even if the cork has been drawn, although of course it should be securely replaced before the bottle is turned upside down.

The Crémants d'Alsace are bottled in a slightly fatter sloping shouldered bottle with a shallow punt; they are made of thicker glass than the table wines because the bottle has to withstand the pressure of the carbonic acid gas in the wine. The pink wines of Alsace are bottled in the usual *flûte*. The white spirits can be bottled as the producer thinks suitable.

Roofs of Riquewihr from the nearby vineyard

7

A Who's Who of the Main Firms

The Alsace vineyards maintain a fierce independence from the rest of France, with their own grape varieties and methods of cultivation; but there is one way in which they do quite closely resemble the vineyards of Burgundy-in their extreme division. For the vineyards of Alsace are, like those of Burgundy, the product of a peasant economy. Though the breaking up of the vast estates of the church and the nobility at the time of the French Revolution at the end of the eighteenth century exacerbated this situation, it by no means caused it.

As Lucien Sittler, in *L'Agriculture et la Viticulture en Alsace* (1974) comments: 'The Revolution brought about changes to the benefit of the peasant and gave him a great deal of land. But the splitting up of property, which went back several centuries, continued. It became even worse with the marriages that involved sharing out land among several families and distributing it through inheritance, as established by the Code Napoléon. Thus, in 1852, the Public Prosecutor of the Colmar Appeal Court was able to say: "Alsace is rich in the fertility of her soil, but she is poor because of the extreme division of her land".'

Perhaps it is for the best that, over the past few years, there has been a definite trend towards the concentration of the vineyards and the accumulation of the holdings of commerical houses in fewer hands; but before anyone begins to rail against the pernicious power of capital and mentions monopolistic tendencies, the situation should be seen in perspective.

Today, there are still over 9000 vineyard owners in Alsace with an average holding of just over one hectare each. While the average is so small, there are still a few *domaines* of some size; many *négociants* are reluctant to state the area of vines they actually own, giving, in preference, a figure for the area they vinify, including grapes that they buy each year under contract. The most important holdings, with their approximate sizes, are: Schlumberger, based on Guebwiller-140 hectares; Jux-Jacobert (which is now Dopff & Irion, a recent amalgamation), based on Colmar and Riquewihr-115 hectares: Dopff 'Au Moulin', based on Riquewihr-75 hectares; Léon Beyer, Eguisheim/Preiss-

Henny, Mittelwihr, another recent grouping – 65 hectares. Among some other domaines that may be mentioned are: Louis Klipfel – 30 hectares; Zind-Humbrecht – 29 hectares; Willm – 25 hectares; Hugel – 22 hectares. Schlumberger and Zind-Humbrecht sell only wines produced from their own *domaines*.

Before mentioning some of the more important firms in detail, it may be helpful to recapitulate on the six different groups that comprise the Alsace wine trade, explaining in more detail how they work: *Manipulants totaux* (complete handlers) are those who produce and sell only what, in Bordeaux, would be called *château*-bottled wines, or, in Burgundy, *domaine* bottlings. Thus they make wine only from grapes coming from their own vineyards, bottle it and sell it themselves. Though they have been responsible for one-fifth of the overall vineyard area, this proportion may now be falling, because of the aggressive recruitment tactics of certain co-operative cellars. The average size of a vineyard holding in this category is as low as 3.5 hectares, not even the area of a somewhat small farm in Britain. The *manipulants partiels* (partial handlers) own more than one-third of the total vineyard area, which is not surprising if one considers that this category includes all those vineyard owners who cannot be placed into any other of the six groups. Thus a grower who, in a very abundant year, such as 1982, has not adequate equipment to press his grapes or ferment his musts and, as a result, has to sell to the *négociants* either grapes, or, on occasion, wine, is transferred to this category. Though there is a substantial proportion of growers who, each year, sell either grapes or wine in bulk, there is also another significantly high number who might be included in this category in one year, but not in the next.

The *vendeurs en vrac* (bulk wine sellers) is a group that is diminishing rapidly; there is now less than half the number of them than ten years ago. They are mainly small-scale growers, with average holdings of less than a hectare each. Although they have the equipment to make the wine and stock it in vat, they have no facilities for bottling and so they sell it in bulk to the merchants; the grower's name, therefore, will never appear on the wine's ultimate label. The wine will be blended to appear anonymously, under the colours of the *négociant*. More than a quarter of all the growers in Alsace are *co-operateurs* (members of co-operative cellars) and the number is growing fast for, by judicious use of government-backed loans at preferential rates of interest, the cellars are in a position to guarantee a satisfactory return for their members. Thus they are squeezing those growers who are still trying to sell under their own labels by a systematic undercutting of prices and they also threaten the *négociants*, who are finding that the number of their potential sources of supply is dwindling.

From its small beginnings at the turn of the century, the co-operative movement in the vineyards of Alsace is now very important, eighteen cellars now being responsible for 29 per cent of the total crop. Some of the sales are made in bulk to merchants, but one-quarter of all the sales of Alsace wine is under the label of a co-operative cellar.

The strength and influence of the cellars can be shown by the fact that, in the past two years, they have absorbed a number of long-established merchants, including Kuehn of Ammerschwihr (by the Ingersheim co-operative) and Heim of Westhalten (by the local co-operative there). This rapid expansion of the cellars is of great concern, particularly to the merchants, who tend to dismiss the enormous investments by such concerns as the Eguisheim co-operative as no more than foolish megalomania. As evidence for the favoured status that the cellars enjoy is the fact that, in 1981, grants of 13.5 million francs were made to the co-operatives. In the same period, one grant only was made to a merchant – a mere 180,000 francs. On the other hand, it is true to say that the technical know-how and modern equipment available to the cellars has meant that much better wine has been made on a number of occasions than otherwise would have been possible.

Not long ago the *producteurs-négociants* (merchant growers) were the source of more than half the total sales of Alsace wines. Now the figure is down to 42 per cent and still falling. Only 10 per cent of their requirements come from their own vineyards, the rest being bought either as grapes or wine from the vineyard owners or co-operatives. On export markets, however, they are still all-important, with almost two-thirds of this business being still in their hands.

As Philippe Laugel says in the periodical *La Revue Vinicole*: 'It must not be forgotten that it is the merchants who have created the reputation of the wines of Alsace'. The fact that they are not tied to members for sources of supply of grapes, as are the co-operative cellars, means that they should be able to produce better wines. Indeed, in the merchants' own vineyards the proportion of 'noble' grapes is 50 per cent above the average.

Finally, there are those who only make wine for their own family consumption. As in other vineyard regions of France, their number is in rapid decline. Some evidence of this is provided by the fact that, during the 1970s, the number of growers with less than two hectares of vines dropped from 10,630 to 7300. Traditionally, their vineyard holdings have often been little more than allotments in the town suburbs – many of these now having been absorbed by the urban sprawl.

Here are notes on a few of the 9000 growers of Alsace. Many are very important, some less so. The interest of a region such as this lies in the variety of its wines, first, because of the number of different grapes and then because of the styles of each individual grower and merchant. It is easier to say when a wine is bad – and, alas, there is bad wine in Alsace, though fortunately little reaches foreign markets – than which is the best, or the most liked. Hugel has his fans, Beyer his. The styles may differ, but the ultimate quality is present in both instances.

These notes may add to the interest and enjoyment of drinkers selecting

127

Alsace wines from the list of a merchant or restaurant and, of course, to travellers in the region. Christopher Fielden has compiled most of the factual information, after having had twenty years of tasting and travelling there. I have appended some notes (appearing in brackets), where possible, on the predominant house styles of certain of the establishments, plus bits of history, supplied by some firms. Where I have either not gained sufficient experience of a firm's wines to be able to define the general characteristics of their products, or simply lack knowledge of the wines in general, there are no comments– which is not to say that any criticism is implied, only my limited personal experience.

Emile Beyer (succ. Luc Beyer), Eguisheim

Alsace is full of wine families with long histories and there are records of the Beyers having owned vineyards at Eguisheim since 1580. The present company was founded in 1867 and is now managed by the fourth generation; recently there has been some amalgamation with the firm of Preiss-Henny in Mittelwihr, which belongs to cousins. Jointly, they will own one of the largest domaines; that traditionally belonging to the Beyers has been of 20 hectares.

Their marketing policy has been firmly based on an image of quality and their wines are well represented in the top restaurants of France. To help maintain their contacts at this level, particularly in Paris, they award a trophy annually for the most capable openers of shellfish; this is commemorated in the Cuvée des Ecaillers Riesling. Their other specialities include a Gewurztraminer Cuvée des Comtes d'Eguisheim. Wines that have made a particular impression on me (Christopher Fielden) include a Tokay Réserve 1976 and a *vendange tardive* Gewurztraminer, also of 1976.

Home sales account for 70 per cent of their turnover and they are important in the very limited market of Alsace wines in the United States. This house is one of the great producers of fine wines.

(Firm, very definite style, with plenty of detail to appreciate about the wines, which, if drunk leisurely, reveal themselves rewardingly.)

E. Boeckel (F. & A. Boeckel Succ.), Mittelbergheim

This house has long possessed a reputation for good wines, both in France and abroad, where their principal market is Holland. Their important vineyard holding of more than twenty hectares include portions of the two outstanding vineyards of Mittelbergheim, the Zotzenberg (Sylvaner) and the Brandluft (Riesling). Their cellars are in a charming 'olde worlde' building on the main street of the village.

(Although I have not a wide knowledge of the different wines of this house, their character usually seems sound, slightly 'meaty', four-square and substantially good for many foods.)

Above: Vintaging up steep slopes, weighed down by the *hottes*

Below: Picking from vines trained high – note the changing colour of the foliage

Early spring–the vines seem dead, but the special 'tulipes des vignes' flower between them. Note how the new shoots spring from the old stock, itself above the graft.

Co-operative de Beblenheim, Beblenheim

This is an important modern co-operative, capable of stocking as much as 10 per cent of the total production of Alsace. The front of the cellars is the old Château de Hoen. There are more than 180 members of the co-operative, with more than 200 hectares of vineyards between Bennwihr and St Hippolyte.

One of their specialities has been an Edelzwicker from the Sonnenglanz vineyard, but, as this will no longer be a name able to be used under the new laws relating to *grand cru*, a brand name 'Storchengold' is being substituted. This co-operative is also known for its Pinot Blanc wines and for its Crémants d'Alsace. Considerable capital has been invested in the sparkling wine plant, even including automatic and computer-controlled *remueurs*, or frames to turn and shake the sparkling wines, obviating manual attention.

(Very clean, direct wines, making an immediate impression, but the finer examples revealing detailed quality.)

Co-operative de Bennwihr, Bennwihr

This is another rapidly expanding co-operative cellar, with 235 growers owning 300 hectares of vines between them, in eight communes. Bennwihr has a long and very proud history. The excellent brochure produced by the Co-operative states that it gets its name from the 'Domain of Beno', first recorded in AD777 as 'Beno Villare', although no one seems able to decide who 'Beno' was. However, excavations here indicate a community established in the Stone Age. It may later have been ruled over by a Frankish chieftain; it became a centre of the quarrels between the Bishop of Strasbourg and the Court of Württemberg. Then, in the seventeenth century, with wine becoming of supreme importance in the area, there were many recorded 'oaths' relating to this – not mere swear words, one supposes, but affirmations of fidelity, uttered at civic (and vinous) occasions. There is the oath of the coopers, the oath of the gourmets, the oath of the wine carriers and the oath of the country policeman in charge of surveillance over the grape harvests.

Bennwihr wines became big business in the 1870s, the little railway station becoming the most important in the region for sending off wine to distant markets. But in 1940, at the outset of World War II, Bennwihr was totally destroyed – it is entitled 'the most devasted village in France'. Reconstruction of the village was simultaneous with the creation of an association of growers – and the people of Bennwihr, nicknamed 'Mondfänger' (catchers of the moon – that is, those who attempt the impossible) perpetrated their reputation. Today, the impressive establishment includes seven centres of fermentation, with six huge pneumatically operated automatic presses, 218 vats, four large cellars, air-conditioned, to hold as many as 5.2 million bottles.

About a quarter of the Bennwihr wines go to export markets. Equipment is so modern as to be intimidating, were it not that the regular tastings of the wines by a commission have established both a human as well as a commercial tradition. The cellar is on the main street of Bennwihr, itself something of a tourist attraction, a chunk of the formerly destroyed church having been preserved as a monument in front of the new one. The co-operative is well organised to receive visitors and it has its own restaurant, which has recently re-opened, after management problems obliged it to close. It therefore can, if advised, usually receive groups of visitors; guides are intelligent and able to cope with even that potential bore, the wine-wise tourist.

Among the outstanding wines here are an Edelzwicker based on the Chasselas and the Pinot Blanc, a Riesling from the Rebgarten vineyard and sparkling wines. The best I have tasted from this cellar was a Tokay 1971.

(Neat, well-made wines, displaying their characteristics clearly. They are easy to like and appreciate and usually possess a mouth-filling style.)

Co-operative de Cleebourg, Oberhoffen, Rott, Steinseltz et Environs

This is the smallest and most individual of the co-operatives of Alsace. It is situated well away from the rest of the vineyards, in pleasant, sometimes wooded countryside, in a small enclave of vines close to the German frontier, near Wissembourg. All the growers of the region – 240 of them, controlling 130 hectares of vines – are members.

Before World War II there were 350 hectares of wines here, of which the majority were hybrids. These were all grubbed up during the German occupation and replanting was carried out in Sylvaner, Gewurztraminer and Tokay. Now the production is mainly Pinot Auxerrois, for which the makers regularly win medals, also Tokay and Gewurztraminer. Two styles of Pinot Noir are made, one the traditional rosé and the other, definitely 'red', much deeper in colour and with a lot of body. A sparkling wine, Duc Casimir, is made for the co-operative by the *cuve close* process at the Caves de Wissembourg establishment. Half the cellar's production is sold directly to passing tourists and a further 20 per cent is exported to Germany.

The cellar is well designed, with facilities for tasting and also a small bar, decorated with modern sculptures in metal, showing vines and wine activities. It is well worth a visit and there is a nearby small hotel and villages in which to stop a short drive away.

(These wines are light-bodied, trim and easy drinking, the Pinor Noir examples likely to please the visitor very much – but serve them coolish.)

Co-operative d'Eguisheim, Eguisheim

This co-operative was one of the first to be founded, early in the twentieth century. As a result of a very aggressive policy during the past fifteen years, it has now become the largest seller of the wines of Alsace. Building goes on apace, equipment is ultra-modern. This rapid expansion has caused much criticism in the neighbourhood and there are allegations of a decline in quality of the wines, plus a ruthlessness in the recruitment of new members. Eguisheim, particularly picturesque as a village, is naturally concerned about the vast amount of building and the numbers of visitors attracted to the premises, where large reception and tasting rooms and bars cater for the entertainment and refreshment of several coachloads at a time.

Less than ten years ago this co-operative had 220 members, with 220 hectares of vines. Today there are more than 550 growers, with 650 hectares. The total production is now more than five million bottles per year–even more in the abundant vintage of 1982–and one-third of this is sparkling wine. It is especially concerning this that there have been some production problems; at Christmas in 1982, for example, demand became so great that bottles were being disgorged in the morning and sold before lunch time! Vast investment is currently being made in plant, including a *machine à dégorger*, which will handle 5000 bottles an hour. Three qualities of sparkling wine are produced, one from the Riesling, one from the Pinot Noir, also a vintage wine.

Of their table wines, the Gewurztraminer Cuvée Saint Léon is generally outstanding and they make some excellent *vendange tardive* wines. Particular efforts have also been made to improve the quality of their Pinot Noir and their Rouge d'Alsace is aged for two years in small oak casks.

Even though the capacity of this cellar is enormous–and likely to double within the next year or two–15 per cent of their wine is sold, at full retail price, through their own five retail outlets. This, plus generous grants, have enabled them to finance this expansion.

Recently the cellar has taken over the Jux-Jacobert distillery in Colmar and its spirits are sold under the brand name Wolfberger, as is a range of wines and various luxury gastronomic specialities, such as *foie gras*.

(The still wines in general are straightforward and pleasant, the Pinot Noir seeming to possess marked fruit and body. The sparkling wines are somewhat varied–as is inevitable when such vast quantities are produced–and may seem a little hard and lacking in bouquet, although this is made up for by the vintage sparkler, which is definitely good. Anyone buying these sparkling wines in quantity might be well advised to give them some additional bottle age, so that both bouquet and flavour can expand.)

Co-operative de Ribeauvillé et Environs

This is the oldest co-operative cellar in France and was founded in 1895. The grapes come from less than 200 hectares of vineyards in the communes of Riquewihr, Bergheim, Rorschwihr and Rodern, as well as Ribeauvillé. Their speciality is the Clos du Zahnacker, of which they have the monopoly, which comes from Ribeauvillé itself. It is claimed that the wine was tasted by Louis XIV as long ago as the end of the seventeenth century.

(It is certainly an experience to taste the Zahnacker, although difficult to describe, because the vines, most of which are of considerable age, far older than would these days be considered practical, are of various kinds, being replanted vine by vine instead of in blocks, when a single one has eventually to be pulled up. Overall, the wine tends to have fair weight and fullness of body and, in some years, the bouquet is both marked and fascinating – although this may be mainly because it is a challenge to the drinker to attempt to determine the preponderance of the grape contributing to it! In general their wines are firm, moderately assertive, and, well-defined – definitely for those who like 'breed' in a wine.)

Co-operative de Westhalten

This is another co-operative cellar with an aggressive outlook about the marketing of Alsace. To reinforce their possibilities of selling top quality wine, they have recently purchased the local merchant Heim, who was known for the depth of his stocks of fine wine. This cellar has made something of a speciality of single vineyard wines, with outstanding Gewurztraminers from the Zinnkoepflé and the Vorburg, and Muscat from the Bollenberg. Traditionally, too, its Pinot Noirs are deep in colour.

Dopff 'Au Moulin', Riquewihr

This company belongs to one of the great families of Alsace, tracing its wine history back to the seventeenth century, when Balthazard-Georges Dopff became a master cooper in Riquewihr. Early in this century Julien Dopff became the first merchant to sell the wines of Alsace in bottle and, following a period of study in Champagne, he began to make sparkling wines from the local grapes. Until the quite recent creation of the appellation 'Crémant d'Alsace' the local field was dominated by this firm and their product is still perhaps the best on the market. In order to cope with increased demand, they have recently formed a joint production company for sparkling wines with Dopff & Irion and Laugel.

Their estate is also one of the most important, with over 75 hectares of vineyards, including 18 hectares of Pinot Blanc in the plain, specifically for the production of sparkling wines. They also have holdings in the famous Schoenenberg for Riesling, and in the Eichberg for Gewurztraminer.

The company is fortunate to have its premises just outside the walls of Riquewihr, so this has left them room for expansion at their headquarters. The presshouse must be one of the most modern of any *négociant* in Alsace and automation is used to the utmost – all the work being done by just three people.

(The wines of this firm usually possess a close-knit and impressive intensity, even when they happen to be light bodied. Their still Pinot Blanc is usually an important and far more interesting and complex wine than is sometimes so, capable of being long-lived and most impressive and their sparklers can be very fine – delicate but assertive, presenting a charm and finesse that makes them delicious, both as regards bouquet and flavour.)

132

Dopff & Irion, Riquewihr

This is another of the important houses of Alsace. Their head office is in the Château de Riquewihr and many of their domaine wines are sold under that name. This château used to belong to the Counts of Montbéliard and Württemberg and was built in 1539. Not much of the original now remains and part of the building houses a postal museum–said to be the only one of its kind in the world and certainly worth a visit.

Dopff & Irion has been considerably restructured over the past few years; it has taken over the sister Riquewihr company of Ernest Preiss and is associated with the Colmar firm, Jux-Jacobert. Dopff & Irion's own vineyard holdings run to 35 hectares, mainly in Riquewihr, but also with small plots in Hunawihr, Zellenberg and Kientzheim. Their specialities are Les Murailles (Riesling), Les Maquisards and Les Sorcières (Gewurztraminer) and Les Amandiers (Muscat). Until recently these appear to have been sold as vineyard wines, but this is no longer so. The company also produce some good *vendange tardive* wines.

The U.K. 1983 *WHICH? Wine Guide* (published by the Consumers' Association) says 'This company's best wines often appear dumb as they need plenty of time to develop in bottle and there is no malolactic fermentation in this house.' (By which is presumably meant that the makers do not allow it to take place.) Although I cannot vouch for the technical reasons for this, I can certainly say that Dopff & Irion wines have frequently shown disappointingly over the years. I myself put this down to lack of character, but it may be that they have been still too young.

(Although I would generally go along with this comment, it is fair to say that the Muscat, Les Amandiers, is usually both pleasing and gracious. The general house character does seem to result in wines that give an impression of more promise than performance although this, again, may be because they have been drunk too early and have too immediate a flavour–followed by some disappointment.)

Faller Frères, Kientzheim

These growers own the Clos des Capucins, between Kaysersberg and Kientzheim and are generally considered to be making some of the greatest wines of Alsace. M.Faller died recently and the vineyards are now run by his widow. Particularly highly rated are their Pinot Noir and Tokay. The Clos, known as the Domaine Weinbach, belonged to the Abbey of Etival in the thirteenth century, before passing into the hands of the Capuchin order in the seventeenth century. The firm market only wines from their own vineyards.

(Although my experience of these wines is somewhat limited, they are usually both aristocratic and fine-drawn in detail, both as regards bouquet and flavour, with considerable length. 'Gracious' and 'impressive' are perhaps appropriate adjectives for most, notably those from the Schlossberg.)

Willy Gisselbrecht et Fils, Dambach-la-Ville

The Gisselbrecht family seem widespread in Dambach and this branch of it has a small merchant's business based around a domaine of about eight hectares. Much of their business is done with passing customers and about one-fifth of their output is exported, mainly to Germany. Their Rieslings have an especially good reputation.

Hauller, Dambach-la-Ville

This company is typical of many of the smaller houses of Alsace, where efforts are made to stress the family welcome: 'Our customers are considered as friends and seldom fail to pop in and see us if they are passing through Alsace, either on business or holidays'. Behind their folksy approach, however, is a stock of fine wines, mainly from their own fourteen-hectare domaine in Dambach, Scherwiller and Châtenois.

Hugel et Fils, Riquewihr

For many people in Britain the name 'Hugel' is synonymous with the wines of Alsace. It is only recently that the portion of their sales in the U.K., as expressed as a fraction of the total Alsace sales on the British market, has fallen below 50 per cent. This predominance has not come about by chance: Jean Hugel, who died recently, frequently visited Britain and his Riquewihr cellars were always open to visitors. One son, 'Johnnie', is carrying on this noble and warmhearted tradition, and two other sons and younger members of the family are actively engaged in the business. Hugel is known throughout most of the English-speaking world, also, it should be noted, having many friends in the other different wine regions who appreciate both their wines and their success. There export business accounts for at least 80 per cent of their trade and they send wines to 120 countries.

The first Hugel – then Hugelin – came to Riquewihr in 1637, from Dannemarie, south-west of Mulhouse. During the frightful period of the Thirty Years War, the walled town of Riquewihr would have seemed to offer some protection. The family prospered and became much respected. Their houses were fine and, by the nineteenth century, they were rich and successful, several Hugels adopting a 'second' trade of coopering and travelling widely to study casks. Throughout their recent history – and Etienne Hugel today is twelfth in line from the founder – the Hugels have voyaged outside Alsace, so as to acquire knowledge of all classic wines, giving them a perspective as to making wine that is not usual. They know the new world as well as the old.

The Riquewihr cellars, below the offices and the house to which the family moved in 1902, are one of the oldest buildings and the enchanting sign, by Hansi, is evocative of 'old Alsace', but the Hugels do not hesitate to use the most modern techniques in the production of their wines. Reference has already been made to Jean Hugel's insistence on the use of stainless steel screws for the presses and inside these there is a sprinkler system, so that they can be self-cleansing. The Sainte Cathérine cask, made in 1715 and shown on page 97, is, they proudly claim, the oldest cask in the world that has remained always in constant use.

The Hugel domaine consists of twenty-two hectares, just in Riquewihr, including part of the Sporen and Schoenenberg vineyards. Their plantations of vines are all done with shoots that they have grafted themselves. Their philosophy – 'A wine that is well treated, is not treated at all', as Jean Hugel used to say – is well known. The style of their wines is somewhat rich and they have made a speciality of *vendange tardive* and *sélection de grains nobles* wines, indeed, they are probably the only house to make the latter on a regular basis when the climatic conditions permit (at least, to offer the wines for sale), and they are the quintessence of richness. The making of sweet wines is a somewhat controversial topic in Alsace, but the Hugel family have no doubts.

At present, Hugel seem to be turning their attention towards making fine and great wines from the Pinot Noir. The bunches are totally de-stalked, natural yeasts are added and heated plates are submerged in the must so to extract the maximum amount of colour from the pigments on the skins; the wine is pumped over the skins twice a day and ferments for a week at 26°, before being drawn off and left to age in second-hand casks – from Mouton-Rothschild.

In all, Hugel sell five qualities of wine. Starting at the bottom of the ladder, there is their standard range, then Cuvée Tradition, Réserve Personnelle, *vendange tardive* and *sélection de grains nobles*. The higher qualities will only be made in the best vintages and in minute quantities.

(Hugel wines are invariably easy to like. They are perfect wines for anyone beginning to study Alsace. Indeed, this very asset of charm may cause some who love them to find it difficult to understand and appreciate the wines of other growers, however fine, because the house style here is so definite and individual. They have a 'smile' to them, both as regards bouquet and flavour, a clear-cut style, exemplifying the grape from which each is made, plus a warmth and depth that makes them fairly full in body and lingering on the palate. In certain years their Gewurztraminer can be opulent, almost 'heady', certainly able to stand up to many rich foods. Their Riesling is usually markedly fruity, accentuating the round, flowing style of wines made from this grape. The Muscat can be very compact and aromatic as it unfolds its bouquet and taste. The *vendange tardive* and *sélection de grains nobles* wines are giants, but gracious and amiable, their balance commanding much respect and requiring leisurely appraisal on the part of the drinker. They stand up amiably to many recipes – from *haute cuisine* of the world to simplified family fare.)

Institute Viticole Oberlin, Colmar

Although this property is scarcely of much commercial significance in the wine trade of Alsace, it does, nevertheless, play a very important rôle. It was founded in 1895 by the noted ampelographer, Chrétien Oberlin, to carry out research into the best varieties of grapes for the region. Since the beginning it has belonged to the town of Colmar and, at present, it has a triple existence: it is still a research station, then it produces wine for all the municipal banquets and receptions and, finally, sells to the general public. In all it has 8.45 hectares of vines on the Harth, to the west of the town of Colmar.

(A single visit and sampling do not qualify anyone to pronounce on the character of the wines offered, but their uncompromising, clean-cut, well-bred style was obvious. Anyone able to try them should note the 'correct' balance and discreet quality. I found them 'classic Alsace'.)

Charles Jux-Jacobert, Colmar

This is an important company, with a domaine of some eighty hectares on the plain, outside Colmar. The vineyards have been planted to facilitate ease of cultivation and the presshouse is at their centre. Much has been planted with Pinot Blanc, for the making of Crémants d'Alsace. The company passed through a difficult period financially in the 1970s and is now linked to Dopff & Irion of Riquewihr. Their white alcohol distillery has been sold. Among their specialities is the Tokay d'Alsace Baron Schwendi.

Eugène Klipfel, Domaine Louis Klipfel, Barr

The Klipfels are one of the few quality wine *négociants* of the Bas-Rhin and have built up a fine reputation for their wines. One competitor described them as being the only people, apart from the Hugels, who fully understand the making of *vendange tardive* wines. They have a domaine of more than thirty hectares, including five hectares of Gewurztraminer in their exclusive property, Clos Zisser; another of their best wines comes from the Freiberg. Only a quarter of their business is with export markets and they are proud that they can sell their quality wines in the best French supermarkets. The Klipfel family is linked by marriage with the Lorentz family of Bergheim and, perhaps confusingly, André Lorentz is a secondary name for Klipfel wines.

(Amiable, well-structured wines that provide pleasure, both in detail and by the general impression they make, although the Gewurztraminer seems especially good in most vintages. They are not 'obvious' but they can appeal to both the novice drinker and the knowledgeable.)

Emil Koenig, Goxwiller

This is a five-hectare domaine in the small village of Goxwiller (famous for its *pain d'épices*, where many shops display different shapes of this cake), just to the north of Barr; it produces mainly Edelzwicker, Pinot Blanc and Gewurztraminer. Its main claim to fame is that it is one of the very few vineyards in Alsace where kosher wine is made, much of it going to the large Jewish community in Strasbourg. The Koenigs are responsible for all the work in the vineyards and for the collection of the grapes, but the making and bottling of the wine is carried out by a rabbi with the help of theological students.

Vins d'Alsace Kuehn, Ammerschwihr

Recently this company has been purchased by the co-operative cellar at Ingersheim but little seems to have changed and the management still remains in the hands of the amiable M. Schielé, whose forefathers used to live on the site of the present Kuehn cellars. (One of them, Jean-Jacques Schielé, who died in 1772, must have been a man of some substance, as his estate included three horses, nine oxen, two bulls, seven cows, one heifer, nine pigs and more than 125,000 litres of wine, from a variety of vintages from 1760 to 1772. The importance of his vineyard holdings can be judged from the fact that also in this inventory were eighty wooden baskets for the use of the grape pickers.)

Also unchanged is the domaine, which consists of eight hectares of vines, including two of Riesling and Gewurztraminer in the Kaefferkopf. Their range of wines begins with their 'Charme d'Alsace', which has a Chasselas base, and also includes the excellent Gewurztraminer Saint Hubert.

The Kuehn family started in the wine trade in Ammerschwihr in the seventeenth century, when they owned the local and trendy-sounding inn 'L'Enfer' (Hell); the cellars of this are still in use and are among the deepest in the village; during World War II hundreds of the inhabitants spent more than a month there, sheltering during the heavy bombardments which largely destroyed the village.

(I admit to being partial about Kuehn wines which I find are usually both impressive and attractive, possessing an amiable but important style, with numerous subtle shades of bouquet and flavour. The adjectives 'beautiful' and 'alluring' may often be found suitable when trying to describe them. Always well balanced and proportioned, their multi-stranded and well-bred character means that most of them merit steady and leisurely appraisal, when they will unfold their enjoyable but subtle and individual taste. In a ripe year they possess great charm, plus delicacy. They can partner many substantial dishes.)

Kuentz-Bas, Husseren-les-Châteaux

Like some of the best companies in Alsace, this house is the result of the coming together of two families by marriage. It is now directed by Jean-Michel Bas, ably assisted by several other members of the family. The cellars, at the end of a narrow, flower-covered courtyard, with the house above, present one of the most beautiful and traditional establishments of Alsace, conventional in historic layout but modern in essential equipment.

The reputation of the company is greater than its size – for it is quite small, with a domaine of just seven hectares in Husseren, Voegtlinshoffen and Eguisheim. This is responsible for approximately one-third of their grape requirements; the balance is purchased as grapes or wine. They have been selling on the British market for more than forty years and are proud to be the smallest member of the promotional group called 'Les Grandes Maisons d'Alsace', which includes several famous establishments and also their U.K. representatives.

In ascending order of quality, their range of wines includes the Cuvée Réservée and Réserve Personnelle. A limited number of *vendange tardive* wines are also made in the better years and, when he is pressed about them, M. Bas will admit that the Muscat would be considered to be the house speciality.

(The wines are generally very well balanced and possess a compact, sleek discreet charm, never seeming obvious but being most rewarding to the drinker who allows them to reveal themselves gradually in the glass. They also have a firmness of construction and are usually endowed with a very clean, trim finish. The *vendange tardive* wines have an impressive balance and intensity.)

Device of the
Grandes Maisons d'Alsace

Michel Laugel, Marlenheim

The first Michel Laugel appears in Marlenheim in 1650, owning vineyards and increasing his holdings by marriage. The firm was established as important commercially in 1889 and, in 1919, the Michel Laugel of the time with his son Paul set up today's Marlenheim premises. They formed a grower's association in the 1960s and the family decided to attack export as well as national markets with particular concentration. They are very important in the U.S. today. The company has the largest turnover of any in Alsace, but this is mainly because it is the distributor of a number of other products, including the locally popular German schnapps, Jägermeister. Perhaps their best wine is a Pinot Noir from Marlenheim, sold as Cuvée du Mariage de l'Ami Fritz (the reference being to a popular Alsace romance). However, I must admit to not being a fan of Laugel wines, which may be sound but are rarely inspiring. In a region where so much store is set by medals, I was once amused to find a Laugel wine in a French supermarket bearing the Silver Medal of the Club Oenologique of the U.K., awarded at one of the Bristol Wine Fairs! At present much publicity is being given to their locally made sparkling wines, of which a range is produced.

(The wines please–but sometimes seem to try too hard to do so. They may appear somewhat superficial in character, but many people find them extremely pleasant, especially drinkers who do not want what may be described as too cerebral a wine. The sparkling wines are available.)

Gustav Lorentz S.A., Jérôme Lorentz, Bergheim

Though these two companies operate separately, they are both under the same management and control. Jointly, they constitute one of the larger Alsace establishments. Their domaine is of 25 hectares and is strong in Gewurztraminers from the Altenberg and the Kanzlerberg; they also have an excellent Riesling from the latter vineyard. This company is not for those who appreciate a florid style in wines, as those of Lorentz are generally rather restrained and introverted.

(The Gewurztraminers do tend to be 'turned in' and stiff at first taste, rather than fluid in style. They need sympathetic handling to show their quality. The Rieslings require some aeration for the bouquet and flavour to emerge satisfactorily–although this judgment is possibly somewhat superficial. They are rewarding to the drinker who will persevere, but perhaps are not wines for the beginner.)

Jos. Meyer, Wintzenheim

It is always interesting to ask wine men whose wines, apart from their own, do they most respect in the region and, in Alsace, the name of the firm of Jos. Meyer is one frequently mentioned. Despite his relative youth, the present head Jean Meyer is not afraid of controversy; he opens the booklet he has written about his wines with the heading 'A Few Generalities' then, straight to his personal beliefs: 'Alsace is the best keeping dry white wine in the world.' M. Meyer does not make a Pinot Noir; he does not believe in them. If his customers insist, he will buy one for them, but, one gets the impression, with less than good grace. For him the term *vendange tardive* in itself means little; on his labels the actual date of picking appears and the wine will be as dry as possible. He does not believe in apeing German wines. To fly against convention so much in Alsace is not easy–unless you are making exceptional wines. M. Meyer does make exceptional wines. His great-great grandfather founded the firm in 1854 and it is still very much an individual concern.

The house of Jos. Meyer is also different from others in that it restricts its purchasing of grapes to the villages of Wintzenheim and Turckheim, so all the wines offered have a distinct regional style. The domaine itself consist of 14.5 hectares and this accounts for about 40 per cent of their needs. When to pick? 'I seek the greatest maturity, while keeping the style of the grape variety.'

The company's best wines are based around the Hengst vineyard at Wintzenheim, which has a chalky soil. From here come Les Lutins, made from the Pinot Auxerrois, and the best Rieslings. His blended Rieslings are sold under the brand 'Les Pierrets' and the Gewurztraminers as 'Les Archenets'.

(Very complex, very tautly constituted and usually rather profound wines. The Rieslings in particular seem generally to have a rich, undulating charm and most of the wines have considerable length; if they are compared with wines from a site distant from Wintzenheim and Turckheim, the region's characteristics are immediately perceptible – firm, warm hearted, well defined. Many examples have a particularly beautiful fragrance, which should enable drinkers to register certain of the grapes' characteristics. Drinkers should take their time about forming opinions.)

A. & O. Muré Clos Saint Landelin, Rouffach

It is generally accepted that, after Perpignan, Colmar is the driest town in France, but the charmingly energetic Mlle Reine-Thérèse Muré would have us believe that, by comparison, the Clos Saint Landelin, which she owns with her brother, is a positive Sahara! The vineyard takes its name from an itinerant Irish labourer – a monk as many were generally termed at that period – who came to convert the Germans in the fourth century and established a monastery in the Black Forest. In due course this vineyard came into the possession of the Diocese of Basle and, during the German occupation of the eighteenth century, was considered to be a model property of its type. The Muré family, who have been growers in the neighbouring village of Westhalten since 1630, bought the Clos Saint Landelin in 1935.

The vineyard is on a steep slope, facing due south. There are eighteen hectares of vines, with some of them dating back more than sixty years. The bottom of the slope is planted in Riesling, the middle in Gewurztraminer, and the top and the plateau in Muscat, Pinot Noir and Tokay. The soil is basically stony chalk and the average yield is between 60 and 70 hectolitres to the hectare. In the exceptional vintage of 1982 this figure rose to 95 hectolitres per hectare.

Neither Mlle Muré nor her brother (a statistician) have had any formal training in wine making, but the results they achieve are outstanding. After studying comparative production figures and the details of vineyards around the world, he, in consequence, makes big, firm wines that are rather tight and closed when young, but which open out with age. Besides the domaine wines, there are also wines that are bought locally in the Rouffach region; these are sold under the A. and O. Muré label. Another speciality of the domaine is its range of marc brandies. They distil one from the Gewurztraminer, one from the Pinot Noir and one from a blend of varieties of grapes.

(Ample, elegantly consititued wines, that possess an instant charm and lightness that has great appeal; they do not reveal themselves completely until they are mature, but their sunny character is evident and the inner zip and crispness delightful. Wines are sometimes curiously akin to the personalities of those who make them – Muré wines are enthusiastic, get up and go, vigorous examples, with plenty of finesse in reserve.)

J. Camille Preiss-Henny, Mittelwihr

This important company now operates in conjunction with cousins Léon Beyer at Eguisheim and jointly they are now among the largest vineyard owners in Alsace. Also in the family is the important distillery of Théo. Preiss.

The Preiss-Henny domaine is of 45 hectares, spread over seven villages and accounts for 90 per cent of the wines that they sell. Behind the cellars rises the Mandelberg vineyard, which claims to be the warmest spot in Alsace: 'Mandel' means almond and this is supposed to be the only place in the region where they will ripen.

(Mandelberg wines are usually charming, welcoming, flowing, light-textured drinks.)

J. Preiss-Zimmer, Riquewihr

This company with its delightful wine-taster on the wrought-iron signboard is installed in the former Auberge de l'Etoile, built in 1685. From the outside it may seem of little importance, but behind the entrance lies a succession of courtyards and cellars, one of which belonged to the Guild of Wine Growers.

The company owns a domaine of about 10 hectares, but believes firmly that vineyard names are of no importance – what must be done is to promote that of the company. In France this is done by selling direct to private customers.

The firm has a high reputation for their Rieslings, even from the less fashionable vintages. Their Gewurztraminers also have a number of admirers.

Typical wrought-iron coloured sign outside the Preiss-Zimmer establishment in Riquewihr

The huge Domaines Viticoles Schlumberger, extending above Guebwiller. The various sections of the vineyard are enclosed in this terraced vineyard in the south of the region

(Sometimes these wines seem a little stiff and reluctant to please, but their firm, defined style can be rewarding, especially with the older wines. They are robust and good for registering grape styles. As with others of the wines from this area, they can be appealing and good with many recipes.)

Domaines Viticoles Schlumberger, Guebwiller

The town of Guebwiller must be among the least attractive in Alsace – most are so delightful that this, dominated by the textile machinery factories of the Schlumberger group, comes as a surprise. The eye does not linger on the grey streets of Guebwiller, lacking in obvious appeal, but is rewarded by looking upwards. Here, dominating the town, indeed soaring above it in curves and terraces reminiscent of some of the vineyards around the towns of Tain-Tournon in the Rhône Valley, is the largest single domaine in Alsace and, in addition, the largest single vineyard property on slopes in France. This majestic site also belongs solely to the Schlumberger family.

The Schlumberger firm express some regret that they tend to be unvisited by Alsace enthusiasts, even including those who write about the region. But for those who penetrate the rather dull façade of their premises and are admitted to the simple, utilitarian reception room, the rewards are great.

Wine has been important in the Guebwiller area since very early times. A Gallo-Roman villa indicates this and the firm relate how the Roman tradition of vine growing became allied to the Gallic cooperage to make a profitable trade with the Roman garrisons in the Rhine Valley.

It was in the Middle Ages that the vineyard of this region became of great importance, the great Abbaye de Murbach, powerful since the eighth century until the Revolution in the eighteenth, dominating the Florival area. But the upheaval of 1789 was the end of the Prince-Abbots of Murbach and the influence of the church. This period, it must be remembered, was the beginning of the Industrial Revolution too and, after a more tranquil period was established in France after 1815, manufacturing concerns began to spring up. The vineyards formerly belonging to the Abbey of Murbach came onto the market after the French Revolution and about 20 hectares were bought by the local mill owner, Nicolas Schlumberger. By the end of the nineteenth century this domaine, now the largest in the area, had doubled in size. At the beginning of the twentieth century, however, first the phylloxera plague and then World War I had almost totally destroyed the vineyards of southern Alsace; it appeared unlikely that vine cultivation would be a rewarding occupation in this region, especially with the lack of labour to work the vineyards. Between 1920 and 1935 Ernest Schlumberger bought cheaply all the vineyard land that had been allowed to return to scrub; from this he created a holding of 120 hectares. Today, this is a single vineyard of 140 hectares, planted on terraces that are retained by 50 kilometres of dry stone walling; the establishment of these and their maintenance is something in itself to admire – even more so when the labour problems during and after World War II are remembered. In all, there are 750 kilometres of vines and the slopes are often so steep that they cannot be worked by tractor, even the modern tractors of today; twelve horses are therefore kept for vineyard work and there is a full-time team of 45 men engaged in the vineyard.

Although the vineyard area of the Schlumberger domaine represents 1 per cent of the total Alsace vineyard, the production percentage is much lower, due to the small yields on the terraced slopes. Because of the varied terrain and the different curves and undulations of this huge property, the vintage can be spread over as much as two months. The vineyards have a variety of different expositions, ranging from east to south-west. The different site names are Kitterlé (perhaps the best), Kessler, Spiegel and Saering. The good exposition of the vineyards enables very rich wines to be made and a 1976 *vendange tardive*, Cuvée Anne Schlumberger claims to have the highest must weight of any Alsace wine ever recorded. In general, Schlumberger wines are full-bodied and heavy in texture.

(Imposing, weighty, lengthy are all suitable adjectives, but there is also a warmth and comfortable style to many of the wines – they nuzzle the drinker gently, without assaulting the palate or nose. They exemplify the region clearly – try one against a wine of equal quality from the Bas-Rhin to see the difference! The favoured aspect of the big vineyard is shown by the ample character – the wines give gradually of themselves with an underlying cosiness that makes them enjoyable both to beginners and the experienced and their somewhat massive flavours make them good with many full-flavoured foods. The astonishing *vendange tardive* wines, notably those of 1976, are unlike any others – they are perhaps best described as essences of a great summer, great grapes and, certainly, adroit and sensitive wine making.)

Albert Seltz et Fils, Mittelbergheim
Pierre Seltz is perhaps the most outward-looking of all the growers of Alsace. He prefers to consider the wines he makes in a global context rather than as simple regional wines from France. The fact that he studied at Davis, in

California, and that his wife is an American have no doubt helped form his philosophy. His reason for studying abroad, previously quoted, was that 'by learning as much as I could, I could completely return to nature', although his father warned him, before he left 'not to tell them everything I knew'. Despite being welcome at any time to call in and lunch with the Gallo Brothers (whose winery is the largest in the world), California wine making has not over-awed him. He thinks it is most important for the growers of Alsace to realise their potential to the full, while also making wines such as are wanted by the consumers of the world, but 'every grape variety has its limit'.

The Seltz domaine is about eight hectares, of which around two are in the Zotzenberg, where the finest Sylvaners of Alsace are made. Outstanding, too, is their Riesling from the Brandluft. Pierre Seltz is very aware that the consumer does not want a wine that 'tires' – one that makes the drinker suddenly realise he cannot or does not want to drink any more, however enjoyable the wine seems initially. So, as much as possible, he limits the use of any additional sugar and sulphur and goes out of his way to make wines with a well-balanced acidity. This is probably one company whose wines should be more widely appreciated.

(Too little experience on which to base a generalisation, but clean, unobtrusively pleasant wines, with underlying charm is probably a fair comment to add here.)

R. Sick–P. Dreyer, Ammerschwihr

The wines from this domaine have been familiar to me for a long time and their clean, fruity style is something I particularly like. Regular favourites are the Côtes d'Ammerschwihr P.M.G. (the wine is pure Chasselas and the 'P.M.G.', for largely unexplained reasons, stands for 'Pour ma gueule', signifying 'For my gob') and the Riesling and Gewurztraminer wines from the Kaefferkopf vineyard. Initial tasting of their *crémant* suggests that the extra bottle age it has had over many of its competitors makes for a more enjoyable wine – as will be appreciated when it is released to the market. (I am less happy about the family marc de Gewurztraminer!)

René Sick and his nephew control about ten hectares of vines, of which two are in the Kaefferkopf.

(I have had limited experience, but much pleasure here, because the wines provide the appeal and multi-stranded texture that is possibly typical of Ammerschwihr style, with a brisk, taut freshness.)

Pierre Sparr et Ses Fils, Sigolsheim

Traditionally, this company has up to now sold all its production on the French market, though they now believe that the future must lie in the export trade. Each year they process grapes from more than 120 hectares of vines, in addition to the sixteen hectares of their own properties. Single vineyard wines have always been something of a speciality and they make excellent Rieslings from the Kaefferkopf at Ammerschwihr, the Altenbourg at Katzenthal and a Gewurztraminer from the Mambourg in Sigolsheim itself.

(Straightforward, direct, slight underlying richness, usually definitely mouth-filling.)

E. Trimbach, Ribeauvillé

This is one of the companies in Alsace whose wines are respected by everybody. In Britain, Trimbach is generally considered as being on a par with Hugel, though the styles of the wines that they make are very different. The magnificent austerity of a Trimbach wine is a complete contrast to the fuller richness of one from the friendly rival at Riquewihr (and Hugel would certainly agree). The two Trimbach brothers have today built up a great renown for their wines, especially in the Benelux countries, the United States and Britain.

Trimbach were founded as Alsace wine makers in 1626. They are yet another of the family firms who can boast that the present generation is the eleventh in direct line from the originator. It was Frédéric-Emile Trimbach (after whom one of their wines of outstanding quality is now named) who showed his wines at the 1898 Brussels International Show, where he took the highest awards. The personal involvement of the present generation, brothers Hubert and Bernard, is constant and extends to every aspect of vine growing and wine making; in talking to them, one receives the impression that every single cask or vat in their cellars contains a wine as individual as a human being as far as they are concerned – and they are concerned to let it realise its utmost potentialities. It is a Trimbach Riesling that represents Alsace at the Elysée Palace in Paris.

The jewel in the diadem of their reputation is the Clos Sainte Hune vineyard, which produces probably the finest Riesling in Alsace. This minute vineyard, of a mere one and a half hectares at historic Hunawihr, has belonged to the family for more than two centuries. In an average year it yields no more than 8000 bottles. Its true merit is shown in certain lesser vintages, such as 1977, when it still produced great bottles of fine, forceful wine.

Other specialities from the Trimbach's own vineyard include the Riesling Cuvée Frédéric Emile, from the Osterberg vineyard, directly behind their cellars in Ribeauvillé, where the unassuming offices are above some of the most impressive and beautiful collections of old casks – containing, of course, equally impressive and beautiful wines. Another fine wine is the Gewurztraminer Cuvée des Seigneurs de Ribeauvillé, from a small part of the Osterberg vineyard that is called Trottacker.

(The reserve, breeding and tantalising aloofness of many Trimbach wines is definite – though not always to the taste of drinkers who prefer immediate early charm. But the detailed elegance and nobility of the wines is likely to be remembered by any who sample them. They insinuate themselves into the senses involved with tasting and make a lasting impression – precision-balanced, tantalisingly knit, but challenging in their finesse. The delicacy and poise of the house style and adroit ability to make a good wine into something memorable is exemplified by a Sylvaner of 1973 from this establishment: it was and remains to me a supreme example of this grape – until I was able to taste their 1982! The fine wines in their range are complex and capable of making an effort even against somewhat challenging foods.)

A. Willm, Barr

To sell snails as well as wine may seem an unhappy or at least unlikely marriage of activities, but this has been the successful achievement of the Willm family. With a domaine of 25 hectares, all in Barr apart from a couple of hectares at Mittelbergheim, thriving export sales and an output of 100,000 snails a day, the company is certainly busy! Recently control has passed out of the hands of the family into those of a large general wine company, but at present little seems to have changed.

The company offices are rather like the sort of hunting lodge one might see in a film of *The Prisoner of Zenda*, even the cellars having wooden shelving dating back to before World War I. The wines of which Willm are most proud are those from the seven hectare Clos Gaenzbroennel, and the Sylvaner from the Kirchberg, which must be among the best of Alsace.

(Sound, firm, possibly a little facile, but out to provide pleasure and demonstrating the slightly four-square character of wines from this area.)

Domaine Zind-Humbrecht, Wintzenheim

The founder of this firm was Sonntag Humbrecht (1620-82) and the present Leonard Humbrecht is twelfth in line from the beginnings in 1658. It was both good fortune and good business when, in 1959, Mlle Zind of Wintzenheim married Leonard Humbrecht of Gueberschwihr. Also, by this alliance, an important viticultural domaine of eighteen hectares was established, spread between these two villages and Turckheim. Since then, this holding has been increased to 29 hectares, the latest acquisition being the four hectare Clos Saint Urbain, part of the Rangen vineyard in Thann, bought from a schoolmaster in 1978.

The firm have now a powerful range of single vineyard wines, each with its own style, due to the differing soils: the Clos Saint Urbain is the only vineyard in Alsace on volcanic soil; the Brand, at Turckheim, is granitic; the Clos Hauserer, part of the Hengst at Wintzenheim, is chalky clay, and the neighbouring Herrenweg is on the richer alluvium of the bottom of the valley. Each of them is vinified separately, often in two or more grape varieties. This domaine can, therefore, offer the most instructive tastings of all Alsace – and it seems a pity that its finer wines are not currently available in the U.K.

Great care is taken with the making of the wines and the answer for temperature control was found as far away as Australia: thermal plaques are fitted inside the fermentation vats. Zind-Humbrecht were the innovators of this technique in Alsace, although Hugel have now followed and make use of it. Not at all in accordance with the Hugel philosophy, however, is the style of the Zind-Humbrecht *vendange tardive* wines: every effort is made to ferment out all the sugar and this results in extremely masculine wines, as, for example, their Gewurztraminer Hengst *vendange tardive* of the 1981 vintage.

The care and enthusiasm of Mme Humbrecht and her husband – she is always eager to impart information and her love of wines is equalled by her knowledge – plus the care they take in production makes their wines always good, often great.

(The wines of ordinary quality from this firm are sound, good, enjoyable – but it is in the higher ranges that they can be exciting. Big, almost swashbuckling wines result, always balanced and contained by the good taste of the makers, so that they are well proportioned, yet impose themselves delectably for the detailed appraisal of the knowing. Unfortunately the British public won't pay for quality wines of this type, so the British shipper is reluctant to buy them – then to risk letting them sag into the 'bin end sales'. But these finer wines are well worth attention.)

The above list cannot include all the great wine makers of Alsace. Among others, Christopher Fielden has also appreciated the wines of producers Schleret, Louis Gisselbrecht, Marcel Mullenbach and Lucien Tempé. Other excellent co-operatives include those of Kientzheim, Ingersheim and Turckheim.

In my experience Louis Gisselbrecht have made very agreeable wines, notably their Rieslings, which are light bodied but fruity and well balanced. The Sipp wines are also pleasing.

Christopher Fielden's 'top ten' favourite Alsace wine producers includes the following (in alphabetical order): Léon Beyer, Faller Frères, Hugel, Schlumberger, Trimbach, Zind-Humbrecht. The other four places he thinks would be difficult to allocate, but would come from Kuentz-Bas, Clos Saint Landelin, Dopff 'Au Moulin', Preiss-Zimmer, Sick-Dreyer, Albert Seltz, Jos. Meyer and Klipfel. I shall likewise venture my 'top ten' with the caveat that my experience has not included sufficient of the wines that have been commented on here to give an overall opinion about certain of them. My 'top ten' (in alphabetical order) would be: Léon Beyer, Dopff 'Au Moulin', Hugel, Kuehn, Kuentz-Bas, Jos. Meyer, Preiss-Zimmer, Schlumberger, Trimbach, Zind-Humbrecht.

8

Gastronomy

Alsace has bred a nation of robust trenchermen. Those who live in a mountain region have had to eat well to survive and the resources of Alsace in the lakes, rivers, forests, plain plantations and the lush river pastures, has always offered varied fare. In many ways the people of Alsace have eaten a better and more nutritious diet than those living in apparently more obviously profitable surroundings. The small population of the region, the autonomy of the towns and villages, the necessity of being able to defend oneself against aggressors and invaders from all sides, have resulted in the average Alsace person displaying exuberant delight in the good things of life, whether these feature at memorable feasts or are part of humbler everyday fare.

Historically, religious occasions – the church festivals, installations of bishops, baptisms, weddings, funerals, blessings of all kinds – were invariably celebrated by eating and drinking. So were more secular events: birthdays, especially the fiftieth anniversaries, victories in war, class reunions and, certainly, the killing of a pig. This animal, the mainstay of much Alsace cooking, is rightly valued by all who keep it, for, in accordance with the English saying, it is 'the gentleman who pays the rent', because every scrap of it except, possibly, the curly tail, can be utilised either for eating or to turn to profit in the form of hides and horn. In the fifteenth century there were at least 1500 pigs kept within the city of Strasbourg by the Bakers' Guild alone. People rejoiced when a house was built and the cooking pot was hung over the kitchen fire – the expression 'pendre la crémaillère' (to hang up the pot) signifies a housewarming.

For large-scale festivals booths selling food and cooked dishes were set up in the streets; fountains ran with wine. At the funerals of important persons all the dishes would first be offered to the corpse – often present in considerable state – and then be bestowed on the local poor. These funerals could last for several days, especially for great nobles or a sovereign. When Strasbourg Cathedral was consecrated the 'cathedral warming' was such that a scandal echoed down the centuries: of course, one tends to remember and pass on bad or shocking news rather than the good, but it is startling to hear of a huge cask being set up and tapped in one of the side chapels and the actual buffet being arranged on the high altar.

In 1580 the great Bordeaux essayist, Michel de Montaigne (1533-92) commented, when visiting Alsace, that the most trivial meals lasted for three or four hours. Some attempts at restrictions were made: in 1544 wedding parties in Strasbourg were allowed to include only 50 guests for a mere couple of days. Otherwise, such gatherings might have gone on–and on. As recently as 1896 there was a wedding in Ribeauvillé that lasted for a whole week one April; then, when the guests got on the train to Strasbourg, they all felt it was a shame to say goodbye, so the caterer, who was also going home, invited them to his house, where they continued eating and drinking throughout the night! Although in 1634 a Confrérie des Maigres was established at Ensisheim (a type of forerunner of Weight Watchers), it does not seem to have flourished.

A fillip to local gastronomy was given when, in 1738, the former King Stanislas of Poland was made Governor of Alsace; the King of France had to establish his father-in-law in some style. The courts of Nancy and Lunéville were appreciative of culinary delights. In *Voltaire in Love* (1957), Nancy Mitford describes some of the pleasures the courtiers enjoyed at this time. Chefs were kept up to the mark by the production of the sweetmeats and delicacies coming from the chic convents of the region, where the cooks vied with each other in making sought-after specialities; at least these skills stood the religious in good stead when, at the Revolution, they were turned out of their convents and had to fend for themselves, often becoming cooks.

King Stanislas himself was much interested in food; he is credited with the idea of soaking the traditional *Kugelhopf* sponge in rum–hence the *rhum baba.* From his kitchens the cheese puffs known as 'bouchées à la reine' were sent to his daughter at Versailles and it was his cook, Madeleine, who is said to have first made the small, orange-flavoured spongecakes that bear her name and were made the focal point of Proust's huge novel *A la Recherche du Temps Perdu.*

Although big feasts created topics of conversation for generations and important events were marked by banquets that were recorded by those chronicling the doings of the nobles and the rich bourgeoisie, the ordinary folk did not eat so lavishly. However, except in times of war there do not seem to have been serious famines; people might not have eaten meat daily or even every other day, but, in many instances, they would have had some form of it during most weeks.

Also, the small population ate sensibly. A variety of foods composing a balanced diet, with vitamins to counteract seasonal afflictions, were in use. Salads played a big part, so did dried fruit (often incorporated in meat dishes), vegetables from the cottage gardens, many root vegetables as well and, of course, the great white cabbage, a staple that has dominated Alsace home cooking for centuries, notably as *choucroute.*

Preparing the moulds for the sponge cake *Kugelhopf* at the Hôtel du Parc, Obernai

The people of Alsace were eating potatoes–a source of Vitamin C–considerably earlier than the rest of France. It is recorded there in 1625, according to Lucien Sittler and although peasant farmers were somewhat hesitant about planting this 'earth apple', from 1700 cultivation of the tuber began to spread and, by 1740, it was well established. This shows rapid progress. Pizarro is thought to have discovered the potato in Peru around the first quarter of the sixteenth century and, fifty years later, a German botanist described it as a 'little truffle', although no one appeared keen on eating it. Sir Walter Raleigh brought it to England around 1585 but again, it wasn't quickly accepted as a food. Attempts were apparently made to publicise it in the Vivarais region of the Rhône Valley, but although botanists and horticulturalists realised its potential, Louis XIV expressed dislike for it, so it didn't catch on.

151

Parmentier was keen to develop it, seeing how valuable a food it might become, but, at the Revolution, he had to call in the army to protect his laboratories as the French shouted for 'Bread!' The people of Alsace were not so conservative (like the English, who, just before Napoleon's attempted blockade of Britain, had begun to plant potatoes in quantities); it was appreciated that, even if the grain crop were not good, potatoes might save many from starvation and in addition provide useful fodder for pigs.

Several pioneer landlords helped to set up orchards and nursery gardens in Alsace after the devastation of the Thirty Years War; these did not only supply table fruit, but fruit for drying. Tobacco also began to be cultivated at the beginning of the seventeenth century, it seems, as the result of someone visiting England and bringing back tobacco plants; there was an 'Englischer Hof' plantation on the banks of the River Ill in 1620 and, although the frightful war interrupted this trade, the crop became well established later, Alsace tobacco being known in many export markets, including Russia, until competition from France itself reduced the crop.

In the mid-eighteenth century beet, vetch, lucerne, sainfoin (for forage) were introduced, indicating the willingness of the people to accept new products. Already there were many inexpensive staples: pulses, such as lentils, beans, rice and barley, noodles in various forms, such as the delectable 'spätzle', all of which eked out such meat and fish as was available. Most people ate only vegetables in the evenings.

Today, there are two distinct types of food. There are the refinements of many traditional recipes, as exemplified by the great restaurants. Many of these have a considerable history. *Foie gras*, the liver of specially fattened geese, is possibly the best known. Many kinds of pâté have certainly been made in Alsace since early times, from meat, fish, snails, crustacea; *presskopf*, a type of brawn, was known in the sixteenth century. The eighteenth-century governor of Alsace, the Maréchal de Contades (whose beautiful château at Montgeoffroy, outside Angers in the Loire, still contains all the original furniture), brought his chef, Jean-Joseph or Jean-Pierre Clause with him and it was this young man who, in 1775, made a *pâté en croûte* (in a pastry case) using goose liver. Clause had a great success with this and, leaving the Maréchal's service, he prudently married the widow of an Alsace *pâtissier* and set up in business in Strasbourg. One of his trainees, Nicolas Doyen, formerly chef to the first President of the Parlement de Bordeaux, added truffles to the recipe. He invariably used the truffles of Périgord although there are truffles in Alsace; indeed, during the German occupation in the latter part of the nineteenth centry, they forbade truffle hunters to use the pig (usually a young sow) for this trade, so the search had to continue with dogs, poodles being found most adept at finding the 'black diamonds'.

Foie gras is served, with the wine jelly with which it has been cooked, usually at the beginning of the meal, although sometimes it is presented later, in place of some form of salad. It is generally served cold, but there are recipes for it as a hot dish. Always rich, it melts in the mouth.

There are many lake and river fish, often combined with superb sauces and the region's wines. Trout today, alas, will come from a *vivier* or trout farm. The pike (*brochet*), pike perch (*sandre*) are only two of the fish likely to feature on menus, but there may also be carp, sometimes served *à la juive*, for the Jewish community in Alsace introduced many recipes, often incorporating sweet-sour flavourings and sometimes fruit.

Game is also plentiful, venison and pheasant being cooked in many ways. Chicken is poached in wine and, of course, roast pork (although the French do not know of the joys of crackling) is often served.

In any good restaurant the sweet trolley will be irresistible: numerous cakes, *petits fours,* sponges, the region's grooved cake, the *Kugelhopf,* in addition to beautiful fruit tarts, gleaming with colour and based on feather-light pastry and, these days, a range of ices and sorbets, the latter often flavoured with the fruit brandies.

There is also the great cheese, Munster. The *fermier* version is the traditional type, but Munster *Laitier* made from pasteurised milk and available all the year round, is made in response to demand. Traditional Munster – both types are made from cows' milk – is supposed to be at its best in summer and autumn. Munster is flattish and round in shape, but varies in size, and has a tawny exterior. The small cheeses are kept to mature in a cheese cave for about three weeks, the larger sizes for two to three months, according to Monsieur Androuet's mighty directory of cheeses. These days Munster is made in places other than the Munster Valley from which it gets its name. When Munster is fresh, it is sometimes eaten with sugar and cream or, just after the vintage, with nuts and the new wine. Otherwise it dominates the cheeseboard – because, though its flavour cannot be truly described as more than 'strong', its smell is a veritable stink, penetrating and wafting through a dining-room. It is useless trying to keep it in any enclosed space because the odour will certainly get out. However, it is certainly a fine cheese, although, for the first-time taster, it is worth bearing in mind that its smell is almost a shield for the flavour and, if hesitant, one should sample a small portion that has been cut off from the extremely strong-smelling whole cheese. It is almost always served with grains of cumin.

Then there is the wide range of more homely Alsace dishes that the traveller should try. It is one of the delights of this region that one can have a light meal, a true snack or some cold meat and salad at almost any time, whereas in other regions of France the traveller – wishing to eat copiously only once in the day – may either have to accept a 'petit menu' or put up with 'un sandwich'. Alsace *winstube* cater for this public, so do many of the dishes they can provide.

The huge variety of sausages is bewildering: *Knockwurst* is blood sausage; *saucisse de Strasbourg* a smoked pork sausage, a little akin to a Frankfurter (these are made in Alsace as well); *saucisses de Montbéliard,* which come from Franche-Comté are somewhat similar to the pork 'banger' of the U.K., though they contain more pork and are slightly smoked; *un andouille* is a tripe sausage; *cervelas* is our saveloy, often quite spicy; and *saucissons secs* are dried sausages, usually rather hard and similar to salame. There are sausages flavoured with anis and many herbs and spices, galantines, *hure* (head cheese, a type of brawn), versions of sausage made with meat, fish, game and, sometimes, even snails; some of all these may be featured in an *assiette anglaise* or plate of cold cuts, which is usually accompanied by a jar of gherkins and possibly some salad.

The *salade de Gruyère* is diced cheese in a dressing, now widely known, as is the savoury tart, quiche Lorraine. The Alsace speciality is onion tart – *zewelwai* or *tarte à l'oignon.* 'Tart' is supposed to be a direct descendant of the Roman 'torta', meaning various things combined with a type of custard and served on a pastry base. Pancakes, too, are sometimes made with meat as well as fruits and also utilise pastry when it's necessary to eke out the filling. Pancakes (*crêpes* or, in German, *Pfannkuchen* or *Eierkuchen*) with cream and seasonings and *petits pois* alongside used often to be served on fast days.

Tarte flambée is a dish widely advertised these days and there are informal eating-places that specialise in it. It is a dish without a history and was, as far as anyone knows, made in the bakers' ovens before serious baking was started on a Saturday. Today it is as popular and chic as pizza but thirty years ago I only remember seeing it on the signboards of very small village restaurants. Essentially, it is bread dough, spread wafer-thin on a wooden, floured shovel, topped with a mixture of eggs beaten with oil and milk, *fromage blanc* (see below) and, possibly, bacon and/or onions, then cooked very quickly in a wood-fired oven. The crisp, fan-like sliver of the 'tarte' is eaten with the fingers and relays are brought to the enthusiastic diners. Where *tarte flambée* is well made, the locals congregate so, to enjoy this truly Alsace dish, it's worth finding somewhere enjoying a reputation for making it.

Another country dish is *fromage blanc*, which seems to be a very old regional recipe. It's what the British would call curd cheese, made by letting full cream milk drip through a sieve or muslin, leaving a solid behind; 'Bibeleskäs' is the name under which to find it in supermarkets – so-called because the white cheese used to be fed to chickens to fatten them. *Fromage blanc*, glistening white, is served in a large bowl, with accompanying dishes of chopped parsley, chives, onions, garlic, shallots, plus potatoes, sautéed in bacon fat, or boiled, or simply baked in their skins, sometimes with sliced radishes. Diners mix up the cheese with the herbs and other things, plus salt and pepper, as they wish. This is the sort of coarse country fare to enjoy at the type of inn where people sit at long tables, much as they would have done centuries ago. It is Alsace informality and great fun.

A type of stew of lamb, pork and beef is *baeckeoffa.* It is simmered for hours with potatoes, onions and seasonings – another dish for which the baker's oven

Ribeauvillé. Fête des Ménétriers or Pfiffertag (8 September) with the wooden
tubs ready for the vintage. The Seigneurs of Ribeauvillé were proud of the title 'Lord of
Fife Players' so, annually on the feast of the Nativity of the Virgin, they received
the fiddlers, dancing bear leaders, jugglers and musicians, after a ceremony at a local
shrine

would originally have been utilised. This too may be advertised outside a small eating place when it has been cooked for the day.

But the great Alsace dish is *choucroute*. Some suppose it to have been brought to the region by the Romans, but historians cite it as being known to the ancient Egyptians and the Tartars. The big round white cabbage is to Alsace what leeks are to Wales and *choucroute* has always been family fare – very satisfying even in its simplest versions. The cabbage is finely sliced and, until comparatively recently, each village would have a man who, equipped with a special slicing device, made a living by cutting up the vegetable. After being sliced it must be pressed with salt and herbs and left for about three weeks. Sometimes casks were used, sometimes, for big celebrations, a virtual tank. The *choucroute* begins to ferment and is then ready to be used in a recipe – this is the stage at which the pre-prepared cabbage should be bought. Wine, onions, seasonings of various kinds are added and the delectable mountain of hot cabbage is eventually adorned with all kinds of extras: smoked pork loin and ham, many other pig products may be cooked with it, including sausages of several kinds. There is one recipe that substitutes sliced turnips for the cabbage. Boiled potatoes are the traditional accompaniment. It used to be such a Sunday dish – left to cook during the morning service – that the humorist Hansi tells of the somewhat scatterbrained housewife who put her missal into the *choucroute* casserole and arrived at church carrying a chunk of bacon! For *choucroute royale* a split of one of the Crémants d'Alsace is often poised on the top of the mighty pile and the wine then dowses the dish – though I don't know that it makes much difference to the flavour. Connoisseurs of *choucroute* – tons of the stuff are consumed at the annual *choucroute* festival in Colmar – affirm that, reheated, it gets better and better. Many find it a wonderful *purée* with roast pork or game; there are those who make it into a salad. It is definitely a gutsy dish, has always been very much a family favourite and also something prepared in the home for a special visitor. Although the great restaurants usually have it on their menus, *choucroute* is something to eat out in the country, in the sort of little eating-place where men take off their jackets and loosen their ties and women abandon all notions of keeping to a diet.

Among the more homely sweet dishes are the little dumplings, which can also be made savoury. The most famous is possibly the recipe called *pets de nonne* (nun's farts). *Pain d'épices* (spiced cake, rather like gingerbread), fruit bread often made with dried fruits (sometimes associated with the religious festivals) are only some of the delights that make up a little of the Alsace menu. But only a little.

9

Serving and Drinking the Wines

Alsace wines are often the problem children on the wine lists of export markets. Those who know and love them drink them frequently – but these wines need knowing and they must be served with understanding. They are not – it cannot be sufficiently stressed – more than *very* vaguely similar to the German wines and this, I think, is where so many who would enjoy them hesitate and, sometimes, fail to place them in their proper context.

The wines of Alsace are to be enjoyed both by themselves and, certainly, with food and with a range of foodstuffs that might well prove taxing, even overwhelming to many wines, on account of their robust, often *piquant* and highly flavoured tastes. Although the finest examples of *haute cuisine* in Alsace stand comparison with any in the world, displaying delicacy and often a remarkable adroitness in balancing unctuousness with crispness and freshness, such dishes are not, even for the wealthy Alsace gourmet, everyday fare. The food the Alsace housewife or, even, the self-catering Alsace bachelor or career girl prepares and eats is the type of simple but sustaining fare that, in the region, may be referred to as 'cuisine bourgeoise' or even 'cuisine paysanne' but which relates to the true 'home cooking' of many households elsewhere. The person who goes out for a treat is nevertheless equally capable of being critically appreciative of, say, the *tarte flambée* or a dish of meat and vegetables, and one could hardly think of a dish that comes more aptly into the category of delectable 'coarse food' than a *choucroute*. It is these agreeable, cosy recipes, prepared from first-rate ingredients (the older generation in Alsace as elsewhere begin to sigh and shake their heads over the short cuts: packet, frozen and so-called 'convenience foods' that are found in the supermarkets) that have for generations been the accompaniments to Alsace wines and will continue to be so.

Many of the admirable books and booklets on Alsace *cuisine* err, in my view, because they stress the luxury foods too much. I think that Alsace wines stand up just as well to the more common as to the finer foods and recipes. Whereas the finer German wines are probably best appraised by themselves, top quality Alsace wines will withstand even the assault of smells and flavours of a closely packed restaurant, where people may be smoking at some tables, the flambé pan active at others, and wafts of garlic, spices and liqueurs assailing the nose from many sides. Their alcohol content, usually slightly higher than that of German wines, makes them more robust. In domestic surroundings the wines of Alsace can transform very humble fare – I venture even to say baked beans on toast, fish fingers, certainly cheese and biscuits – yet will go happily along with many of the finer traditional Anglo-Saxon recipes. They have, too, an additional 'plus' these days, when it has been discovered that a number of people suffer from a curious reaction to red wine. Known colloquially as 'Redhead', this causes the sufferer to feel sick, giddy and incur all the symptoms of a fairly bad hangover if red wine is drunk, even in small amounts. So considerate hosts are advised to provide for guests who may really not be able to enjoy red wines by serving something white as well – and something white that will stand up even to grills, roasts and spiced casserole dishes.

Alsace wines are subtle with flavours and bouquet aromas in the finer quality ranges, but they all possess a robust character. You are well advised not to swill the finer wines. But they possess a 'push' and definition that asserts itself on the palate and can be retained, even when foods are equally assertive. The balance of the wines, even from makers who opt for a light, even delicate style, gives them tremendous resilience; indeed, they may retain this delicacy – but it's the delicacy of the steel spring!

There is another 'plus' that should appeal to the host who plans a meal including some Alsace wines. The wines make an immediate impression. Of course, the finer wines go on unfolding their charms with aeration and, as the palate changes under the impression of food, they change too, often most rewardingly. They don't 'die in the glass', they don't need a lot of preliminary handling and presentation to be at their best, they soar out of the first glass poured and say 'Like me? Drink me!' This is a great asset to anyone selecting wines for a dinner-party in a restaurant, or for the host at home who may be coping singlehanded with the food as well, or who doesn't know the detailed preferences of guests, or who has had to rush home and has no last-minute opportunity to do much more than present the wines at reasonable temperature and draw the corks.

One point that can make a great deal of difference: even with inexpensive white wines, sometimes even more so when serving them, it is always wise to pull the cork and, either leaving it out for a few minutes or replacing it lightly, wait for five to ten minutes before pouring the wine. This dissipates the 'bottle stink', or stale air that has been shut into the bottle between the cork and the wine. An initial impression of this can occasionally suggest that the wine is defective, on many instances the whiff of bottle stink can adversely effect the first smell and taste of the wine as it is poured. It is surprising how much difference this minute additional aeration can make, so it's trouble worth taking.

Temperature

What about temperature? Inevitably, I must stress that 'cool' is not 'frozen stiff'. The purchaser of a bottle of wine has paid for all the enjoyment it is capable of providing and this includes the smell, the bouquet and the aroma (all three different, all three of interest). To semi-freeze a wine is to deprive the drinker of the smell and, indeed, most of the flavour; a cool liquid is all that enters the mouth, any subtleties having been overwhelmed, so that neither nose nor palate can welcome them. Wines that are slightly sweet or definitely sweet and luscious can, and sometimes should, benefit by a little lower temperature than the light, dry type, but in general a quarter of an hour in a deep bucket of ice and water (not ice alone, which merely chills patches of the bottle) or an hour in the middle or door of an ordinary domestic refrigerator will bring down the temperature to a refreshing point. On a very hot or extremely stuffy day it may be more agreeable to serve white wines at a slightly lower temperature than usual, but this is something for the individual to decide.

Having said this, it follows that wines in the various late-picked categories may be chilled a little more than those of the ordinary qualities, also that a Gewurztraminer of a particularly ripe year will benefit by a slightly lower

Square in Kaysersberg, where one of the fountains warns of the risk of drinking water – 'which chills the stomach' – and recommends 'old and complex wine'

temperature at serving than, for example, an ordinary quality Sylvaner; the weight and ripeness of individual wines should be considered, also the house styles. Makers of full, rounded, rather 'open' wines, that, as it were, come eagerly to meet the drinker will, I hope, not disagree with my suggestion that these can, on occasions, take a little more chilling than the wines made in accordance with a house style that is reserved, close-knit, shy, somewhat delicate, for such wines need bringing on gently to the palate. But too many caveats may inhibit the drinker. If he or she concentrates on cooling the wine to what is most agreeable and seems best to bring out all the qualities, that is the aim – how it is achieved is a matter of individual practice and individual experimentation.

The late M. Jean Hugel particularises a little more, while warning that the subtle aromas of a fine wine are released as it warms up, or takes on something of the temperature of the surroundings. He advocates that 'Alsace wine should generally be served between 7° and 9°C (44-48°F). For great Gewurztraminers or Tokays d'Alsace of *Réserve Personnelle* or *Vendange Tardive* level, for example, the temperature could be slightly lower (5-7°C or 41-44°F), but the bottle should not be replaced on ice afterwards, once opened.' I would certainly agree with the last sentence, but M.Hugel probably had no experience of the type of wine cooler that will hold the bottle and *maintain* the cool temperature at which it came from fridge or ice bucket for a considerable period and I do not think this harms even the greater wines, as it will not bring down the temperature – which is what he warns against.

Apéritifs

Considering the wines in relation to various settings of social drinking, there are several possibilities for an apéritif. Jean Hugel gives many ideas, but I am not sure that everyone could go along with his recommendation of Muscat as a pre-prandial drink: the people of Alsace themselves are keen on this and I certainly can enjoy it myself, but anyone who finds the Muscat difficult to like will probably find it *very* difficult to like before a meal. In addition, its intense grapiness sometimes gives the impression that the wine is going to be sweet on the palate; so strong are immediate reactions to smells and they so condition a subsequent reaction to tastes, that someone who – mistakenly – supposes that they do not like sweet wines at all, may be put off from the moment they stick their nose into a glass of Muscat.

There is another caveat about Muscat. If you serve it as an apéritif, then it does tend to be somewhat firm and robust, overwhelming the possibly lighter wine that is going to be served with the first dish of the meal or even all through. If you start with something definite and impressive, then you must go on with wines that are even more definite and impressive and this is not always easy – or economical.

Where Muscat is first rate before a meal is when the sort of canapés are served that, in themselves, can tax a very delicate, light-bodied wine–certain slightly *piquant* 'dips', stuffed eggs, sausages and salame high in pepper or other seasonings, or, in a British context, the matured hard cheeses, which are certainly taxing to many delicate wines. Muscat is robust enough to go well with these and, for those who enjoy its particular style, truly delicious as an opening wine on a pleasant occasion.

For informal entertaining, Sylvaner is acceptable–a good example can be extremely refreshing and it has the advantage of being able to accompany many first courses. M.Hugel suggests a 'Chasselas or a Sylvaner such as one may drink to quench one's thirst rather than to get any special gastronomic satisfaction' with salads, *crudités* and the sort of foods that make agreeable starters to a meal, but which are not wholly sympathetic to very fine wines. As an apéritif, Sylvaners can be somewhat light in body unless you take one from a particularly good year and, certainly, from an establishment known for making fine examples. Especially if guests are not heavy smokers, this is the wine for pouring generously and drinking with gratitude. In the past, I recall my own teacher, the late Allan Sichel, giving a 'Silver Sling' to American friends, who expressed a desire for a spirit-based apéritif; this drink was a measure of gin, topped up with Sylvaner, in the proportion of about one to two or three.

Nor, in my opinion, is there any reason why an Edelzwicker or a Riesling in the 'everyday' category and price range should not serve as apéritif, but then subsequent wines or wine must be slightly up in quality and weight. For any occasion of importance, however, a *crémant* would seem an excellent choice–providing that people do truly like bone dry sparkling wines; some may say they do, but insincerely! The weight and 'push' of this wine will also mean that any wine coming immediately after it should be equally weighty–possibly a continuation of the same *crémant*. As eggy and similarly unctuous sauces are well partnered by a dry sparkling wine, which will cut through the richness, this is a possibility.

Fruit, such as melons, smoked ham and figs or pears, at the beginning of a meal need not, of course, be accompanied by a wine, but Muscat does go well with the perfumed character of Ogen melon. Smoked fish, however, pose big problems: Christopher Fielden is firm that a Gewurztraminer is the only possible choice with smoked salmon–if you must have a specific wine with it. Smoked fish in general are usually inimical to wines, although the individual must experiment and see.

Foie Gras and Pâtés

Alsace recipes often recommend wines of various styles with *foie gras*–not that the ordinary household is likely to serve this often. M. Hugel, recommending, as do the makers, that *foie gras* should come at the beginning of a meal suggests 'a light Tokay d'Alsace', mentioning that, at this stage, no very rich or full-bodied wine should be served, as this might overpower and detract from a fine but lighter wine following on. The richness and unctuousness of *foie gras* is obvious, but also it is of a complex and refined flavour, so that the Pinot Gris would certainly seem suitable. If pâtés, both of meat and fish – and, these days, vegetable versions – are served, then the choice of Alsace wine is wide: I think that the softening of smoked fish in making certain of them into a pâté – smoked mackerel, trout, eel – can enable them to be partnered by the Pinot Gris or, if the seasonings are fairly strong, then a Gewurztraminer is a possibility. If a very light, almost fluffy taramasalata is made (or bought), then this too is something with which the Gewurztraminer can be served, though one should go easy on any accompanying lemon juice.

Meat pâtés are richer. Gewurztraminer will go with some, but with any game I think a fairly assertive Riesling is better, bearing out the 'rich with rich' theory that a wine should either complement or contrast with a dish. Or, if the pâté is very light and rather delicate in flavour, then the Pinot Gris or even a very good Sylvaner is possible – and, for the lovers of Muscat, this is another possibility. But recipes vary so much that the choice cannot be arbitrary. Similarly, with a pie or pâté composed of vegetables, the ingredients must dictate the choice of wine: some vegetables, such as tomatoes and certainly peppers tend to dominate any mixture, also the copious use of spices and perhaps a sauce that is moderately *piquant* may also affect the wine.

Cold Meats, Salads, Fish and Quiches

The Pinot Blanc is a wine that is extremely useful with a variety of 'cold cuts', brawn, veal and ham and chicken and ham pies, and the cold sausages and salame platters so popular today. It is moderately resistant to gherkins, even to mustard and pickles – as witness the way the people of Alsace enjoy this type of food. Mixed salads, both of fish and meat and poultry, are suitably accompanied by Pinot Blanc, but it is also a good wine with hot poultry if stuffed or flavoured with herbs and spices, stuffed veal and roast chicken with 'trimmings', including sausages and a herby stuffing, plus gravy, should anyone prefer white wine to red.

The Pinot Gris, however, is good with many dishes of baked fish, a possible choice with veal cutlets or escalopes, a selection of shellfish of the modest type, and most types of quiche. I have thought it successful with blanquette de veau, a rather lightly flavoured casserole of lamb and even with pigeon casserole – but much depends on how much seasoning is in the gravy.

Fine Foods

The Riesling is such a very varied wine that one could devote an entire section to particularising vintage, style and maker apropos various dishes. It is certainly superb with poached trout, also with grilled salmon – if the vintage is an opulent one – and poached turbot, halibut, salmon trout, almost any fine fish served very simply with melted butter and possibly one or two plain boiled potatoes. I have known people enjoy a moderate type of Riesling with oysters, too. What it partners best is fine but essentially simple food, in which delicacy of texture and taste combine with the nobility and subtlety of the wine; any complications introduced via strongly seasoned sauces, stuffings or accompanying vegetables will detract from the harmony of the food and wine. It is also good with that rarity today – a poached chicken – and I have tried it successfully with duckling, even with orange sauce! The Riesling should be rather more 'important' than a good everyday wine for this. There are also those who say that it can accompany certain pork dishes, but this depends very much on the dish – certainly a fruity Riesling will 'cut' the fattiness of the pork, but it may be somewhat swamped in detail; it is sometimes also suggested as a possible choice with some of the light game birds, but here any stuffings, sauces and extras such as meatballs, sausages, bacon and so on, have to be taken into consideration. But the versatility of this wonderful grape is such that I have known Alsace wines made from it drink well with ham poached in a wine sauce (Riesling), some forms of *choucroute*, pheasant, cold partridge, even liver and bacon! It is the way in which a fine and, certainly, a great Riesling seems to bring out the flavour of many fish and meat and poultry dishes that cause people to aver that it is 'the' great wine grape of the world and, I admit, at times I waver myself in thinking that the Chardonnay, certainly of the white Burgundies, makes the most multi-purpose wines of all.

The Pinot Noir of Alsace is not really a substantial enough wine to stand up to roast beef or the gamier forms of game, although it is worth making the experiment if you are in the region. It is an appropriate wine for many cold foods, especially in stuffy weather: cold game pie, chicken and ham pie, galantines and, certainly, many cheeses, notably the light goat cheeses, and the sort of cosy dishes based on potatoes (*gratins, galettes, pommes Anna*) and any of the combinations of noodles with cheese. Its character is such that it stands up quite well even to eggs, so it could be a wine for a cheese or spinach soufflé, eggs with spinach, ham mousse, and it will pleasantly 'cut' the richness of, for example, mushrooms in a cream sauce, or kidneys cooked in red wine.

The Gewurztraminer is also a versatile wine. M. Hugel suggests it with lobster, in the *à l'Américaine* or Thermidor recipes and I think that it would be a good choice with most crustacea (not, perhaps, dressed crab, which may be taxing, because of its dressing, better with a Pinot Gris or Pinot Blanc), even if mayonnaise is involved. With plainly cooked langouste, crayfish and so on it is a good partner. Fatty meats are also something that it can accompany – even ham or gammon steaks (but choose a wine of ordinary character), pork chops and, if you wish, certain forms of kebab – the Gewurztraminer is sufficiently spicy to stand up to them, but I may say this because I don't like peppers so omit them in such recipes – they really are somewhat strong for any wine. I have also had Gewurztraminer with black pudding, recipes involving quite a lot of garlic, tomatoes, onions, aubergines (all a bit strong in flavour), smoked salmon pâté and smoked turkey, but although it is very much the 'when in doubt' Alsace wine, there are so many gradations of quality, style and the variations of the vintages that generalisations are even more tricky with this wine than with most!

Cheese

Some recommend the Gewurztraminer with cheese, notably the Munster that dominates the Alsace cheeseboard. It is also possible to drink a really big Gewurztraminer with a matured British hard cheese, though not, I think, one with a pronounced 'bite'; it can go with blue cheese, again, if this is not too aggressive – I have had it satisfactorily with Bleu de Bresse, even with a fairly creamy Stilton or Roquefort.

If you do offer Gewurztraminer with cheese, then try to have at least one sample that is fairly creamy and not too strong – a Brie that is *à point* (alas, so seldom) or one of the cheeses of at least 75 per cent *matière grasse*; this will not only balance the cheeseboard, but enable you to decide with what Alsace wine or wines certain styles or cheese can be served.

Sweets

Then the sweet course. Here I must state that the term 'dessert' is, and will remain for English-speaking people of my generation, nothing to do with puddings, pastries, ices and creams. Dessert is traditionally the course that is offered once that, in traditional style, the cloth has been removed and the board is *desservie* – in other words, dessert is fruit and nuts, the final foods provided at a formal dinner. The sweet course is rather different – and comes earlier. (The whole notion of calling a sweet course 'dessert' is ridiculous once one thinks of the great dessert wines – notably port; do they accompany puddings, pies, tarts, ices? Alas, I have the menu of a supposedly 'fine wine dinner' in which the vintage port was partnered by a chocolate cake, so I feel one must be ready firmly to defend 'dessert' and dessert wines for the nonce.) With the sweet course, serve sweet or sweetish wines – unless the 'sweet' includes anything based on chocolate, which as M. Hugel says 'annihilates the flavour and bouquet of any wine'. I would not only agree, but say that chocolate, delectable as I find it, so affects the palate that, for at least a couple of hours after eating anything chocolate-y it is virtually impossible to appraise a table or dessert wine – this is the time when spirits come into their own. But I may be old-fashioned; one of my young colleagues actually advocates Marsala with chocolate – but why? One could, indeed, combine chocolate peppermint creams with a *vendange tardive* wine – but could one truly enjoy either except as a somewhat unbalanced taste experience?

The beautiful fruit tarts that bejewel so many sweet trolleys in Alsace are well partnered by the sweeter wines – if these are available and can be afforded – the *vendange tardive* and even higher categories. Go easy on the cream, however. In British culinary traditions, I would think that a wine in the *vendange tardive* category could be wonderful with apple pie (with or without the cheese, but very few, if any, cloves), some of the light sponge puddings, not, maybe, treacle pudding or roly-poly, but certainly summer pudding, maids of honour or any almondy pudding or tart, and, of course, fresh raspberries and strawberries – again, go easy on the cream – but it is fair to say that some people find the acidity of strawberries too aggressive for delicate wines. Citrus, pineapple and gooseberries tend, in my view, also to be too acid, but, when made into fools, syllabubs and ice-creams, they need not be inimical to a fairly assertive wine.

If in doubt, however, it is probably fair to say that any of the late-picked fine wines merit appraisal by themselves – even if this means that you pick up your pudding spoon after ten minutes' delay. As a very high note on which to end a meal, they will stand alone and make a great impression. Possibly a few slightly sweet biscuits or plain spongecake are adjuncts if there has been no pudding. But, for serious students of wine, the chance to compare, say, a pair of *vendange tardive* wines, either from different makers or different vintages, is a rare and appreciated pleasure that should not be forgotten by anyone planning a meal around fine Alsace wines.

This sixteenth-century street cryer
is holding a *trognon de chou* beaker,
a traditional drinking vessel shaped
like the stump of a cabbage

Dignatories of the Confrérie St-Etienne in session at the Château de Kientzheim, now seat of their order. Note the glasses prepared for a blind tasting by the prospective candidates for membership

10

The Confrérie Saint Etienne

The fraternities or associations that are well known today in many wine regions frequently had their beginnings in the Middle Ages. The trade guilds or associations of growers, wine makers, coopers and related trades were formed so as to train apprentices, control methods of work, define standards of quality and organise the way in which business might best be done. The wine orders, however, were not always quite such serious bodies, although there are notable exceptions: the Jurade of St Emilion, for example, founded in 1199 in the Gironde, was the governing body of the wine growers in that area, exercising much power and there are others equally influential. Mostly, however, groups who joined together in these bacchic clubs seem to have been more concerned with social and promotional events – as happens today; members would gather to feast and enjoy the wines, often celebrating seasonal occurrences, such as the end of the vintage, the flowering of the vine in the spring or, sometimes, the visit of someone particularly distinguished. Sometimes they could and did exercise some form of control over the quality of the wines, but in general they seem to have been formed from a number of people who might be in daily competition with each other, but who found it agreeable and useful to gather from time to time so as to promulgate the pleasures of their wines and the attractiveness of their region.

The Confrérie Saint Etienne was first formed at Ammerschwihr, probably in the fourteenth century. The first records date from 1440, when the Herrenstubengesellschaft, as the fraternity was then called, appears to have been well established. The 'Stephen' (Etienne) with which it was associated as patron will, by many, be assumed to be the first martyr, stoned outside Jerusalem as related in the Acts of the Apostles, and whose feast is celebrated on 26 December. But there are other Stephens, including Saint Stephen, King of Hungary (c. 975-1038). He worked to convert his subjects to Christianity and to restore order in his kingdom and, in 1001, was crowned as Hungary's first monarch, receiving his crown from the Pope; it is this crown that is still regarded almost as a holy relic in that country.

The Ammerschwihr group consisted of only about twenty men; it was quite powerful and, although the sons of deceased members could join, daughters were not admitted. Anyone else wishing to join had to have been established in business in Ammerschwihr for at least three years, be of good reputation – and be married; the wives of members were apparently 'tolerated' by the fraternity – who probably had no alternative – and their rôle was presumably to ensure a certain stability of conduct in members. Most reunions, however, were for the men only.

Regular meetings were held in the town hall and, although wine was the prime purpose of the gatherings, food was served and cards and gambling might be enjoyed. The rules governing the proceedings were, however, strict: no shirt sleeves, even for the servants present, so jackets had to be kept on. There was to be no swearing, no hurling of cards or dice out of the windows. All these actions were subject to fines. Anybody who so thoroughly lost control of himself as to draw a weapon was severely punished. The local councillors, plus the priest and the Rector of Meiwihr were members as of right, so a fairly high tone was maintained. Members seem to have looked after colleagues who fell on hard times; masses were said for the dead, who were regularly commemorated. Over the years the members acquired a quantity of plate and furniture for their two main halls, where the meetings took place and where they undertook the organisation of a number of public events, including the weddings and funerals of members. They and their activities were financed by certain vineyards belonging to the fraternity, a portion of one of these being the property of the Curé of Ammerschwihr in recompense for his services to the group.

Then, in 1848, all the activities of the Confrérie ceased; no one seems to know exactly why. It was certainly the 'year of revolutions' throughout Europe and perhaps the civil authorities feared that riot and sedition might result from gatherings of what had been quite respectable groups, especially the long sessions in the winter evenings, when hard times can make people restless and discontented. Some authorities suggest that the abandonment of the Confrérie was due to the young and progressive members of the local community, who felt that many old traditions should be scrapped; others put forward the theory that, as 1848 was a very bad vintage, no one felt inclined to get together to drink the wines in the following autumn and winter. Jean-Louis Gyss, in a recent but undated publication *Le Vin et l'Alsace* thinks that maybe the women of Ammerschwihr were tired of their menfolk deserting them for the evening meetings, so they put a stop to these club-like activities. Anyway, the Confrérie appeared to have ended its existence.

Then, in the aftermath of World War II, when the appalling destruction of at least three-quarters of Ammerschwihr (including the deaths by drowning of several hundred people sheltering in a cellar, which was bombed by Allied planes, shattering the vats which poured their contents over the wretched men, women and children) might well have resulted in the decay and eventual end of life in the little town, the sturdy survivors and their neighbours formed a Society of the Friends of Ammerschwihr. Their aim was to attract attention to the vast plans for building and reconstruction, to encourage those attempting to resuscitate their blasted and bombed homes and places of business and create interest in Ammerschwihr in general. It was this society that, in May 1947, revived the Confrérie Saint Etienne.

From the outset, the organisers of the re-formed fraternity determined that it should be more than a group of people who regularly met to eat and drink together. Members were only to be admitted after demonstrating that they really did know something about the wines of Alsace and the higher ranks of the order could only be attained after a period of 'apprenticeship' in a lower grade and after a further test that established their superior qualifications. It was decided to have three grades: apprentices, who were to wear a blue ribbon with a little cask hanging from it; 'compagnons' or members, who would wear a red ribbon, and masters of the order, who would wear green ribbons.

All this was finally decided in 1949, when the Confrérie's first dinner was held. Gastronomical history was made, because, in the planning, the dishes to be served were chosen specifically to accord with the wines, instead of the other way round. Astonishment greeted the service of the cheese – Munster of course – at the end of the meal, because this was accompanied by a Gewurztraminer! Before each course, a member had been deputed to 'present' the wine about to be served and explain its suitability with the food. The member responsible for accouncing the Gewurztraminer with the Munster had to resort to forceful phrases to persuade the company to sample what was, for them, an unprecedented partnership . . . and then, afterwards, it was universally admitted and agreed that never had a Gewurztraminer drunk so well, never had a Munster cheese been so superb!

By 1951 the Confrérie Saint Etienne was sufficiently important to assume the form in which it is known today. Its officers, who wear robes and chains of office, administer the fraternity's activities, exercise control over various sub-committees and groups who are concerned with promoting Alsace wines, gastronomy and the countryside as a setting for both. Chapters of the Confrérie are now frequently held in various parts of the world and there are also special sessions devoted to serious tastings of the wines of the previous year.

Famous people and 'personalities', women as well as men (confrères and consoeurs), are admitted to the Confrérie, but everyone applying for membership must be approved by the Grand Council and pass the requisite tests. For the beginner, applying as an *apprenti*, this is to distinguish between 'un vin ordinaire, un vin mi-fin, un vin fin'. Then, after a year, the member may apply to be received in a higher grade as 'compagnon' but the test this time is to pick out in a blind tasting the four top grape varieties – Riesling, Gewurztraminer, Tokay d'Alsace and Muscat. After another year anyone wishing to become a *maître* must pass a tasting that establishes they have a sound knowledge of all the Alsace wines.

Since 1973, the Confrérie has had its headquarters and holds many of its meetings in the restored Château de Kientzheim, which, with its attractive garden, is a particularly pleasant setting for the reunions. It is now referred to as the Château de la Confrérie Saint Etienne and a wine museum is located alongside. The two tasting sessions, of great importance, are held in June and September. One of the special treasures of the order is its *oenothèque* or wine library; this, first being a collection of old and rare bottles, some dating from the early part of the nineteenth century, now receives gifts of wine from members and regular samples of newly made wines. If these last are approved, after being tasted by members, the Confrérie can award its special seal, *Sigille,* to the particular wine, but this is difficult to acquire as growers, shippers and co-operatives may only enter five wines each, and all of these have to be tasted and wholeheartedly approved by two different juries. The *Sigille*, therefore, is something makers display on their bottles with pride. At the banquets of the Confrérie members wines are served bearing neutral labels, merely carrying a number, so that only the *Receveur* of the Confrérie can identify them. Penalties are still exacted for breaches of the rules – anyone smoking during the course of a reunion is fined three bottles. Indeed, the procedure is according to the rules drawn up in 1561.

Each session of the Confrérie concludes with an exhortation known as the 'Strasbourgeoise', because it is a version in modern French of what was written by a native of Strasbourg, Jean Fischart (1546-90). The impressive, sonorous – and lengthy – citation expatiates on the styles of the members of the assembly, euologises the wines, proclaims the long list of the names of the wine villages and, in rotund phrases, urges drinkers to 'swallow, absorb, ingurgitate, consume, taste, appreciate' what is before them. There is plenty of good humour too, for each of those present is exhorted to raise 'glass, mug, ceremonial goblet, chalice, beaker, pot, jug, little barrel, bucket, cask, vat and tank' so as to drink! The activities of the Confrérie demonstrate that it is possible to be serious about wine without ever becoming solemn.

11

Spirits and Liqueurs

Alsace revels in eating and drinking and the people are by no means single-minded about what they eat and drink. If you do not enjoy wine, then they can offer a beer from one of a number of local breweries – an excellent beer, too, made with locally grown hops. At the end of the meal there is a large family of *digestifs*, the *alcools blancs* or white spirits.

Although Alsace has developed a style of wines all its own, as far as the colourless spirits are concerned, the region is just part of a much larger area of production. As Hugh Johnson says in *The World Atlas of Wine* (1977) 'Distilling nowadays is nearly all big business. There are bootleggers still – probably more than most people suppose – but in most countries the old cottage industry has been taxed out of existence. Only where the results are exceptional does it still flourish. That place, above all, is the stretch of Europe east and south of the Vosges; the Black Forest and the northern half of Switzerland. In the valleys of the Vosges mountains, where the rivers rush down to the Rhine and its tributaries, the art of distillation is still very much alive and, despite heavy additional taxes recently imposed in France on all spirits, it appears to be flourishing and not merely big business.'

This tradition of distilling is a long one. As early as the sixteenth century there was an important market in Strasbourg for the sale of fruit spirits and these were exported as far as the Low Countries, Scandinavia and England. They were known generically as 'Strasbourg waters'. This indicates a remarkable rapidity of production and demand from the time when the method of distilling was introduced to Europe in the fourteenth century by Arnaud de Villanova; some information about the process had been known previously, notably in the medical schools of Italy, but distilling, evolved by the Arabs, possibly originally in the preparation of perfumes and cosmetics, came late to the drinking scene. However, an Alsace army surgeon, Hieronymus Brunschwig (*c.* 1450-1533) wrote *The Vertouse Boke of Distyllacyon*, in which he was able to state, concerning brandy, that 'It heleth also all stynkyng woundes when they be wasshed therwith'. The famous Swiss, Aureolus Theophrastus Bombastus von Hohenheim (1493-1541) better known as Paracelsus, was a native of Basle and it is not perhaps assuming too much to suppose that the work of these two would have become famous within the Alsace region. What had been originally medicinal also became enjoyable and social.

For reasons of safety, the stills in which the 'waters' were made operated outside the towns. The highly inflammable spirits were, it should be remembered, made in buildings largely consisting of wood. At the beginning of the seventeenth century Colmar could count as many as thirty-seven distillers, or 'Brennherren' as they were known, along the banks of the Logelbach. The special risk of the distiller occurred in time of war or civil strife, when the stills were exposed to attack by besieging troops or marauding bands of lawless persons. As a result of this, four distilleries were operating within the walls of Riquewihr itself by 1691 – no doubt much to the concern of neighbours. The eighteenth century saw a major decline in the number of distilleries, mainly due to the arrival of sugar from the colonies in the New World, and the serious competition from grain spirits, especially from the Baltic.

Today, the spirits of Alsace may be divided into three categories. First there is the local wine brandy, eau-de-vie de marc de Gewurztraminer; second the other fruit-based white spirits, and finally the liqueurs. The first two types are completely dry and colourless, the liqueurs are sweet – and are the colour of the fruit involved in their making.

MARC DE GEWURZTRAMINER

To be charitable, this is an acquired taste. It has a very aggressive flavour, the strength of the spirit and the taste of the grape seeming to be locked in mortal combat. After the vintage, the skins and pips of the Gewurztraminer grapes are put in an air-tight container and allowed to ferment for two or three months. They are then distilled twice, in a pot still. The first time the spirit comes off at about 25° Gay Lussac, the second time at about 60°. Gay Lussac gets it name from a French chemist, Joseph Gay-Lussac, 1778-1850, who evolved a system of measuring the strength of alcoholic beverages, in terms of percentage of alcohol by volume (see also page 102). On both occasions, the 'heads' and 'tails' of the impure spirits at the beginning and end of the distillation are extracted and sent back to be redistilled. (All these spirits must be distilled twice if they are to get the *appellation contrôlée*.) The spirit is then aged in glass carboys.

The leading distiller of marc de Gewurztraminer is Théo Preiss of Mittelwihr and one of their attractive presentations has a bunch of grapes in the bottle. This effect cannot be achieved, as it is with the pear spirits, by placing the bottle over the buds and letting the fruit grow inside, so the bottom of the bottle actually unscrews and the bunch of grapes is inserted. What is more, it is rare that the grapes are actually from the Gewurztraminer vine, because they soon shrivel up in the spirit; more often they are Muscat grapes, which appear more attractive.

Records indicate that marc, made by the final hard pressing of the accumulated grapeskin, pips, stalks and stems left after the wine had been made, has been produced for a considerable time. (Today this debris either contributes to the making of the 'house wine' of an establishment, or else is sold for making industrial alcohol and, finally, the residual cake is used for cattle food and manure for the vineyards.) But there are some curious variations. A drink known bilingually as 'Warmer-Vin-chaud-Wyn' appears to have been a means of using the remains of both wine making and distilling: it seems to have been made both with red wine – that of Ottrott is mentioned in one account – and white, although a contemporary writer says Muscat is too dry to be satisfactory. According to old recipes this drink consists of two-thirds wine, one-third water; it is heated with cinnamon bark, a little sugar and slices of lemon and simmered for a couple of minutes before serving.

Thrifty countryfolk also knew the value of wine lees – as a poultice. This was recommended for relieving rheumatic pains and, one may suppose, the sufferer might also have a tot of spirit at the same time.

There is also an interesting reference to the way in which the people of Alsace found this type of spirit multi-purpose. In the 1890s, the traveller Henry W. Wolff, in *The Country of the Vosges* (1891) is described as inspecting the premises of a somewhat suspicious cheese maker near Munster. Mr Wolff knocked a milk pail off its hook with his hat – one imagines him wearing a high-crowned one – and the farmer insisted that he should pay for the damage to the pail in which a chip was found. The man 'had the generosity to throw in a half-pint of vinegary wine . . . which, not to give offence, I swallowed. He himself, he declared, could not drink that sour stuff. Traberschnapps for him – eau de Marc. That was "good for the wholesomes" and he helped himself to a good half-pint at a time. Next to wine, traberschnapps is the liqueur that Alsatians swear by. There is no occasion to which it is not held to be appropriate . . . It "sets their thoughts" of a morning, and it lulls them to sleep at night. It sees the young infant into the world at the christening; it sees the old body out at the funeral. The French government, sympathising with the local peoples' weakness for this peculiar kind of alcohol – distilled from grape-husks – used to allow them to make it themselves for domestic consumption – tax-free. The German [remember Alsace was mainly German at this date] levies a tax, and has imposed ever so many restrictions. It impounds the still-lids, and exacts special notice whenever they are wanted, levies an impost on the still, another on the distilling, a third on the product – at least so Alsatians tell me – and altogether makes the whole thing unworth their while. "It is all to compel us to drink that beastly poisonous pétrole" say the Alsatians, pétrole being the slang name for German potato fusel.'

There is another pleasant reference by a twentieth-century writer of how marc de Traminer (*sic*) superseded 'the old Traber the vingerons liked'. He relates how an elderly lady he knew would drink a full, generously sized glass of marc every morning, dipping a fresh roll into it and then, announcing that her roll had drunk her 'trab', ask for another – and this she did daily until an unfortunate slight accident brought her to the end of her days – at the age of 95.

White Spirits

Cyril Ray in *In a Glass Lightly* (1967) says that he and a director of the Dolfi distillery at Strasbourg counted as many as seventeen varieties of Alsace white spirits. Nowadays it is not difficult to find even more, as there seems to be a feeling that an enjoyable drink can be made from almost any fruit or root. In the past the wild fruits of the land were utilised in this way; sugar was expensive until comparatively recently and it was cheaper to distil than to make jams and jellies and there was nothing unusual about having a still in the home. Indeed, during World War II, many farmyard antiques of this sort were brought back into use – those who could run the businesses and keep the farms going were not inclined to let natural produce go to waste. 'We made spirits of all sorts of things!' says one jovial wine-maker of the Haut-Rhin, looking back to this time. 'The old family recipes were revived – we knew the customs officers were simply sitting in Colmar and wouldn't come prowling!' Mountain countryside and the foothills are usually abundant in a variety of herbs, berries, barks and fruits and it should be remembered that, until it was realised how animals could be fed during the winter, many beasts would be slaughtered before the really cold weather set in, meat being preserved by salting, drying or in some fatty conserve. Then during the bad weather the inhabitants of the more remote farms could do little outside – and the still provided them with additional drinks that might be incorporated into recipes for dishes and gave warmth and tonic sustenance in the dark days.

In *Spirits & Liqueurs* (1983) Peter Hallgarten describes the spirits as 'dry fruit brandies, usually bottled at higher alcoholic strength (approximately 45° Gay Lussac = 79° [British]) than liqueurs and infrequently aged before bottling'. He also states that the majority of popular flavours of the Alsace liqueurs of this type, as made commercially, 'are made by distillation of the fermented fruit, but many are prepared by maceration in neutral *eau-de-vie* for several weeks, to extract the delicate flavour, which would be destroyed by the heat of the distillation process'. He lists the distilled *eau-de-vie* spirits as: quetsch, Mirabelle, poire Williams, prunelle; those made by means of maceration are framboise, fraise, mûre, sureau, sorbier, baie de houx and aubépine. (For translation and accounts of these, among others, see pages 176-181.) With fruits possessing sufficient flesh and sweetness to produce a natural fermentation, this is a straightforward process. Apricots, for example, may simply be left to ferment and are then distilled. For others, such as the holly (*baie de houx*) and any roots, the process of maceration is more complicated, the spirit used prior to distillation being a young Cognac in the best distilleries, such as that of F.Meyer at Hohwarth.

Whereas the fruits were, in the past, gathered locally, today most of them come from elsewhere: the wild raspberries from Roumania, apricots and pears from the Loire and the Rhône Valley, gentian from the Auvergne. The cost of the final spirit cannot be low – because it takes about eight kilos of fruit to make one litre of pure alcohol. (At the time of writing in 1983, the market price of a kilo of hollyberries is approximately fifteen francs – including a nuisance premium for the pricks.)

In general, the fruit, berries, herbs or whatever are put into large wooden vats or casks, sometimes old wine or spirit casks being used, where they ferment slowly. The mash produced is distilled, sometimes during the winter following when the fruit was picked, but some fruits take a long time to ferment and may be in the vat – today often glass-lined for ease of cleaning and disinfecting – for a year or more.

The still used is a type of pot still, similar to that used for Cognac and malt whisky, with a long 'swan neck', leading from the first 'pot', which is somewhat like a large copper casserole, over to another vessel in which the distillate resulting from the heating of the pot is received in the form of vapour; it is then cooled, so that it again becomes liquid. The 'heads' or first part of the distillate, and the last part, the 'tails' are usually kept apart and subsequently redistilled. Once the still is heated and has begun to run the process must not be arrested until the operation is complete and all the material has been used up. The control of the still while it is running involves great skill and experience, so that the resulting liquid is neither raw nor weak and is wholly suited to the matter that is being distilled and endowed with all its properties. It should be appreciated that the house style of each distillery will be individual – and that the home-made spirits that the privileged visitor may be offered in someone's house may be even more so, sometimes much stronger.

But distilling in Alsace is generally somewhat of a small family business. There are even some *alembics ambulants* or travelling stills that go around making the spirits for some small firms. The valley of Giessen, leading up to the small town of Villé, has eleven distillers, of which probably the best known is Massenez, whose speciality is a spirit made from the wild raspberry; their shop, Cave des Trois Eglises, in the main street of Riquewihr, makes it easy for the traveller to view a variety of *alcools blancs*. On a smaller scale is a company such as Mehr, run from the family house – with Madame complaining that her sitting-room has been taken over by the computer – and a small-scale but impeccably arranged installation.

Even smaller is the Schmidt-Mehr distillery; this is literally at the bottom of the garden of the Restaurant Au Lion at Breuschwickersheim, near Strasbourg – unlikely to be frequented by many tourists but usually packed by knowing locals. Here only five fruits are distilled and it's useless to ask to inspect the stills after an evening meal – for there is no electric light in the shed where, as elsewhere, the spirit ages in glass jars. Monsieur Mehr says that he will close the stills in about five years, when he retires as there is no one to take over from him.

Most Alsace wine houses have a range of white spirits, but they do not usually distil these themselves, buying them from the various distillers or from such specialist wholesalers as Radmacher, at La Wantzenau. In addition to the installations that have been mentioned, it is also worth noting the name of the firm of Nussbaumer and Wolfberger, which is the former Jux-Jacobert distillery, recently purchased by the Cave Co-operative at Eguisheim.

Here are brief notes on some of the spirits that travellers may find worth trying.

KIRSCH (cherry)

Certainly the best-known *alcool blanc*, because of its popularity in fruit salad, on pancakes and many flambéd dishes, this is also a good drink in its own right. Opinions seem to differ as to whether the cherry stones are or are not crushed and included in the fruit mash prior to fermentation and distillation. There is also a 'kirsch de commerce', intended for use in the kitchen, with only about 15 per cent of kirsch in it.

Kirsch is very much associated with Alsace – indeed, Henry W. Wolff in *The Country of the Vosges* (1891) tells a touching story of how, on 14 July (Bastille Day), in the 1890s numbers of Alsaciens travelled up to the frontier at Sainte Marie-aux-Mines (then named Markirch by the Germans); here they congregated at a 'very fourth-rate café' where 'the tricolour floated over the miserable little auberge' which was actually on the dividing line and where, it was said, the village baker kneaded in one country and baked in another. Mr Wolff later met 'a Germanised Alsatian from Barr' who had noticed him on that day and proudly announced: 'My son and I were in France, too. We walked across and when we had passed the frontier, we stopped and drew out flasks of kirsch, and drank on French soil to the welfare of France! Vive la République!'

FRAMBOISE (raspberry)

This is thought by many to be the finest and most delicate of all *alcools blancs*. It also tends to be more than usually expensive, both on account of its being difficult to make (few people are willing to go and pick the local fruit these days) and because it is often higher in alcohol than the others of this kind.

MIRABELLE (plum)

This is made from the Mirabelle golden plum. It is lightly luscious and the fruity bouquet is delectable.

QUETSCH (plum)

This is also made from a plum, but the purple variety known as the *switzen* or *zwetschen*. It seems usually to have a slightly more intense flavour than Mirabelle.

176

Both Mirabelle and quetsch are ideal accompaniments or conclusions to the beautiful open tarts that glisten jewel-like on the sweet trolleys of many restaurants, in which the fruit is often Mirabelle or quetsch.

FRAISE/FRAISE DE BOIS (strawberry, ideally, wild)
The smell of this drink is immediately evocative of the fruit-fresh, crisp, intense, never obviously sweet.

MYRTILLE (bilberry)
This is a very fruity drink, often recommended as a 'pousse café', or digestive, possibly a good partner to a rather rich creamy sweet dish.

MURE/MURE SAUVAGE (wild blackberry)
The French do not use *mûres* for cooking to the same extent as the British do-but the drink is fruity and evokes the flavour of the ripe fruit squeezed against the palate from the days when one went blackberrying along the hedgerows as a child.

BRAMBLE/BRIMBELLE (bramble)
This is not often found, but it really is the fruit of the bramble-it's pronounced 'bromble'-and Alsace friends relate how this particular *alcool blanc* was recommended in the past as a convalescent's tonic and warming drink.

POIRE WILLIAMS/WILLIAMINE/POIRE (William pear)
This is a remarkable drink-instantly smelling and tasting like a prime pear, crisp and delicious. Many who have come to know it will opt for it above all other drinks of this type.

REINE CLAUDE (greengage)
This gets its name from Queen Claude, wife of François I of France, who is supposed to have loved the fruit, which was introduced in her time, the early sixteenth century.

EAU-DE-VIE DE POMME (apple)
This, as its name implies, is made from apples, but seems rather unimportant-one French writer says it must not in any way be associated with Calvados (the Normandy spirit made from apples), which it doesn't resemble and that it is 'without pretensions'. It is often used as a base for the other drink, Tutti frutti, which is a mixture, probably originally made with any leftover fruit. Tutti frutti is not particularly distinctive in style but a local recommendation is to pour a little of it into a coffee cup when you have drunk the coffee-the warmth apparently brings out the fruity aromas agreeably.

SORBIER/BAIE DE SORBE (sorb apple)

This, *Sorbus domestica,* gets translated variously as 'sorb apple' and 'service tree', but the *Oxford Book of Food Plants* says that it is 'a relative of the rowan' and Alsace friends have said it is virtually a crabapple (*Malus pumila*). The fruit is small, hard and brownish-green and the drink slightly bitter, definitely digestive.

The service tree is one of the 'Forgotten Fruits' described in Francesca Greenoak's enchanting book of the same name (André Deutsch, 1983). Thanks to this, I am able to state that the fruit in Britain went back probably before even Anglo-Saxon times into pre-history. The wild service is apparently a most beautiful forest tree and its berries are supposed to be 'binding'. The other type of service described by Miss Greenoak is the sorb apple, *Sorbus domestica*, of which there appear to be many varieties; what used to be known as 'the service tree of Fontainebleau, after the woods where it was found in the early part of the eighteenth century' has large white cherry-like fruits. In Britain they were known as whitebeam. Only a botanist could work out which of these is used for the *alcool blanc*. Miss Greenoak says that *Sorbus maliformis* has a 'delicious winey taste', that wild service fruits, which turn brown in autumn, 'are eaten bletted' (sleepy – as in 'sleepy pear'). The reference to their use for medicinal purposes is possibly significant.

ALISIER (rowan)

This is the mountain ash or rowan, (*Sorbus aucuparia*) whose bright orange berries are used in many countries to make jelly, or to flavour other preserves, especially those based on apples, to which they give a pleasant colour and acidity. There is a vaguely marzipan-like flavour to the drink – reminiscent of Christmas cake.

NEFLE (medlar)

The *nèfle* in warmer climates can be eaten as a fruit, but in cool countries must be allowed to get slightly rotten before it can be used. It is also utilised for jam. It is a relation of the quince.

COING (quince)

The quince is a hard, somewhat pear-shaped fruit, uneatable when raw but making a delicious pinkish jam, or a conserve – in French this is *cotignac*, in Spanish *marmelo*, in Portuguese *marmelado* (served with cheese). As an *alcool blanc* it is direct, fresh and interestingly fruity.

PRUNELLE/PRUNELLE SAUVAGE (blackthorn or sloe)

This is the wild plum of Western Europe, used in some countries to make sloe gin or 'winterpick wine'. It is a good *alcool blanc*, concentratedly fruity, finishing fresh. Readers of Georges Simenon's stories about Inspector Maigret may remember that the detective and his wife often take a mouthful of prunelle after dinner, as Madame Maigret comes from Alsace and is sent it–presumably home-made–by her family.

SUREAU/BAIE DE SUREAU (elder)
The elderberries form in clusters, hanging from a central stem and are very dark red, almost black. It was these berries that, in the nineteenth century, were used to give a richer tone and a certain zip and fullness to port wine. In many countries elderberries are used to make wine, as well as jams and jellies, and in Britain the flowers can be made into a very pleasant country wine which, being sparkling, is sometimes referred to as 'Elderflower champagne'. In the form of an *alcool blanc*, there is not a very obvious fragrance, but the flavour is full, lingering and intensely fruity.

EGLANTIER/EGLANTINE (briar rose, dog rose sweetbriar)
Rosehips are used for making jelly and syrup in many countries–a valuable sauce of vitamins and eglantine is one of the flowers in Titania's bower in *A Midsummer Night's Dream*. The slightly sweet *alcool blanc* does not, however, smell of roses. It has the bizarre nickname of 'Gratte-Cul' (scratch arse) but no one seems to know why. The pips of the dog rose are covered with a substance that causes irritation, so maybe the name was invented by those who ate them raw.

AUBEPINE (hawthorn)
Aubépine is a rarity today, because the small, hard berries have to be picked after the first frost and few people can be found to do this.

GENTIANE (gentian)
This herb gets its name from the King of ancient Greece, Gentius, who apparently was famous as a herbalist. The dark blue flowers are found in many mountain regions and there is also a gentian with yellow flowers. The extract of the gentian root is bitter and has been known for centuries as a tonic, antidote to poisons and a remedy for liver complaints and severe vomiting; it was even worshipped for its medicinal properties by the American Indians. Gentian is used to flavour several proprietary brands of drinks, of which the bright yellow Suze is possibly the best known, another being Arvèze, from the Auvergne, from which region some Alsace distillers buy the root. A purée of this is made prior to distillation and then this is combined with the *eau-de-vie de vin* of the Charentes; it takes eight kilos of gentian root to make a litre of *alcool blanc*. In smell, gentian is vaguely warm and dusty, in flavour the rootiness comes out– it's an obvious digestive and, as the first-time drinker is unlikely to find it very agreeable, it may be worth trying a sip from someone else's glass before ordering.

HOUX/BAIE DE HOUX (holly berry)

This is very much a speciality of Alsace, distilled from the bright red berries - and a kilo of berries costs more than a kilo of other fruit of similar type, because the pickers run the risk of being pricked by the leaves! It makes a very good *alcool blanc*, the bouquet being extremely fresh and crisp, the flavour slightly herby and complex - unlike anything else. One Alsace enthusiast describes it as 'the smell of the forest in your glass, the aroma of undergrowth after rain in summer, all in that scent known to all lovers of nature - but which is indefinable'.

SAPIN (pine)

This is distilled from pine tree buds, but it is rarely found today and should not be confused with the Liqueur de Sapin, made in the Jura Mountains and which is not an *alcool blanc*. One comment is that the pronounced flavour of resin has to be cut by adding neutral alcohol.

CUMIN (cumin)

Cumin, according to some herbals, is *Carum carvi* or caraway, famous for centuries as a remedy for flatulence - there is a reference to this in an Egyptian papyrus of about 1500 BC - and the gripe water given to 'wind' babies is based on caraway. But cumin is *Cuminum cyminum*, a plant not unlike caraway but more aggressive in flavour, so this may be the basis of this particular *alcool blanc*, as it is for the liqueur kümmel.

Liqueurs

Many liqueurs are made in Alsace but, although the *alcools blancs* must rank among the great spirits of the world, the liqueurs are, as Cyril Ray says in *In a Glass Lightly* (1967), 'pretty little liquid sweetmeats compared with the potent hard stuff'. These are made in all parts of France and Alsace has no special reason to be proud of them. They are made by infusing fruit in spirit and adding sugar; naturally, as a result they are sweet. The best have a clean, fruit flavour, but they lack the distinction of the white spirits - for sugar can hide much, but natural spirit can hide nothing.

Serving and Drinking

How should the white spirits be drunk? The fashion seem to serve them straight from the deep freeze, in a rime-encrusted bottle. The glass, too, is often chilled, usually with ice-cubes being swirled in it before being emptied out and the spirit put in. Many people will have been informed - and may have agreed - that this chilling brings out the remarkable aroma and flavour. This is all quite wrong, according to M. Mehr of Villé. To be appreciated at their best, these

180

Sign of the Crown Inn, now a museum piece

spirits should be served at the same temperature as a white wine – that is, cool rather than chilled. And Xavier Dumoulin, in *La Gastronomie Alsacienne* (1969) condemns 'those snobs who imitate the Anglo-Saxon lovers of refrigeration'. (It is Monsieur Dumoulin who advocates pouring Tutti frutti into a still warm empty coffee cup.) He goes on: 'Chilling kills the finesse of the volatile elements in fruit *eaux-de-vie*. This is one of the symptoms of what may be called the century of whisky – they (presumably he means the despised Anglo-Saxons) drink, we (here he speaks for the discriminating people of Alsace) taste; they knock back something that is a shock to the gullet – indeed, it is often an adulterated mixture.' So – cool, but not iced.

There may be some who claim that a spirit drinker is not a wine drinker, but in Alsace that is never claimed to be true. The wines and the spirits cohabit in harmony, they complement each other to the full. The local gastronome will have a glass of Muscat before the meal, at the end an *alcool blanc*: they are the alpha and omega in the Alsace feeding cycle. Each family has its old bottles of Mirabelle and kirsch, as often as not from the fruit of their own trees. But the distilling right of each owner of fruit trees comes to an end with the present generation. It will be a contribution to Alsace hospitality that will be sadly missed.

181

Celebrations with plenty of folklore at Barr

12

The Route du Vin

The Alsace wine road or *Route du Vin* is particularly well planned and signposted so that travellers can make détours from the big main roads and see at least something of the wine country. Of course, there are vines planted and wines made off the principal itinerary, but this, with its winding about through the vineyards and villages, includes all the main areas of production. Although it would be possible to cover the 90 miles or so of the main *Route du Vin* in a day, this would not allow for any stops and it is a pity to miss seeing some of the more picturesque villages and towns and, perhaps, making a few excursions to view some of the great works of art or, simply, wandering around, getting the 'feel' of the region. This, it should be mentioned, varies within quite small areas, so those who restrict their exploration to one segment of the *Route du Vin* are depriving themselves of many enjoyable experiences.

Anyone looking upwards along the *Route du Vin* will see the numerous castles, or ruins of their keeps, perched above the vineyards. In more than one place these are still the features that formed the subject of a saying dating from 1644, now something of a proverb:

Three castles on one hill,

Three churches in one churchyard,

Three villages in one valley —

That's Alsace!

But in the early medieval period there were even more castles on the flatter ground as well, rectangular, chunky fortifications, usually slightly elevated so as to dominate the surroundings and be more easily defensible, often with a moat. Increasing numbers of these buildings are mentioned in documents between the eleventh and thirteenth centuries. It is possible to find traces of them, such as the one at Eguisheim, but the buildings as such have completely disappeared, the stones probably being used for more humble purposes. One piece of comfort that is typical of the region still, is the big stove, which seems to have been in use from about the eleventh century, first constructed in stone, then in

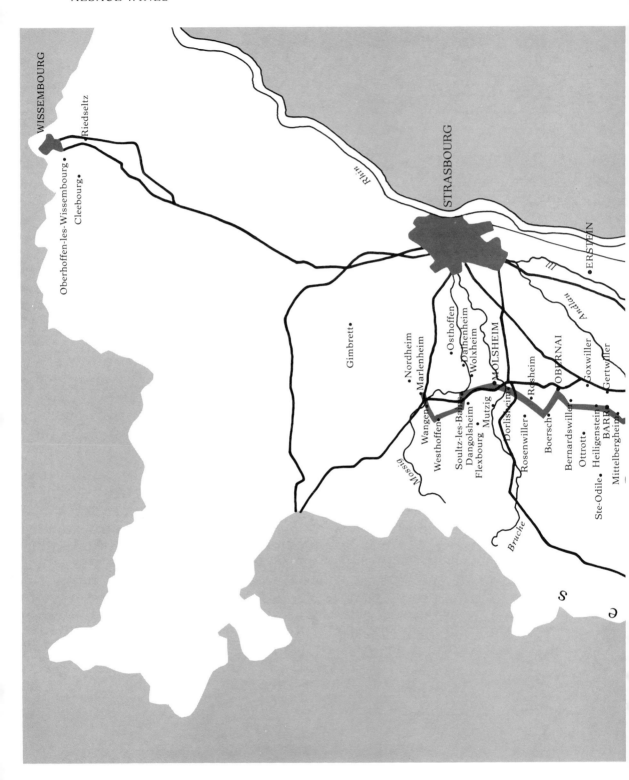

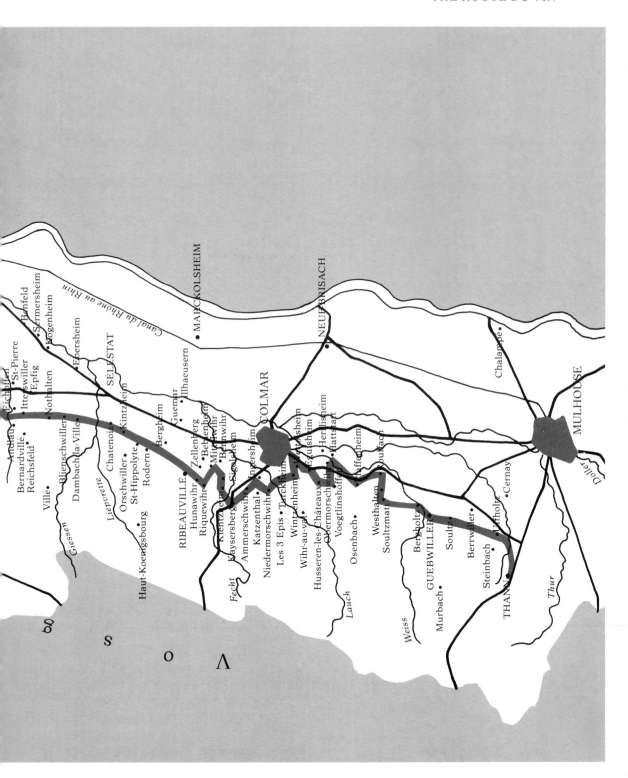

porcelain, allowing the aristocracy and important ecclesiastics of Alsace to enjoy warmth without dirt and smoke eddying throughout the room.

The wine road extends from Marlenheim in the north – or, for the exact, from slightly to the north-east as far as Urdenheim – and, in the south, it ends just beyond Thann. It would be possible to see at least a large section of it for a traveller based in Mulhouse in the south, or Strasbourg, towards the north, but many people will probably opt for a base either in Colmar or maybe up in the mountains to the west; there are a few comfortable hotels and inns to the east of the main route as well and, certainly, plenty of accommodation in many of the villages, although choice of any of these depends rather on what is required: the tourist unable to speak French or requiring a certain degree of luxury may prefer to opt for a larger hotel, such as in one of the mountain spas. But the hotels and guesthouses are all listed and categorised, so this need be no problem for anyone with their own transport although of course anyone depending on trains and buses will be obliged to stay in a town or where excursions can be easily arranged.

The names of many villages indicate something of their origin. Lucien Sittler, in *L'Agriculture et la Viticulture en Alsace* (1974), points out that, of the settlements founded in the early part of the Middle Ages, the majority have Germanic names; the oldest often end in 'ingen' or 'heim'. The names of many wine villages ending in '-wiler', '-wihr' (in German these would be '-weiler' and '-weier') may be survivals of either the Latin '-vilare' or the German 'Weiler', the last meaning a hamlet. Sometimes the first part of a place name is that of an individual – 'So-and-So's village'.

A little later, village names may indicate, by their endings, something of the character of their site: the suffix '-hof' means a farm, '-hausen' houses, '-bach' a river, '-tal' a valley, '-kirch' a church, '-feld' a field; the latter can also be indicated by '-au', which means a meadow. Some names suggest that the land has been pioneered for cultivation; the German 'roden' or 'reuten' surviving in such place names as Ottrott, Hohrod, Rott. Others indicate the presence of a spring – 'Brunn' or 'Bronn', or where certain tribes settled: Sassenheim (Saxons), Friesenheim (Friesians).

Another thing to note is the way in which many of the churches could serve as a place of refuge for the peasants in disturbed times, both the church itself and the churchyard often being surrounded by a wall that could be defended. Some of the remnants of these fortified sites date from pagan times, but the church at Hunawihr, one of the most famous, is both commandingly placed as a lookout position, difficult to attack, and has walls of particular stoutness, still mostly intact.

Throughout the *Route du Vin* there are a number of 'villages fleuries' which at any time are delightful to the view and, in high summer, glorious with blooms. Tubs and beds are laid out in the squares and public open spaces, plants border the roads and spring in clumps around the fountains; pots, windows boxes, hanging baskets and swags of climbing plants garland steps, terraces, and the fronts of houses and balconies, all carefully arranged and tended; it restores faith in human nature that the hand of the modern vandal does not spoil them. These flowers and foliage are offered in goodwill both by the villages as corporate bodies and by individuals. They were inspired by the touching thought of a parish priest at the end of World War II.

Because of the destruction caused by the final action of the occupiers as they fought their way back to Germany, many villages were, literally, a heap of ruins (look at the pictures of Ammerschwihr, with the single battered tower alone standing), or the completely rebuilt Bennwihr. Damage was widespread everywhere and, as part of the rehabilitation programme, workers were drafted from the south, especially from the bottom of the Rhône Valley, to assist in the rebuilding. 'How can we welcome these strangers who have come to help us?' the priest inquired. 'What can we offer them that they may miss, away from their own homes? They will long for sunshine and flowers. We can only give them the warmth of our hearts – but flowers! We can give them flowers to remind them of their own country!' So the people of the villages brought out their pot plants, built window boxes and set up beds and sowed seeds wherever it was possible for flowers to grow. The result is wonderful.

Hochwiller, a 'village fleurie'

Local Architecture

In general, the architecture of the villages is worth noting, even if it is not always fairy-tale picturesque, but traditions are strong and even quite new buildings are usually constructed at least to resemble the old or, if they are of modern design, this tends to be subdued and to make use of local materials. In some of the more famous villages, the details of new buildings are strictly controlled – height of house, whether it stands up above its neighbours, the angle at which the roof slopes, the colour of the paint that can be used on the exterior and so on. The beauty and the charm are not arrived at by chance. Yet although a destroyed building may blend with its neighbours in its rebuilt form, the devotion of those who have resisted any temptation to introduce discordant styles has to be admired profoundly. The mayor of one northern village relates how, during the first part of the German occupation in World War II, the entire population of several villages were compelled to leave their homes: animals were turned loose from the farms to run wild, only the basics of personal possessions could be taken away. When, after more than a year, the people were allowed to return, grass and vegetation was pushing between the stones of the pavements, the weather and neglect had begun – far more swiftly than could have been anticipated – to destroy human habitations. Yet today the trim houses, orderly gardens, well-arranged farms and fields make it difficult to believe that reconstruction had to be on such a vast and radical scale. Note, too, the way in which even the new roads do not – possibly with the exception of the autoroutes that facilitate travelling – distort the countryside; the original paths and tracks, often followed by animals either being taken from one set of pastures to another or driven to market, with the necessity for finding grazing and water along the way, are still those that may be traced on the oldest maps.

The different styles of Alsace houses should be noted, whether these are in the villages and towns or out in the country. The frequently terrifying history of the region necessitated that in many instances a building that housed a family and its animals should be able to shut itself off from casual marauders even if it couldn't resist definite attack: so the basic house, prior to the seventeenth century, is constructed, together with the outbuildings – barn, stables, stores – forming a rectangular unit, able to be shut off by high walls and very strong doors. This applied also in the villages and towns but, out in the country, it can still be seen as a small settlement, containing family, servants, workers and beasts.

After the appalling wars of the seventeenth century, the buildings became more open, easier to inspect; courtyards, which still enable vehicles to unload, where equipment and machines are kept and maintained even if the animals no longer live there, still have their huge gates, but the houses in which the owners live tend to have more storeys and, with balconies and wider window frames, to look out more than in. The galleries inside the courtyards of many of these

Sélestat, the Clock Tower, built in the fourteenth century, with the top sections added in 1611

houses are extensive-anyone who longs to reconstruct a replica of an Elizabethan inn yard, with balconies around would acquire infinite inspiration from getting inside some of the more modest-seeming Alsace houses along the *Route du Vin!*

It should also be remembered that, in the majority of houses in towns and villages where the owners are wine makers, the cellars are also under the houses, sometimes the equivalent of several storeys down. If it were possible to take an aerial photograph by some form of X-ray, showing the below ground installations of the villages, this would probably reveal almost as much cellar space as otherwise visible habitation. Often a firm will have acquired cellars extending far beyond their own premises, running below streets and nearby blocks of dwellings and, in the compact area of many villages, there must be occasions when someone inadvertently breaks in to someone else's subterranean establishment.

In most of the villages, too, the fire services-of additional importance anywhere near large stocks of wines and spirits-are manned by volunteers and it can well be imagined how, in a seventeenth century alley, no modern fire engine can easily manoeuvre. The somewhat extended and enlarged streets of some of the rebuilt villages and towns at least give space for public services, although there are many 'pedestrians only' areas, preserving the charm of ancient buildings. The sign that indicates no vehicular traffic, apart from delivery vans at certain times, is frequently seen.

189

The Storks

And the storks–they are shown on every poster, postcard and pictorial representation of Alsace. The device of the Grandes Maisons is a stork and an Alsace glass. They are so much part of the region's history that it's worth knowing a little about them.

The storks fly, it has been said, along the two great routes of the dispersion of the Jews: from the Middle East, one set of birds will migrate along the north coast of Africa and up through Spain and Portugal to Scandinavia, another will fly north, across those central European countries whose folk lore and legends so often include them. Both routes have been known to traders since very early times and the stork seems always to have been a bearer of good fortune, whether in the form of a child or success in business. In Alsace, for centuries, they have made their nests at the peak of many high buildings, perching on the top of partially ruined masonry after many wars, their large, rather untidy nests appearing to afford little protection to the inhabitants and their young. Their conjugal devotion and willingness to sacrifice their lives in the protection of their young are often recorded and there's an eighteenth century account of a stork's nest on the spire of Strasbourg Cathedral where, when a bird of prey advanced on the mother returning to her young, her mate fought off the attacker and, when he was being defeated, the female threw her young family out of the nest so that they might escape, and then lay there to be killed as a diversion.

Yet even in the mid-twenties of the present century the travel writer, B.S. Townroe, in *A Wanderer in Alsace* (1926) comments that storks are disappearing, being 'replaced by the aeroplanes' because, as he notes, the draining of many of the previously stagnant marshes is depriving the stork of a supply of frogs; today, the use of detergents is also said to have so polluted the streams and rivers (trout is from a *vivier* now, although I suppose that, in the higher and more remote Vosges, one might be able to find 'the real thing' from a stream) that frogs do not multiply and so the storks do not visit. However, *Parcs aux Cigognes* or stork nurseries have been established, one of them along the *Route du Vin*, just north of Riquewihr, to breed the birds; such has been the success of these that apparently the creatures are unwilling to leave the region at all, even when their wings are not clipped to prevent them migrating, and some are now seen flying around, apparently at home and adapting themselves to their year-round environment. Some big circular nests, often erected on a wheel or round platform, are still to be seen poised on the highest point of many buildings, although few churches bear them today; they are, sometimes, occupied in the stork season–although a mere quarter of a century ago the huge birds, clacking their beaks, were far more frequent and friends of mine even complained of the noise they made at night. Some hopeful householders, however, have even installed model storks as a type of lure to the real thing–rather akin to the gnomes in suburban gardens, but perhaps slightly more appealing.

Storks on the nest

Some Places of Interest

The section north of the *Route du Vin* is given in the Michelin Green Guide as extending from Marlenheim to Châtenois. Anyone based in Strasbourg could make a number of excursions, also possibly going up to the German frontier – where the end of the Deutsche Weinstrasse of the Palatinate may be seen – and where the plantations of a range of varieties of wines may be seen on the hillside above the customs post. In the forest of Haguenau is the shrine of Saint Arbogast, who built the first cathedral at Strasbourg. The villages specialising in pottery, Soufflenheim and Oberbetschdorf, are other interesting places to

191

see. There you can buy the flower-pot-shaped device with holes, in which *fromage blanc* (see page 154) is made. The countryside is undulating and agreeable, perhaps not very impressive but charming.

Strasbourg itself is so rich in things to see that more than a single day is required; in addition to the several museums that cluster around the cathedral, the Musée Alsacien is worth visiting because of the very well-arranged rooms giving an idea of Alsace houses of former times, plus exhibits of a reconstructed kitchen, pharmacy and a section devoted to viticulture. From Obernai, another delightful town in which to wander, an excursion may be made to the Mont Sainte Odile; a spectacular route to the top of the mountain leads to an impressive church and the shrine of the patron saint of Alsace.

Colmar, viticultural capital of Alsace, has been frequently referred to in this book and it deserves a leisurely visit, with time to explore on foot the admirably restored houses in the squares and pedestrian precincts. The Fontaine Schwendi, with the statue of Schwendi holding up a vinestock is in the Place de l'Ancienne Douane (Old Customs House Square), with the rue des Marchands leading off from it. Here are some of the most picturesque old buildings of Colmar. The Musée d'Unterlinden, in the square of the same name, is second only to the Louvre in Paris for its glorious works of art and special salons. The layout is admirable and crowds do not usually prevent visitors seeing round with ease. One exception is the room in which is displayed the Mathias Grünewald masterpiece, formerly the altarpiece in the Antonine convent at Issenheim; it was here that those suffering from 'St Antony's fire', an appalling infection, were tended, and medical authorities say that Grünewald must have observed the malady at close quarters as he portrays many of the signs in the great painting. A warning – although sections of the double-sided altarpiece are glorious and inspiring, the Crucifixion scene is appalling and emotionally taxing – keep this room until last, as you will probably wish to go away after viewing it. Another religious masterpiece is the Virgin with the rose bushes displayed in the Dominican convent and particularly sensitive and charming.

In the rue des Têtes, the Maison des Têtes is a Renaissance building, now a well-known restaurant, the interior being typical of Alsace.

Mulhouse, in the south, is seldom visited by tourists concentrating on the *Route du Vin* but, especially for anyone arriving via Basle, it too deserves exploration. There are numerous handsome old buildings and several important museums: one of these has printed fabric, from the eighteenth century to the present day. Another, in the north of the town, has a splendid exhibition of railway trains. History and works of art are the subject of other museums.

Sélestat, on the left bank of the River Ill and on the main road between Colmar and Strasbourg, is remarkable for its great library; this, which includes a number of world-famous manuscripts, is the only humanist collection that has survived intact from the time when, at the beginning of the sixteenth century, Sélestat was an important university town.

Most of the villages along the *Route du Vin* merit a stop, but it is especially rewarding to explore tiny Boersch, in the north. Hunawihr is of great interest: walk up to the fortified church, from which there are finè views over the vineyards. There is Kaysersberg, birthplace of Albert Schweitzer, Kientzheim, with its gate with the tongue to poke out at any enemies and the Château headquarters and museum of the Confrérie St Etienne. Also Riquewihr (with its postal museum), Eguisheim and Turckheim (where the night watchman still patrols) are all places in which to stop and wander around – although almost any wine village merits a halt. Just north of Dambach-la-Ville and a hundred metres off the main road the Chapel of St Sebastian contains a remarkable seventeenth-century altarpiece in carved wood, well worth even a short stop. Nor are the rebuilt villages without attraction: opposite the co-operative at Bennwihr there is an impressive modern church, with a shard of the one that was destroyed, preserved as a monument in front; Ammerschwihr is another example of agreeable modern design – and has at least one good and a definitely great restaurant (Aux Armes de France). At Mittelwihr, just south of the village, there is the 'Wall of Martyred Flowers'.

One of the gates of Turckheim, showing the storks' nest. Here, the night watchman still makes his rounds

193

Firms to visit

Many of the wine establishments along the *Route du Vin* are open to visitors, although special arrangements usually have to be made for groups. Many of the local wines can, or course, be sampled by the glass in the *winstube* and cafés and, in the more important restaurants, the sommelier, waiter or patron will usually be pleased to offer advice and make suggestions, frequently recommending wines that may not easily be found on lists outside the region, even in France, and which should therefore be sampled on the spot. In the towns and out in the country, too, the traveller may hear people ordering drinks asking for 'Une schope', an Alsace word sufficiently curious to deserve a small digression. (It should not be confused with the *Alsacien* 'Une echoppe', which is 'a shop'.) 'Une chope' in French signifies a tankard and, therefore, the Alsace word in a drinks context means a large drinking vessel; in fact 'Une chopine' is a French liquid measure – half a litre – and the same word in the Shorter Oxford Dictionary is defined as 'half a pint', its supposed origin being Middle English. However, as readers of 'Hamlet' will recall, the reference to a 'chopine' or 'chopin' in Hamlet's welcome to the players, when he remarks that one of their company is 'nearer Heaven . . . by the altitude of a Chopine', relates to the wearer being taller, either because the boy player had actually grown or was wearing shoes that have thick soles, to raise the wearer above the ground as one might say of an actor today that he wears 'lifts' in his shoes. In fact the *chopine* or *chapin* of the sixteenth century was a type of footwear with a built-up sole of cork or wood, enabling the wearer to walk about above any mud, puddles and dirty ground, just as the wearers of pattens or small stilts could do. The word referring to a type of shoe in English is so similar to that referring to a liquid measure and the tankard in which it would be served, that I do not think it far-fetched to suggest that this may be one of the words that in former times had international significance just as 'a coke' or 'a cocktail' have today. And maybe the height of the tankard was similar to that of the chopine, so that the one became synonymous with the other.

In a producer's establishment or a co-operative, it is not necessary to make any purchases of wines, although you can usually do so. Sometimes small souvenirs, such as the miniature tumblers from which much tasting is done, may also be purchased on the spot. (Don't attempt to tip anyone showing you round, unless this is a paid guide who makes it obvious that some tangible 'thank you' is expected. Otherwise, an expression of gratitude and appreciation is all that is necessary.) Bear in mind that a tour of even a modest establishment will generally take at least an hour, more if you are then able to taste some of the wines; the enthusiasm of the maker tends to make it difficult to hurry and considered appraisal of any wines offered for tasting is essential if one is not to risk seeming discourteous. Also remember that, from about 1 p.m., most establishments will close for lunch, the period lasting from between an hour to two hours, so it is unlikely that you will be able to get in to be shown round at mid-day. Public holidays and festivals, when everything of this kind shuts down are usually listed, but one can always inquire from one's hotel or a local restaurant.

Below is a list of some of the many establishments that are open to visitors along the *Route du Vin*. They are given with addresses – if the place is large enough to warrant this – and telephone numbers, but details of the exact opening hours can vary, so it is wise to inquire in advance. In some instances, cellars may be seen, in others tasting may be offered, in yet others a meal may be available. During vintage, many establishments cannot receive visits.

A complete and up-to-date booklet as to all the wine houses is available from the Centre d'Information du Vin d'Alsace (C.I.V.A.), 68004 Colmar, France, who will supply it on request.

Christopher Fielden and I have selected establishments known to us, who make wines that we consider of interest and good quality. There are, of course, many more and there are a number of establishments that are not open to the public, where we have been fortunate enough to taste and get to know the wines. But the following should provide a basic guide. It is perhaps worth mentioning that, in some of the installations, the cellars may be cool if not actually cold, so a jacket or some form of coat may be advised even in hot weather. The route has been sub-divided, from south to north.

Note: The numbers after the main place names refer to the region and should be used if you write or telephone.

From Guebwiller up to Colmar

Guebwiller (68500)
Domaines Viticoles Schlumberger: 100 rue Théodore-Deck (tel: 76.91.10)
Westhalten (68111)
Cave Co-operative Vinicole de Westhalten et Environs (tel: 47.01.27)
Heim: 'Vins d'Alsace': 18 route de Rouffach (tel: 47.00.45)
Rouffach
Muré A. & O., R.N. 83 (sortie sud de Rouffach) (tel: 49.62.19)
Voegtlinshoffen (68420) *Herrlisheim près Colmar*
Théo Cattin et Fils (tel: 49.30.43)
Husseren-les-Châteaux (68000) *Colmar*
Kuentz-Bas (tel: 49.30.24)
Eguisheim (68420) *Herrlisheim près Colmar*
Maison Emile Beyer, 7 place du Château (tel: 41.40.45)
Cave Co-operative Vinicole d'Eguisheim et Environs, 6 Grand'Rue (tel: 41.11.06)

The terraces and drystone walls of the great Schlumberger vineyard, looking down on Guebwiller

Wintzenheim (68000) *Colmar*
Maison Jos. Meyer et Fils, 76 rue Clemenceau (tel 49.01.57)
Zind-Humbrecht, 18 rue Mal.-Joffre (tel: 49.02.05)
Turckheim (68230)
Cave Vinicole de Turckheim (tel: 49.06.25)
Charles Schleret, 1-3 route d'Ingersheim (tel: 49.06.09)
Colmar (68000)
Institut Viticole Oberlin, 2 rue du Stauffen (tel: 41.29.87)

From Colmar to Ribeauvillé

Ingersheim (68000) *Colmar*
Cave Co-operative des Viticulteurs d'Ingersheim et Environs, 1 rue Clemenceau (tel: 49.05.96)
Ammerschwihr (68770)
Vins d'Alsace Kuehn, 3 Grand'Rue (tel: 47.10.18)
R.Sick – P.Dreyer (tel: 47.11.31)
Sigolsheim (68710)
Société Co-operative Vinicole de Sigolsheim et Environs (tel: 47.12.55)
Pierre Sparr et Fils, 2 Grand'Rue (tel: 47.12.47)

Storks' nest on the ruined remnant of the
church at Ostheim – the modern church
is behind

Bennwihr (68630) *Bennwihr-Mittelwihr*
Société Co-operative Vinicole de Bennwihr et Environs, 3 rue Général de Gaulle
(tel: 47.90.27)
Mittelwihr (68630) *Bennwihr-Mittelwihr*
J.Camille Preiss-Henny, 23 Route du Vin (tel: 47.90.21; 47.93.64)
Baumann-Ziegel, 5 rue du Vignoble
Beblenheim (68980)
Edouard Bott, 1 rue du Petit-Château (tel 47.90.04)
Société Co-operative Vinicole de Beblenheim et Environs, 14 rue de Hoen
(tel: 47.90.02)
Riquewihr (68340)
Dopff 'Au Moulin' (tel: 47.92.23)
Dopff & Irion 'Au Château de Riquewihr' (tel: 47.92.51; 47.92.52)
Hugel et Fils, 3 rue de la lre Armée (tel: 47.92.15)
Preiss-Zimmer, 35 rue Général de Gaulle (tel: 47.92.58)
Zellenberg (68340) *Riquewihr*
J.Becker (tel: 47.90.16)
Ribeauvillé (68150)
Bott Frères, 13 Route du Vin (tel: 73.60.48)
Cave Co-operative de Ribeauvillé et Environs, 2 route de Colmar (tel: 73.60.77)
Louis Sipp, 5 Grand'Rue (tel: 73.60.01)
F.-E.Trimbach, 15 route de Bergheim (tel: 73.60.30)

197

Itterswiller, a village sandwiched between vineyards

From Ribeauvillé up to Barr

Bergheim (68750)
Gustav Lorentz, 35 Grand'Rue (tel: 73.63.08)
Rorschwihr (68590) *Saint-Hippolyte*
Rolly-Gassmann (tel: 73.63.28)
Dambach-la-Ville (67650)
Willy Gisselbrecht et Fils, Route du Vin (tel: 92.41.02)
Louis Hauller, 92 rue Maréchal-Foch (tel: 92.41.19)
Louis Gisselbrecht
Mittelbergheim (67140) *Barr*
E.Boeckel (tel: 08.91.02; 08.91.91)
Albert Seltz et Fils (tel: 08.91.77)
Barr (67140)
Louis Klipfel, 6 avenue de la Gare (tel: 08.94.85)
A. Willm, 32 rue Docteur-Sultzer (tel: 08.94.55)

From Barr to Marlenheim

Obernai (67140)
Société Vinicole et Distillerie Sainte-Odile (tel: 95.58.03)
Marlenheim (67520)
Maison Michel Laugel, 136 rue Principale (tel: 38.36.64)
Cleebourg (67160) *Wissembourg*
Co-operative Vinicole de Cleebourg, Oberhoffen, Rott, Steinseltz (tel: 94.72.14)

Bibliography

Brunet, R. *Le Vignoble et les Vins d'Alsace,* Baillière, Paris, 1932

Couanon, G. *Les Vins et Eaux de Vie de France,* Payot, Paris, 1920

Dion, R. *Histoire de la Vigne et du Vin en France,* Paris, 1959

Doutrelant, P-M. *Les Bons Vins et les Autres,* Editions du Seuil, 1976

Dreyer, J. *Les Harangues du Receveur,* Confrérie St.-Etienne, Colmar, 1977

Duijker, H. *The Wines of the Loire, Alsace and Champagne,* Mitchell Beazley, 1983

Dumay, R. (ed.) *Le Vin d'Alsace,* Editions Montalba, 1978

Edwards, G.E. *Alsace-Lorraine,* Skeffington, St.Paul's, London E.C.4, 1918

Fischer, A. (ed.) *La Gastronomie Alsacienne,* Saisons d'Alsace, 1969

Hallgarten, S.F. *Alsace, its Wine Gardens, Cellars and Cuisine,* Wine and Spirit Publications, 3rd edition, 1978

Hugel, J. *. . . and give it my blessing* (privately printed by Hugel)

Huglin, P. *Le Vignoble d'Alsace et ses Vins,* C.I.V.A., Colmar, 1975

Gyss, J-L. *Le Vin de l'Alsace,* Berger-Levrault/Jean-Pierre Gyss (undated)

Klein, G. *L'Art du Vignoble Alsacien,* Editions Garnier, 1979

Layton, T.A. *Wine and People of Alsace,* Cassell, 1970

Riegert, H. *Où mûrit le vin d'Alsace,* C.O.P.R.U.R., Strasbourg, 1969

Sittler, L. *L'Agriculture et la Viticulture en Alsace,* Editions S.A.E.P., Colmar-Ingersheim, 1974

Sittler, L. *La Route du Vin d'Alsace,* S.A.E.P., Colmar-Ingersheim, 1969

Sittler, L. *La Viticulture et le Vin de Colmar à Travers les Siècles,* Editions Alsatia, Colmar, 1956

Townroe, B.S. *A Wanderer in Alsace,* Methuen, 1926

Viegling, F. (ed.) *La Gastronomie Alsacienne,* Saisons d'Alsace, 1969

Vignobles et Routes du Vin, Librairie Larousse, 1977

Vignes, Vignerons et Vins d'Alsace, Editions Alsatia, Colmar, 1975

Les Vins d'Alsace, Confrérie St.-Etienne, Colmar, 1963

Vins d'Alsace, Guide des Caves Cooperatives, F.C.V.A., Colmar (no date)

Willer, O. and Woutaz, F. *Circuits Touristiques en Alsace,* Solarama, 1975

Wolff, C. *Riquewihr, Son Vignoble et Ses Vins à Travers les Ages,* S.A.E.P.,
   Ingersheim, 1967

Wolff, H. *The Country of the Vosges,* Longmans Green, 1891

Young, A. *Travels in France during the Years 1787, 1788 and 1789,*
   Cambridge University Press edition of the 1795 publication, 1950

Other books referred to:

Androuet, P. *Guide du Fromage,* Stock, 1971

Brunschwigg, H. *The Vertuouse Boke of Distyllacyon*

Forbes, P. *Champagne, the Wine the Land and the People,* Gollancz, 1967

Gosse, J. *Alsatian Vignettes,* Geoffrey Bles, 1946

Hansi, *L'Alsace,* B.Arthaud, Grenoble, 1938

Johnson, H. *World Atlas of Wine,* Mitchell Beazley, enlarged and revised 1977

Evans, L. *Complete Book of Australian Wine,* Paul Hamlyn, 1978

Galet, P. trans. and adapted Lucie T. Morton, *A Practical Ampelography,*
   Cornell University Press, 1979

Mitford, N. *Voltaire in Love,* Hamish Hamilton, 1957

Pongrácz, D.P. *Practical Viticulture,* David Philip, Cape Town, 1978

Schoonmaker F. *The Wines of Germany,* revised ed. 1983, Peter M.F. Sichel

Siegel H. *Guide to the Wines of Germany,* 1978

Simon, A.L. *The History of the Wine Trade in England,* Holland Press 1964,
   facsimile reprint of the 1906 edition - no publisher given

WHICH? Wine Guide 1983, Consumers' Association and Hodder & Stoughton

Willan, A. *French Regional Cooking,* Hutchinson, 1981

Appendices

Appendix I

EXPORTS OF ALSACE WINES—TRENDS IN 1983

Export sales of Alsace wines for 1983 showed an increase of 34 per cent in volume and 22 per cent in value on the previous year. 36 million bottles (255,000 hectolitres) were exported, totalling over 300 million francs. Export sales now represent 30 per cent of total sales of Alsace wines, which, in 1983, exceeded 121 million bottles (850,000 hectolitres) in both French and export sales.

The major export customers are, in order: West Germany, Belgium, the Netherlands, the U.K., the U.S.A., Switzerland, Canada, Denmark and Japan. In fact it is the enormous increase in sales to West Germany that has resulted in the overall high total, for Alsace is now ahead of all other French wines of certified origin in Germany, accounting for 30 per cent of French *appellation contrôlée* wines in the Federal Republic of Germany. Exports to Germany totalled 27 million bottles (189,000 hectolitres), an increase of 46 per cent over the previous year. In view of the big crop in Germany in 1982, the Alsace producers are particularly pleased with the expansion.

Exports to Belgium increased 15 per cent in volume, those to the Netherlands increased 38 per cent. In the U.K. the increase is 21 per cent (27 per cent in value) and in the U.S. the increase is 29 per cent (35 per cent in value). In Canada the increase is 9 per cent, in Denmark 69 per cent (59 per cent in value). The Swiss figures show a regress, due to abundant harvests in that country and a resultant quota system, but Japan's 25,000 bottles recorded in 1982 jumped to more than 60,000 in 1983.

Appendix II

The Alsace vintages 1969-82, expressed in hectares under vines and as percentages of the total, divided according to grape varieties

	1969		1970		1971		1972		1973		1974		1975	
Grapes	ha.	%	ha.	%	ha.	%	ha.	%	ha.	%	ha.	%	ha.	%
Mixed varieties	755	8.0	681	7.1	672	7.1	475	4.8	464	4.5	570	5.6	545	3
Chasselas	1 001	10.6	956	9.9	831	8.7	878	9.1	833	8.1	744	7.3	678	6.6
Sylvaner	2 577	27.3	2 591	26.9	2 571	27.0	2 559	26.5	2 638	25.8	2 587	25.4	2 600	25.3
Pinot Blanc	1 039	11.0	1 116	11.6	1 133	12.0	1 221	12.7	1 375	13.4	1 385	13.6	1 438	14.0
SUB TOTAL	5 372	56.9	5 344	55.5	5 207	54.8	5 133	53.1	5 310	51.8	5 286	51.9	5 261	51.2
Riesling	1 199	12.7	1 270	13.2	1 293	13.6	1 336	13.9	1 450	14.2	1 518	14.9	1 541	15.0
Tokay d'Alsace	387	4.1	410	4.3	418	4.4	430	4.5	458	4.5	448	4.4	452	4.4
Muscat d'Alsace	340	3.6	362	3.8	298	3.1	394	4.1	433	4.2	418	4.1	401	3.9
Gewurztraminer	1 945	20.6	2 006	20.8	2 035	21.4	2 070	21.5	2 266	22.2	2 190	21.5	2 271	22.1
Pinot Noir	198	2.1	233	2.4	258	2.7	280	2.9	313	3.1	326	3.2	349	3.4
SUB TOTAL	4 069	43.1	4 281	44.5	4 302	45.2	4 510	46.9	4 920	48.2	4 900	48.1	5 014	48.8
TOTAL	9 441	100	9 625	100	9 509	100	9 643	100	10 230	100	10 186	100	10 275	100

	1976		1977		1978		1979		1980		1981		1982	
Grapes	ha.	%	ha.	%	ha.	%	ha.	%	ha.	%	ha.	%	ha.	%
Mixed varieties	552	5.1	572	5.1	579	5.1	549	4.8	917	7.9	539	4.6	529	4.4
Chasselas	639	5.9	617	5.5	535	4.8	487	4.3	427	3.7	417	3.5	403	3.3
Sylvaner	2 633	24.3	2 648	23.6	2 608	23.0	2 576	22.4	2 549	22.0	2 500	21.3	2 497	20.7
Pinot Blanc	1 593	14.7	1 808	16.1	1 890	16.7	1 916	16.8	1 949	16.8	2 004	17.1	2 118	17.6
SUB TOTAL	5 417	50.0	5 645	50.3	5 612	49.6	5 528	48.3	5 842	50.4	5 460	46.5	5 547	46.0
Riesling	1 712	15.8	1 840	16.4	1 971	17.4	2 048	17.9	2 159	18.6	2 247	19.1	2 364	19.6
Tokay d'Alsace	477	4.4	494	4.4	502	4.4	521	4.6	526	4.5	547	4.7	559	4.6
Muscat d'Alsace	433	4.0	426	3.8	379	3.4	428	3.7	327	2.8	423	3.6	417	3.5
Gewurztraminer	2 368	22.0	2 368	21.1	2 367	20.9	2 397	21.0	2 169	18.7	2 433	20.7	2 453	20.4
Pinot Noir	412	3.8	449	4.0	402	4.3	517	4.5	577	5.0	639	5.4	712	5.9
SUB TOTAL	5 417	50.0	5 577	49.7	5 701	50.4	5 911	51.7	5 758	49.6	6 289	53.5	6 505	54.0
TOTAL	10 834	100	11 222	100	11 313	100	11 439	100	11 600	100	11 749	100	12 052	100

Appendix III

Changes in the overall plantations of *appellation contrôlée* Alsace wines, according to the grape varieties, expressed as percentages of the total from 1969-82

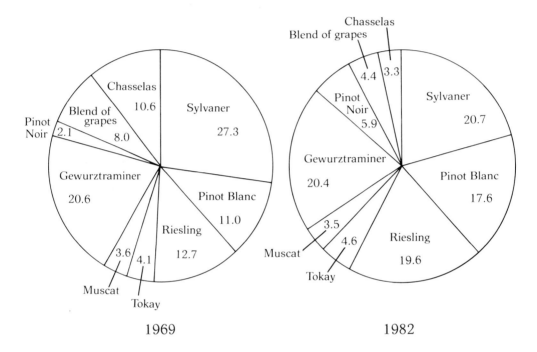

1969   1982

Appendix IV

Sales of bottled *appellation contrôlée* wines, in France, in export markets and as a whole, in hectolitres and as a percentage of the total up to 1982. The steady rise in exports is to be noted.

	1976/77		1977/78		1978/79		1979/80		1980/81		1981/82		Variation
	hl.	%	hl.	%	hl.	%	hl.	%	hl.	%	hl.	%	81-82/80-81
France	716 554	83.5	652 820	78.8	540 592	79.3	552 083	78.2	558 627	76.5	569 823	75.6	+2.0
Export	141 582	16.5	175 994	21.2	140 857	20.7	154 194	21.8	171 927	23.5	183 486	24.4	+6.7
TOTAL	858 136	100	828 814	100	681 449	100	706 277	100	730 554	100	753 309	100	+3.1

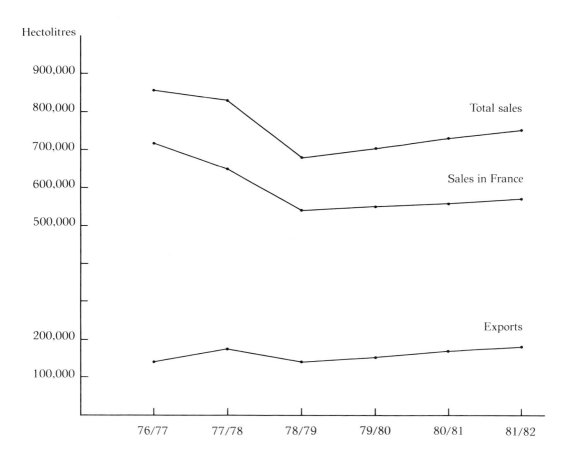

Appendix V

Division of the Alsace crop according to the declarations of the various types of grower, in 1981. The number, total area and volume (in hectolitres) is given with the percentage of the whole each represents.

Categories of wine makers	Number		Area		Volume (in hectolitres)	
	Number	%	Hectares	%	Hectolitres	%
V. Récoltant total	499	5.9	2 440	20.8	184 690	20.4
V. Récoltant partiel	1 378	16.3	3 077	26.2	225 717	25.0
Vendeur vin en vrac	380	4.5	629	5.3	50 209	5.6
Vendeur de raisins	2 832	33.4	1 569	13.3	111 055	12.3
Coopérateur	2 553	30.2	3 511	29.9	297 053	32.8
Producteur-Négociant	53	0.6	444	3.8	31 645	3.5
Consommation familiale	770	9.1	79	0.7	3 380	0.4
TOTAL	8 465	100	11 749	100	903 749	100

Appendix VI

Chart showing in hectolitres the 1982 crop in Alsace in relation to the thirteen preceding years.

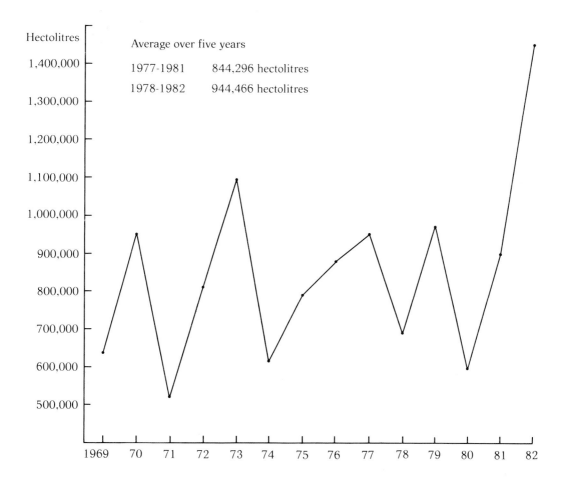

Hectolitres

Average over five years

1977-1981	844,296 hectolitres
1978-1982	944,466 hectolitres

Appendix VII

DETAILS OF THE 1976 *VENDANGE TARDIVE* AND *SÉLECTION DE GRAINS NOBLES* WINES AND PRODUCTION IN 1981 AND 1983

	Date of picking	Racking	Bottling	Deg. oechsle	Must weight	Potential alcohol	Alcoholic deg.	Residual sugar	Acidity oechsle
Riesling vendange tardive	20.10.76	1.6.77	13.9.77	102	236gr	13°05	13°05	13,6gr	4,0
Riesling sélection de grains nobles	20.10.76	26.7.77	12.9.77	117	271gr	16°00	12°24	51gr	4,5
Tokay vendange tardive	18.10.76	26.5.77	27.7.77	106	244gr	14°3	12°8	9,2gr	4,5
Tokay sélection de grains nobles	18.10.76	5.5.77	27.7.77	135	310gr	18°3	13°10	75,2gr	4,7
Gewurztraminer vendange tardive	16.10.76	13.4.77	23.8.77	110	250gr	14°8	13°25	10gr	3,5
Gewurztraminer sélection de grains nobles	16.10.76	11.7.77	22.8.77	130	301gr	17°7	13°81	52,3gr	3,9

All these wines were made from grapes affected by noble rot (*botrytis cinerea*) which occurred, in the remarkable sunshine, between 1.10.76 and 21.10.76.

PRODUCTION OF VENDANGE TARDIVE AND SELECTION DE GRAINS NOBLES WINE IN 1981 AND 1983 (in 1982 the production was minuscule)

1981 Growers making *vendange tardive* wines			Total (in hectolitres)
10			700
Of these	2	made	60 of Riesling
	10	made	550 of Gewurztraminer
	4	made	96 of Tokay d'Alsace

1981 Growers making *Sélection de grains nobles*		
1 grower (Hugel)	made	20

1983 Growers making *vendange tardive* wines			Total (in hectolitres)
102			7,300
Of these	30	made	1,300 Riesling
	94	made	5,500 Gewurztraminer
	22	made	500 Tokay d'Alsace

1983 Growers making *Sélection de grains nobles*		
26	made	750
Of these	5	made	50 Riesling
	25	made	600 Gewurztraminer
	9	made	100 Tokay d'Alsace

Appendix VIII

LAW GOVERNING *VENDANGE TARDIVE* AND *SÉLECTION DE GRAINS NOBLES* WINES

On 1 April 1983, a law governing Alsace *vendange tardive* and *sélection de grains nobles* wines came into force. It is of great importance, setting out the criteria, in certain vintages, for the production of these wines. Wine makers stress that there will be no change in the normal style of Alsace wines, which will continue to be 'varietal, dry and fruity'.

Innovations, affecting *appellation contrôlée* legislation are several: the minimum quality requirements are the highest to be applied anywhere in France, with the exception of the unusual *vins de paille* (straw wines). It is mandatory to declare the intention to harvest wines of this special type; an official quality check must take place before picking begins; there has to be an inspection of the fresh must, both in the press and in the cellar – all these checks ensuring that quality minima really have been achieved. Of course no chaptalisation is permitted, nor the addition of grape juice – such as takes place in the involvement of *süssreserve*. Prior to the commercialisation of the wine in bottle (that is, when it is to be released for the market), the wine must be officially tasted and this may not take place sooner than fifteen months after the date of the harvest. Nor may any wine be labelled with terminology that could in any way be confused with the terms *vendange tardive* or *sélection de grains nobles*.

The minimum quality levels are as follows:

	Gr. per litre	Degree Oechsle	Strength	Brix
Vendanges tardives				
Gewurztraminer } Tokay d'Alsace }	243	105°	14.3	24.4
Riesling	220	95°	12.9	22.4
Sélection de grains nobles				
Gewurztraminer } Tokay d'Alsace }	279	120°	16.4	27.6
Riesling	256	110°	15.1	25.6

Appendix IX

THE 1983 VINTAGE

The preliminary reports on this year indicate that the quantity of wine made is around the average – one million hectolitres – and therefore about one-third less than the total of 1982. The quality is already established as exceptional and outstanding. It looks as if this vintage will be comparable with that of 1976 and even, in certain instances, with the remarkable vintages of 1971 and 1959. It is certainly one of the most successful years of the past quarter century, with the must weights of the Pinots, the Tokay, the Gewurztraminer and even the Riesling, surpassing the level of the best vintages of former times. All the grape varieties appear to have yielded most satisfactorily and it is unusual for growers to be able to record as many *vendange tardive* wines and, even, those made from *sélections de grains nobles,* as in 1938. (The latter category was produced by many more firms than the usual few. See Appendix VII.)

The spring was extremely wet, floods causing dramatic situations in the villages and fields alongside the Rhine and the Ill. There was some damage by hail on about 600 hectares of vines in the plain; some chlorose was suffered during the spring. But the flowering of the vine was early and wholly successful, the summer was blessed with much sun and was warm and dry – sometimes even a little too dry – and the autumn was outstandingly fine, with just a little cloudy weather towards the middle of October. In general – and taking into account the different rates of ripening of the different grape varieties – the vintage came early: for the Pinots and grapes destined to be made into the *crémants* it started 26 September; 6 October for all the grape varieties intended for making wines to bear the *appellation contrôlée* Alsace and Alsace *Grand Cru,* only the Riesling being picked from 10 October.

The C.I.V.A., commenting on the availability of most promising wines, among them definitely being wines to keep for long-term maturation, describes the different grape varieties as they yielded in 1983 as follows: Gewurztraminer and Tokay 'grandissimes' (which might be rendered as 'important'), Pinot Blanc and Pinot Noir 'opulents,' Riesling 'd'une rare plénitude' (unusually complete), Sylvaner and Muscat d'Alsace 'd'une belle rondeur' (beautifully rounded). Coming after the big – and good – vintage of 1982, producers are likely to be pleased that they will have both the quantity to satisfy the 11 per cent increase in overall demand for the wines of Alsace in the past twelve months, together with wines that will maintain high quality throughout their lives.

Index

Note: The numbers printed in bold type refer to the illustrations

Abondant (grape), 60
Adam, Abbot, 29
Aedui (tribe), 28
alcohol content, 102-3, 114-5, 117, 158
alcool blanc see white spirits
alisier (rowan berry spirit), 178
Allen, H. Warner, 56
Alsace: character of region, 13-15, 56; language, 16, 53; vineyard, 17-26; soils, 18-19, 21-2; climate, 22-5; vintage, 22; prehistory, 27; Romans in, 27-9; name, 30; numbers of wine villages, 32; wine exports and trade, 32-4, 37, 39, 44-5, 56-7, 127, 201-2; wine taxes, 33; religion in, 38; in Thirty Years War, 38-9; population, 39; wine quality and viticulture control, 39-40, 52, 55-6, 58; and French Revolution, 42-3; vineyard area, 43, 49, 52-3, 206; under German rule, 44, 50-3; per hectare wine production, 45, 53-4, 82, 120; wine consumption 46-7; return to French rule, 48, 52, 114; wines little known in France, 52; fine wines, 101-2; size and number of vineyards, 111, 125-6; wine laws, 113-20; production control *(rendement),* 120; crops, 151-2; wine production, 207-10
Alsace-Villages, 76
Altenberg vineyard (Bergbieten), 118
Altenberg vineyard (Bergheim), 119, 139
Altenbourg (Katzenthal), 146
Amandiers, Les (wine), 133
Ammerschwihr: vineyard, **20;** town, 53; Tour des Fripons, **54;** vineyard names, 55; sparkling wines, 107; *grand cru* wines, 117-9; Kuehn at, 137, Sick-Dreyer at, 145; Confrérie St Etienne in, 167-9; destroyed in World War II, 168, 187; visiting, 194, 196
Androuet, P., 153
apéritifs, 107, 109, 160-1

appellation contrôlée, 55-7; and grape variety, 59-60; and *crémant,* 106, 108; and wine laws, 114-5, 119, 121; and yield *(rendement),* 120; plantation changes, 204; sales, 205; 1983 vintage, 210
Arbogast, St, 29, 191
Archenets, Les (wine), 140
architecture, 188-9
Ariovistus (chieftain), 28
Armagnacs (plundering bands), 37
Arvèze (brand of gentian), 179
Association of Alsace Wine Growers, 114
aubépine (hawthorn spirit), 179
Auberge de l'Etoile, Riquewihr, 141
'Auslese' wines, 101-2
Australia, 67-8, 73, 147
Auxerre, 32-3

Baccius, Andreas, 37
baeckeoffa (dish), 154
Ban des Vendanges, 115
bangardes (watchmen), 36-7
Barr, 51, 68, 118-9, 147, **182,** 198
Barth, Médard, 32
Bas, Jean-Michel, 137-8
Bas-Rhin, 50, 56, 62-3, 68, 74, 79, 115
Baumann-Ziegel (firm), 197
Baumé scale, 102
Beaune, 56
Beblenheim, 55, 63, 112, 117, 119, 129, 197
Becker, Helmut, 72-3
Becker, J. (firm), 197, 201
'Beerenauslese' wines, 101
Bela, King of Hungary, 66
Belgium, 57
'Bennes' (containers), **85, 92**
Bennwihr, **58,** 111, 129-30, 187, **197**
Bergbieten, 118
Bergheim, 119, 131, 198
Bergholtz, 119
Beyer, Emile (firm), 195
Beyer, Léon (firm), 60, 69, 71; holdings, 125; history and house style, 127-8, 148; and Preiss-Henny, 141; exports, 201
Black Forest, 18-19, 22, **58**

blending, 91; *see also* Edelzwicker
Bock, Jerome (*known as* Tragus), 63, 70, 74
Boeckel, Emile (firm), 128, 198, 201
Boeckel & Seltz (growers), 62
Boersch, **110,** 193
Bollenberg, 132
Bollwiller, Nicholas de, 37
Bott, Edouard (firm), 197
Bott Frères (firm), 197, 201
bottiches, 88
bottles (and bottling): introduced, 51; use, 55, 99-100; regulations, 55-6, 115-6, 121; and sparkling wines, 107-9; form and size, 121, **122,** 123; opening, 158
Brand vineyard (Turckheim), 75, 101, 117, 119, 147
brandies, 140; *see also* spirits
Brandluft vineyard (Mittelbergheim), 74, 128, 145
Breuschwickersheim, 175
Britain *see* United Kingdom
Brix scale, 102
Brunet, R., 60, 67
Brunschwig, Hieronymus, 171
Burger (grape), 43, 50, 55, 60, 114

Caesar, Julius, 28
California, 62-3, 69, 76, 99, 145
Calvados (spirit), 177
Canada, 73, 123
'Capus Law', 55
casks, 54-5, 88, **95,** 96, **97,** 98, 135
Catholics, 43
Cattlin, Théo, & Fils, 195
Cave des Trois Eglises, 175
'Caveau, Le' restaurant, Eguisheim, 59
Centre d'Information du Vin d'Alsace (CIVA), Colmar, 58, 195, 210
centrifuge, 93-4
cépages courants, 114-5
cépages nobles, 114-5
Cernay, Battle of (58 BC), 28
Chais Réunis d'Alsace, 201
Champagne, 106, 108, 113, 120
chaptalisation, 24, 115
Chardonnay (grape and wine), 60, 116, 163
Charlemagne, Emperor, 30
Charles IV, Emperor, 33

Charme d'Alsace (wine), 60, 136

Chasselas: grape, 50, 60-2; white, 60; rosé, 60; wines, 76, 81, 130, 137; and wine laws, 114, 116; as apéritif, 161; *appellation contrôlée*, 204

Châtenois, 74, 134, 191

cheese, 153-4, 164

Chiavenna, 63

chilling: wine, 159-60; spirits, 181

chocolate, 164

choucroute (dish), 75, 150, 156-7, 163

Christianity, 29-30

Clairette de Die (wine), 68

Clause, Jean-Joseph (*or* Jean-Pierre), 152

Cleebourg, 63, 111-2, 130, 198

Clevner (Klevner): grape, 44, 60, 62-3; wine, 80; and wine laws, 114, 119

climate, 22-5, 34, 37, 77, 84

Clos des Capucins ('Weinbach'), 133

Clos Gaenzbroennel, 147

Clos Hauserer, 75, 147

Clos Saint Landelin, 103, 140, 148

Clos Saint Urbain, 75, 147

Clos Sainte Hune, 74-5, 146

Clos de Zahnacker, 131

Clos Zisser, 136

Clovis, King of Franks, 29

cochylis (grub), 45

Cocks, C. and Feret, E., 59

Code Napoléon, 43, 125

Cognac, 174-5

Colmar: museum, 13; climate, 22; arms, 27; built, 32; wine trade, 33, 44; status, 34; old houses in, **35**; wine guilds, 36-7, 43; and wine quality, 39; property-owning, 43; Court of Appeal, 43, 125; Oberlin Wine Institute, 46, 196; as wine centre, 50; and Muscat grape, 68; Viticultural Research Station, 52, 74, 135-6; vineyards, 125; distilling in, 172; visiting, 192, 195

Columella, 28

Confrérie des Maigres, Ensisheim, 150

Confrérie Saint Etienne (*formerly* Herrenstubengesellschaft), 58, 62, 65-6, **166**, 167-70; Château de, 66

Contades, Maréchal de, 152

co-operatives, 50, 77, 111-3, 126-7, 201, 206

Co-operative de Beblenheim, 129, 197

Co-operative de Bennwihr, 129, 197

Co-operative de Cleebourg, 130, 198

Co-operative d'Eguisheim, 130-1, 176, 195

Co-operative des Viticulteurs d'Ingersheim, 196

Co-operative de Ribeauvillé, 131-2, 197

Co-operative Vinicole de Sigolsheim, 196

Co-operative de Westhalten, 132, 195

coopers, cooperage, 32, 36, 96-8; *see also* casks

corks, 109, 158

Coteaux Champenois, 106

Côtes d'Alsace, 76

Côtes d'Ammerschwihr, 61, 145

Côtes d'Eguisheim, 59

Cotte, Robert de, **40**

coulure (disease), 67

Covidal, 112

Crémant d'Alsace, 63, 105-9, 129, 132, 145; bottles, 123; as apéritif, 161; 1983 vintage, 210

Crouchen (grape), 73

customs dues, 37, 44

cuve clos (sealed vat), 105-6, 130

Cuvée Anne Schlumberger, 71, 103

Cuvée Christine Schlumberger, 71, 103

Cuvée des Comtes d'Eguisheim, 71, 128

Cuvée des Ecaillers Riesling, 128

Cuvée Frédéric Emile, 146

Cuvée du Mariage de l'Ami Fritz, 138

Cuvée Réservée, 138

Cuvée des Seigneurs de Ribeauvillé, 71, 146

Cuvée Saint Léon, 131

Cuvée Tradition, 135

Dambach-la-Ville, 34, 50, 111, 134, 193, 198

Dão area, 18

débourbage, 93, 96

Derindinger (brewer), 43

Dietrich, Baron Frédéric de, 42

Dietrich, J. Victor, 99

diseases and pests, 44-7, 67

distilling *see* spirits; *also* individual distillers

Divinal *see* Union Vinicole Divinal

domaines, 125-6

Domaines Viticoles Schlumberger, 142-4, 195, **196**

Domitian, Emperor of Rome, 28-9

Dopff 'Au Moulin' (firm), 51, 107-8, 125, 132, 148, 197, 201

Dopff & Irion (firm), 71, 125, 132-3, 197, 201

Dopff, Balthazard-Georges, 39, 132

Dopff, Guy, 92

Dopff, Julien, 51, 106, 132

Dopff, Pierre, 108-9

'dosage' (sugar), 109, 114-5

Douro, 18

Doutrelant, Pierre-Marie, 63, 67, 76

Doyen, Nicolas, 152

Dreyer, Joseph, 45

Dreyer, P. *see* Sick-Dreyer

Duc Casimir (wine), 130

Dumoulin, Xavier, 181

Durbach, 72

eau de vie de marc de Gerwurztraminer, 72, 172-4

eaux-de-vie, 123; *see also* spirits

eau-de-vie de pomme (apple spirit), 177

Edelzwicker, 59, 61, 63, 91, 101, 129-30, 136, 161

Edward III, King of England, 32

églantier/églantine (rose-hip spirit), 179

Eguisheim: vineyards, 31, 49, **85**; co-operative, 50, 107, 111-2, 127, 130-1; wines, 69; *grand cru* vineyards, 119; Beyer holdings, 125, 128; Kuentz-Bas holdings, 137; fortresses, 183; visiting, 193, 195

Eichberg vineyard (Eguisheim), 119, 132

Eichberg vineyard (Turckheim), 71

Eichhoffen, 118

Eiswein, 101

Elbling (grape), 55, 114

Elsässische Weinbauverband, 50

Ensisheim, 150

Eschenauer, Louis, 201

Etival, Abbey of, 133

eudemis (grub), 45

European Economic Community (EEC), 106

Evans, Len, 61, 68

exports, 201-2; *see also* under Alsace

Exposition de Vins (fairs), 50

fairs (wine), 50

Faller Frères (Kientzheim), 133, 148

Faudel, Frederick William, 70

feasts, *see* food

fermentation: and ripening of grapes, 24, 86, 91; arresting, 86, 93; in manufacture, 93, 95-6, 99; temperature control, 147

fêtes and festivals, **155**, 156

filtration, 100

Fischart, Jean, 170

fish, 153, 162-3; smoked, 161-2

Flambeau d'Alsace (wine), 118

Flûte d'Alsace (bottle), 121, **122**, 123

foie gras, 131, 152-3, 161-2

food: wines to accompany, 104, 157-8; *crémants* with, 109; tradition of, 149-56, 157

Forbes, Patrick, 105

fouloir-égrappoir (crusher-destalker), 108

fraise/fraise de bois (strawberry spirit), 177
framboise (raspberry spirit), 176
France: reclaims Alsace, 48, 52; Alsace wines in, 52; *appellation contrôlée* sales, 205
Franck, Sébastien, 37
Franco-Prussian War (1870-1), 44
Franconia, 62, 80
Frederick Barbarossa, Emperor, 32
French Revolution, 41-3, 125
Froissart, Jean, 32
fromage blanc (Bibeleskäse), 154, 192
Fromentot (grape), 66
frosts, 34, 37, 50, 82, 84
fruit, 161, 165; and white spirits, 174-80
Furmint (grape), 66

Gachon, Jean, 69
Galet, Pierre, 61-2, 64
Gallo E. & J. (California), 76, 145
Gamay (grape and wine), 59, 91
Gaschy, A., 201
Gaul, 27-8
Gay-Lussac, Joseph, 172; scale, 103, 172
Geisberg vineyard, 119
Geisenheim, 72
gentiane (gentian spirit), 179
Gentil Aromatique, 69
Gentil Nature Blanc (grape), 69
Geoffrey, Bishop of Viterbo, 32
Germany: wine production, 44; wine imports, 45-6, 57, 130, 202; rule in Alsace, 44, 50-3; grape varieties, 60; sparkling wines in, 107; wine laws, 114-5, 120, 173; bottles, 123
Gewurztraminer: explained, 15; bottling regulations, 55-6, 116; quality, 60, 68-9; grape, 68-72, 104; yield, 71; spirits from, 72, 140, 145, 172-4; wines, 76, 80, 102-4, 128, 131-2, 135-7, 139-40; maturing of grape, 91, 146; fine wines, 117, 128; serving, 159-60; as accompaniment to foods, 161-4, 169; *appellation contrôlée*, 204
'Giant, The' (Strasbourg building and guild), 36
Giessen (valley), 175
Giraudoux, Jean, 53
Gisselbrecht, Louis, 148, 198, 201
Gisselbrecht, Willy, & Fils, 134, 198, 201
glasses (wine), 107-8, **122, 165**
Gloeckelberg vineyard (Rodern), 119
Gloeckelberg vineyard (St Hippolyte), 119
Goldert vineyard, 119
Goldriesling (Riesling Doré; grape), 60, 73, 86, 114, 116

Goxwiller (village), 136
grand cru wines, 76, 102; legislation and definition, 115, 116-9, 121; 1983 vintage, 210
grand vin, 115
Grandes Maisons d'Alsace, Les, 138, 190
grapes: varieties, 40, 44, 55, 59-76; 'noble', 52, 59, 67, 114, 127; as names of wine, 59; importance in Alsace, 76; maturing of, 86, 91; and *crémant* wines, 108; regulation of, 114; *see also* hybridization; and individual varieties
Gratian, Emperor of Rome, 29
Greenoak, Francesca, 178
grey rot (*pourriture grise*), 23, 70, 104
growers (types of), 112-3, 206
Grünewald, Mathias, 192
Gueberschwihr, 119
Guebwiller: built, 32; status, 34; grapes, 68, 71; *grand cru* vineyards, 117, 119; Schlumberger holdings, 125, 142-4; visiting, 195; view, **196**
guilds, 36-7, 43, 167
Guyot, J., 44, 50
Gyss, Jean-Louis, 79, 168

Haguenau, 32; Forêt de, 29, 191
'halb trocken', 56
Halbfuder (cask), 88
Halbstück (cask), 88
Hallgarten, Fritz, 53
Hallgarten, Peter, 174
Hansi, 13, 156
Harth, 136
harvesting, 49, 92; *see also* vintage
Hatschbourg vineyard (Hattstatt), 119
Hatschbourg vineyard (Voegtlingshoffen), 119
Hattstatt, 119
Hauller, Louis (firm), 134, 198
Haut-Koenigsbourg, 31, **45**
Haut-Rhin, 50, 56, 61, 68, 115
Hecker, Dr, 50
Heidsieck family, 106
Heiligenstein, 63
Heim (firm, Westhalten), 127, 132, 195, 201
Heitz J. (California), 76
Hengst vineyard, 71, 103, 119, 139, 147-8
Hercules, 27
Herrenweg, 75
Herrlisheim près Colmar, 195
Hochwiller, **187**
Hoen, Château de, 129
Hohenstaufen dynasty, 31
holly berries, 174-5, 180
Horbourg, Battle of (378 AD), 29

Hospice Civile, Strasbourg, 98
'hottes' (containers), **85, 87,** 88, **89**
houx/baie de houx (holly berry spirit), 180
Hugel & Fils (firm), 57, 61, 64, 86, 96-8, 127; fine wines, 101, 103-4, 209; blended wines, 118; holdings, 126; history and character, 134-5, 158; visiting, 197; exports, 201
Hugel, Etienne, 134
Hugel, H.U., 39, 69
Hugel, Jean: and hygiene, 91; portrait, **97**; on wine manufacture, 99, 135; on wines, 104; and Britain, 134; on wine temperature, 160; on serving wines, 160-1, 163-4
Hugel, 'Johnnie', 134
Huglin, Pierre, 22, 74
Humbrecht family, 39
Humbrecht, Leonard, 147
Humbrecht, Madame Leonard (née Zind), 147-8
Huna, **frontis**
Hunawihr, **frontis.**, 119, 133, 146, 186, 193
Hunon, **frontis.**
Husseren-les-Châteaux, 137, 195
hybridization (grapes and vines), 48, 51-2, 55, 114
hygiene, 91, 95, 100

'Ice Saints', 84
Ill, River, 17, 28, 30, **40**, 152
Ingersheim, **25**, 127, 148, 196
inns, 34, 36
Institut Viticole de Colmar *see under* Colmar
International Wine & Food Society, 55, 76
Itterswiller, **198**

Jägermeister (schnapps), 138
Jatserberg, 119
Jews, 43, 136-7, 153
Johannisberg, 72
Johnson, Hugh, 171
Julian, Emperor of Rome, 29
Jura, 64, 69
Jux, Charles, 66
Jux-Jacobert, Charles (firm), 131, 136, 176; *see also* Dopff & Irion

Kabinett wines, 101
Kaefferkopf vineyard, 55, 71, 117-9, 137, 145-6
Kantzlerberg vineyard, 119, 139
Kastelberg vineyard, 118
Katzenthal, **70**, 119, 146
Kaysersberg, **159**, 193
Kellermann , F.E.C., duc de Valmy, 42

Kessler vineyard, 119, 144
Kientzheim, 66, 74, 119, 133, 148, 193; Château (Château de la Confrérie St Etienne), 58, **166**, 170, 193
Kirchberg vineyard (Barr), 118, 147
Kirchberg vineyard (Ribeauvillé), 119
kirsch (cherry spirit), 176, 181
Kitterlé (grape), 40, 71
Kitterlé vineyard, 71, 119, 144
Kléber, Gén. Jean-Baptiste, 42
Kleber (grape), 44
Klevner de Heiligenstein (grape), 60, 63-4; *see also* Clevner
Klingelberger vineyard, 72
Klipfel, Eugène (firm), 136, 148
Klipfel, Louis (firm), 126, 136, 198
Knipperlé (grape and wine), 44, 60, 114, 116
Koenig, Emil (firm), 136-7
kosher wines, 136
Kuehn family (and firm), 39, 60, 127, 137, 148, 196, 201
Kuentz-Bas (firm), 137-8, 148, 195, 201
kugelhopf (cake), 150, **151**, 153

lactic acid, 99
Ladhof, the (Colmar), 33
Lamber (grape), 114
Landal (grape), 60
Laugel, Michel (firm), 138-9, 198, 201
Laugel, Paul, 138
Laugel, Philippe, 127, 132
Layton, T.A., 64-5, 69
lees, 95, 173
Leo IX, Pope, 31
Lichine, Alexis, 102
liqueurs, 172, 174, 180-1
Lorentz family, 136
Lorentz, André, 136
Lorentz, Gustave (firm), 139, 198, 201
Lorraine, Plain of, 19
Louis VII, the Pious, King of France, 30
Louis XIV, King of France, 13, 151
Lunéville, 150
Lutins, Les (wine), 139

Maccabeo (grape), 66
machine harvesting, 92
McWilliams (Australia), 67
Madeleine (Stanislas's cook), 150
Mainz, 37
Málaga (wine), 68
malolactic fermentation, 99
Malvoisie (grape), 66
Mamburg vineyard, 71, 119, 146
Mandelberg vineyard, 74, 119, 141

manipulants partiels (growers), 112, 126, 206
manipulants totaux (growers), 112, 126, 206
Maquisards, Les (wine), 133
marc, 173; *see also* eau-de-vie de marc de Gewurztraminer
Maréchal Foch (grape), 60
Marlenheim, 65, 138, 186, 191, 198
'Marseillaise, The', 42
Massenez (distillers), 175
Médoc, 120
Mehr/Schmidt-Mehr, (distillers), 175, 180
Ménétriers or Pfiffertag, Fête des, **155**
Merian, Matthäus, 116
Meyer, F. (distillers), 174
Meyer, Jean, 139
Meyer, Jos. (firm), 103, 139-40, 148, 196, 201
mildew, 84
mirabelle (plum spirit), 176-7, 181
Mirassou (California), 69
Mitford, Nancy, 150
Mittelbergheim, 62, 99, 118, 128, 144, 147, 198
Mittelwihr, **12**, 119, 126, 141, 193, 197
Moenchberg vineyard, 118
Molsheim, 32
Mont Sainte Odile, 192
Montaigne, Michel de, 37, 150
Morio-Muskat (grape), 67
Morton, Lucie T., 61
Mosel, 18
mould, 90-1
mousseux wines, 105
Mouton Rothschild, Château, 65, 135
Mulhouse, 49, 192
Mullenbach, Marcel, 148
Müller-Thurgau (grape), 60, 62, 72, 116
Munster (cheese), 153, 164, 169
Murailles, Les (wine), 133
Murbach, Abbaye de, 143
mûre/mûre sauvage (blackberry spirit), 177
Muré, A. & O. (firm), 103, 140, 195, 201
Muré, Reine-Thérèse, 140
Muscadelle (Muscadet; grape), 67
Muscat: grape, 40, 60, 67-8, 71, 104, 172; wines, 67-8, 76, 81, 103, 132-3, 138, 173; and wine laws, 114; *grand cru* wines, 117; as apéritif, 160-1; as accompaniment to foods, 162; *appellation contrôlée,* 204
Musée Alsacienne, Strasbourg, 192
must, 94, 102, 115, 144, 210
myrtille (bilberry spirit), 177

names, naming, 59-60, 118-20; *see also appellation contrôlée;* place names
Napoleonic Wars, 43, 152
nèfle (medlar spirit), 178
négociants, 112-3, 125-6; *see also* individual names
New Zealand, 62
Ney, Maréchal Michel, 42
Niedermorschwihr, **23**, 119
Nigellus, Ermold, 29, 30
'noble' grapes *see under* grapes
noble rot *(pourriture noble; botrytis cinerea),* 23, 72-3, 103
Nussbaumer (distillers), 176

Oberbetschdorf, 192
Oberhoffen, 130, 198
Oberlin, Chrétien, 46-8, 50, 69-70, 135-6
Obernai, 34, 54, 112, 192, 198
Oechsle scale, 71, 102-3
oïdium (powdery mildew), 44-5, 84
Ollwiller vineyard, 119
Ortlieb, Fernand-Paul, 48, 60, 69
Osterberg vineyard, 71, 119, 146
Ostheim, **197**
Ottrott, 65, 173, 186

pancakes, 154
Paracelsus (Aureolus Theophrastus Bombastus von Hohenheim), 171-2
Parmentier, A. A., 152
'Passe-Tout-Grains' wine, 91
pâtés, 152, 161-2
Pedro Ximenez (grape), 68
pests *see* diseases and pests
pétillant wines, 106
phylloxera vastatrix (aphis), 44-7, 144
Pierrets, Les (wine), 140
Pinkenberg (monastery), 74
Pinot (grape), 59, 114
Pinot Auxerrois: grape, 62-3; wine, 80, 130, 139
Pinot Beurot (grape), 66
Pinot Blanc: grape, 60, 62-3, 76; wines, 80, 129-30, 132, 136, 162; sparkling wines, 108; *appellation contrôlée*
Pinot Gris: grape, 15, 60, 63, 65-6; wines, 80, 103, 108; *grand cru* wines, 117; with *foie gras,* 162
Pinot Meunier (grape), 60, 116
Pinot Noir: grape, 63, 64-5; wines, 76, 81, 91, 104, 130-3, 135, 138; sparkling wines, 117; brandy, 140; as accompaniment to foods, 163; *appellation contrôlée,* 204
pipe (cask), 88
piquant wines, 109
Pizarro, Francisco, 151

place-names, 186
Plaine d'Alsace, 17, 19, 21
Pliny the elder, 28
poire Williams (pear spirit), 177
Pongrácz, D.P., 64-5
pork, 163
porters (wine), 34
pourriture grise see grey rot
pourriture noble see noble rot
Pouilly-sur-Loire, 61
Preiss, Ernest, 133
Preiss, Théo, 141, 172
Preiss-Henny, J. Camille (firm), 125-6, 128, 141, 197
Preiss-Zimmer (firm), 141, **141**, 148, 197, 201
presses, pressing, 91, 93, **94**, 108
Probus, Emperor of Rome, 29
producteurs-négociants (merchant-growers), 127, 206
Protestants, 43
prunelle/prunelle sauvage (blackthorn/sloe spirit), 178
Pulliat, 61
Purschera (grape), 114

quetsch (plum spirit), 176-7
quiches, 162

Radmacher (spirit wholesaler), 176
rainfall, 22, 25
Raleigh, Sir Walter, 151
Rangen vineyard (Thann), 71, 119
Rangen vineyard (Vieux-Thann), 117, 119
Rangen (wine), 101
Rapp, Gén. Jean, 42
Ray, Cyril, 174, 180
Rebgarten vineyard, 130
Reine Claude (greengage spirit), 177
remuage, 109
rendement (yield), 120-1
'Réserve exceptionelle' wines, 101
Réserve Personnelle, 135, 138, 160
Revue Vinicole, La, 127
Rheinriesling, 72-3
Rhine, River, 17, 19, 21, 33-4, 37, 39
rhum baba (dish), 150
Ribeauvillé: built, 32; status, 34; Catholicism, 38; wine-producing, 55, 61; grape varieties, 70; wine quality, 103; *grand cru* vineyards, 119; co-operative, 131; Trimbach at, 146; gastronomy, 150; Fête, **155**; visiting, 197
Riesling: grape, 44, 60, 72-6, 86, 91; bottling regulations, 55-6, 116, 121; future, 76; character and quality, 79, 103-4; sparkling wines, 108, 131; and wine laws, 114; *grand cru* wines, 117; wine types, 130, 133-4, 137, 139-40, 145-6; as apéritif, 161; as

accompaniment to foods, 162-3; *appellation contrôlée,* 204
Riquewihr: Protestantism, 38; wine-producing, 55; grape varieties, 66, 74; vintaging, **89**; fine wines, 104, 117, 119; view, **124**; vineyards, 125, 131, 132-3; Château de, 133; Hugels in, 134-5; distilling, 172; visiting, 193, 197
Rodern, 119, 131
Rohan, Château des, Strasbourg, **40**
Rolly-Gassmann (firm), 198
Rome and Romans (ancient), 27-9
Rorschwihr, 131, 198
Rosacker vineyard, 119
Rott, 130, 198
Rouffach, 46, 103, 140, 195
Rouge d'Alsace, 131
Rouget de Lisle, Claude Joseph, 42
Route du Vin, 28, 183-7, 191, 193-5

St Gotthard Pass, 33
Saint Hippolyte, 65, 119, 198
Saint Hubert (wine), 137
Sainte Marie-aux-Mines (Markirch), 176
salads, 162
Sandherr family, 74
Sang des Turcs, 40
sapin (pine spirit), 180
Saering vineyard, 119, 144
sausages, 154, 162
Sauvignon (grape), 61
Savagnin (grape), 64, 69
Saverne, 32, 34, 41
Saverne, Château de, **41**
Scherwiller, 74, 134
Schielé, J. 137
Schielé, Jean-Jacques, 137
Schleret, Charles (firm), 148, 196
Schlossberg vineyard (Jatsersberg), 119
Schlossberg vineyard (Kientzheim), 74, 119
Schlumberger (firm), 46, 71, 103; holdings, 125-6; Domaine Viticole, **142**, 142-4, 195, **196**; assessed, 148; exports, 201
Schlumberger, Anne, 144
Schlumberger, Ernest, 144
Schlumberger, Nicolas, 144
Schmidt-Mehr distillery, 175, 180
Schmidt, René (firm), 201
Schnidst (dish), 41
Schoenenberg vineyard, 74, 104, 116, 119, 132, 135
Schoonmaker, Frank, 62, 65
'schope', 194
Schweitzer, Albert, 193
Schwendi, Baron Lazare de, 40, 66
sealed vat *see cuve clos*
Sekt wines, 107

sélection de grains nobles, 72, 102-4, 135, 209-10
Sélestat (Scheckstadt), 32, 41, **189**, 192-3
Seltz, Albert, & Fils (firm), 144-5, 148, 198
Seltz, Pierre, 99, 144
Sémillon (grape), 73
Sequani (tribe), 28
Sermesheim, Forest of, 27
Service tree, 178
Seyval Blanc (grape), 60
shellfish, 162-3
Sichel, Allan, 161
Sichel, Peter M. F., 62
Sick, R.-Dreyer, P. (firm), 61, 107, 145, 148, 196
Sick, René, 145
Siegel, Hans, 61, 63
Sigolsheim, 29, 111, 119, 145-6, 196
'Silver Sling' (drink), 161
Simenon, Georges, 178
Simon, André L., 16, 32-3, 55, 75
Sipp, Louis (firm), 148, 197, 201
Sittler, Lucien, 28, 69-70, 125, 151, 186
Société de l'Histoire et de Viticulture de Colmar, 50
Société Vinicole et Distillerie Sainte-Odile, 198
Société de Viticulture pour l'Alsace-Lorraine, 50
soils, 18-19, 21-2, 75, 77, 84
Sommerberg vineyard (Katzenthal), 119
Sommerberg vineyard (Niedermorschwihr), 119
Sonnenglanz vineyard, 55, 63, 117, 119, 129
sorbier/baie de sorbe (sorb apple spirit), 178
Sorcières, Les (wine), 71, 133
Soufflenheim, 192
South Africa, 63, 68, 73
sparkling wines, 105-9, 130-2, 138-9; see also *Crémant d'Alsace*
Sparr, Pierre, et Ses Fils (firm), 145-6, 148, 196, 201
Spätlese wines (late-picked), 74, 101
spätzle (noodles), 152
Special Fruits de Mer (wine), 60
Spiegel vineyard (Bergholtz), 119
Spiegel vineyard (Guebwiller), 119, 144
spirits, 131, 171-81
Sporen vineyard, 71, 104, 117, 119, 135
spraying, 21
Stanislas Leszczynski, King of Poland, 150
Station de Recherches Oenologiques, Colmar, 52

Staufenberg Castle, 72
steel (stainless), 91, 95, 134
Steinseltz, 130, 198
sterility, 91
Stoltz, J. L., 44
Storchengold (wine), 129
storks (birds), 190, **191**
Stosskopf, 14
Strasbourg, **26**; founded, 28; Battle of (357), 29; bishopric, 29; free city, 34; wine duties in, 37; decline, 37, 39; in Thirty Years War, 38; in French Revolution, 42; wine guild, 43; brewing in, 43; 1913 Exhibition, 51; decorated casks in, 98; pigs in, 149; cathedral, 149, 190-2; spirits in, 171, 174; as tourist centre, 192
sugar: content in grapes, 71; residual, 86-7, 91; dosage, 109, 114-5; in distilling, 174; *see also* Oechsle scale
sulphur dioxide, 93
sureau/baie de sureau (elder spirit), 179
Suze (brand of gentian), 179
Swabian Plain, 19
sweets, 164-5
Switzerland, 39, 44, 57
Sylvaner: grape, 44, 50, 60, 62, 71, 74; ripening, 91; wines, 76, 79-80, 145, 147; sparkling wines, 108; and wine laws, 114, 118; serving, 160; as apéritif, 161; as accompaniment to foods, 162; *appellation contrôlée,* 204

'tandelins', 49
'tartar pressings', 48-9
tarte (dish), 154, 157
tartrates, 98, 100
tasting, 77
teinturier (grape having red juice), 48
Tempe, Lucien, 148
temperature: climatic, 22-4, 84; control, 147; for serving wine, 159-60; for spirits, 181
tendeurs (tighteners), 34
Thann, 32, 34, 38, 117, 119, 186
Thirty Years War (1619-48), 38-9, 134, 152
tobacco cultivation, 152
Tokay d'Alsace/Pinot Gris: grape, 15, 40, 60, 65-7; wines, 76, 80, 102, 108, 128, 130, 133; and wine laws, 114; serving temperature, 160; with *foie gras,* 162; *appellation contrôlée,* 204
Tokay d'Alsace Baron Schwendi, 136

Townroe, B. S., 190
Traberschnapps, 173-4
Tragus *see* Bock, Jerome
Traminer (grape), 40, 44, 60, 69-70, 114
Tramyn (Termeno), 70
Trautsohn, Donath, Duke, 66
trellising, 50
Trew, Aileen, 93
Trimbach, F. E. (firm), 71, 75, 80, 146-8, 197, 201
Trimbach, Bernard, 146
Trimbach, Frédéric-Emile, 146
Trimbach, Herbert, 146
'trocken', 56
Trollinger (grape), 60, 114
Trottacker vineyard, 71, 146
truffles, 152
'tufa', 49
Turckheim: status, 34; grape varieties, 60; *grand cru* vineyards, 117, 119; Meyer at, 139-40; Zind-Humbrecht at, 147, 196; co-operative, 148; visiting, 193, 196; gate, **193**
Tutti frutti, 177, 181

Union Viticole Divinal, 112, 201
United Kingdom (Britain), 56-7, 106, 134, 138, 146, 201
United States of America, 57, 72-3, 123, 128, 146, 201; *see also* California
Urdenheim, 186

Vaslin press, 93
vats, 95, 98, 175; *see also* casks
vegetables, 150-2
vendange tardive (late-vintaged), 23, 70, 72, 74, 86, 91; wine quality, 103; as accompaniment to foods, 104, 165; wines, 131, 133, 135-6, 138; Meyer and, 139; Schlumberger and, 144; Zind-Humbrecht and, 148; serving temperature, 160; production, 209-10
vendeurs en vrac (bulk sellers), 112, 126, 206
vendeurs raisins (growers), 112, 206
véroniques, 123
Vieux-Thann, 119
villages fleuries, 186-7
Villanova, Arnaud de, 171
Villé, 175
vin bourru, 60
vin de paille, 47
vines, 20-1, 24-5, 27-9, 84; *see also* grapes

vineyards: size and numbers, 32, 111, 125-6; routines, 82-4; running costs, 82
Vins d'Alsace, Les (magazine), 116
vins de comptoir, 55, 76, 116
vins jaunes, 64
vintage, vintaging, 82, 86-8, 91, 115
vintages: quality of, 24, 44; 'Comet year' (1811), 44; and yield, 120; tables (1969-82), 203; 1983 report, 210
vitis silvestris, 27
vitis teutonica, 27
vitis vinifera, 27
Voegtlinshoffen, 119, 137, 195
Vorburg, 132
Vosges mountains, 17-19, 21-2, 25, 27-8, 82

'Wagkeller', 36
Wannen vineyard, 117
Wantz, Charles, 64
Wantz, Erhard, 64
Warmer-Vin-Chaud-Wyn, 173
Wasselonne, 54
Weinbach *see* Clos des Capucins
Welschriesling (grape), 73
Westhalten, 112, 132, 195
Westphalia, Treaty of, 38
Which? Wine Guide, 133
white spirits, 172, 174-81
Willm, Alsace (firm), 57, 126, 147, 198, 201
Willmes press, 93
Winlute (guild), 36
Wintzenheim, 61, 71, 103, 119, 139-40, 147, 196
wires, wiring, 50, **83**, 84
Wissembourg, 32, 52, 63, 130, 198
Wolfberger, 131, 176
Wolff, Christian, 54
Wolff, Henry W., 173, 176
Wolxheim, 68
World War I, 144
World War II, 52-3, 89, 186, 188
Worms, 37
Wuenheim, 119

yeast, 93
yield *(rendement),* 120-1
Young, Arthur, 41-2

Zellenberg, 133, 197
Zind-Humbrecht (firm and domaine), 75, 103, 126, 147-8, 196, 201
Zinnkoepflé, 132
Zisser vineyard, 71, 119
Zotzenberg vineyard, 62, 118, 128, 145

Rapeßweir

Eunenwir

S.Grim

Bilstem

Zellnberg

Reichnweir

ruchß

Mittelweir

Rhein

Kienßheim

Zeiser ßpg

Gotz acker

Prediger

S. Catarin

Inß tal

Ingersheim
Morßwir

Fäch A

Schlif

Turckheim